"A. Gary Shilling's new book, *Deflation*, is a contrarian's gem and an eye-opener. Paragraph by paragraph, chapter by chapter, chart by chart, Shilling lays out his thesis that the coming problem for investors, business people (and yes, everyone else) is deflation. What is deflation, why it will hit, and what do we do to survive it, these are some of the critical subjects covered in this startling, 'must-read' book. But caveat—take a deep breath before you sit down with *Deflation*. I can almost guarantee that you'll find it a shocker."

> Richard Russell, Editor
> *Dow Theory Letters*
> La Jolla, California

"There are lots of economists making predictions these days about the future course of the global economy, but few are doing the research to get it right. With a clear sense of how the prospect of deflation is dramatically changing the economic environment for consumers, companies and countries, Gary Shilling stresses the importance of growth. This book is essential reading for anyone trying to understand how to enhance the benefits and minimize the costs of major deflationary forces."

> Jerry Jasinowski, President
> National Association of Manufacturers
> Washington, DC

"This excellent book is 'must' reading. Gary Shilling was the first to understand the unwinding of inflation. Now he explores the prospects for deflation, and how investors can profit from it. I think he's right on. You should read it."

> Ed Hyman, Chairman
> ISI Group
> New York, New York

"There is no question but that this book is essential for serious investors who are coming to grips with the changes taking place around the world as inflationary pressures subside and as deflationary pressures grow. The arguments Dr. Shilling puts forth are well made, cogently argued, pleasantly written—and most importantly of all, correct. In the words of Siskel and Ebert, we give Dr. Shilling's new book an enthusiastic two thumbs up!"

Dennis Gartman, Editor/Publisher
The Gartman Letter
Suffolk, Virginia

"After tracking Gary Shilling for over a quarter century, I do not know of any economist who scored more bull's eyes on major turns in the economy—which ultimately affected the stock market. Ignore him if you will, and lament the ravages of deflation later."

Charles Allmon, President
Growth Stock Outlook
Bethesda, Maryland

"Don't fight the last economic war while the next one is bearing down on you. Gary Shilling's new book lays out plainly why half a century of inflation is ready to give way to deflation, how the rules of the game will change, and how to protect your assets and investments from the forces that seem likely to make a new determination of your economic success or failure. Americans need to read this book to know how to navigate the troubled waters ahead."

Charles T. Maxwell
Energy Analyst
Bronxville, New York

"A drinking orgy is followed by a massive hangover. And the way benign inflation in the 1960s was followed by high inflation in the 1970s, Gary Shilling makes, in this brilliant book, a compelling case that recent disinflationary trends, which he was the first economist to identify, will be followed by a painful deflationary period. The beauty of this book is that it explains how we investors who are well positioned can reap huge gains from the coming deflation."

> Marc Faber, Author & Publisher
> *The Gloom, Boom & Doom Report*
> Hong Kong

"When will the sweet spot of deflationary stimulus end? How will it end? Gary Shilling, always well ahead of the crowd, addresses these key questions in his new book, *Deflation*. For those who think the drop in long Treasury yields is over, read on. Shilling sees a further drop to 3%, providing a 62% return, or better than half the return seen from the peak yields of 14%."

> Kiril Sokoloff, President
> 13D Research, Inc.
> New York, New York

DEFLATION

*Why it's coming,
whether it's good or bad,
and how it will affect your investments,
business, and personal affairs*

ALSO BY A. GARY SHILLING

Is Inflation Ending? Are You Ready?
(Co-authored with Kiril Sokoloff)
McGraw-Hill
1983

The World Has Definitely Changed: New Economic Forces and Their Implications for the Next Decade
Lakeview Press
1986

After the Crash, Recession or Depression?
Lakeview Economic Services
1988

DEFLATION

*Why it's coming,
whether it's good or bad,
and how it will affect your investments,
business, and personal affairs*

A. GARY SHILLING

LAKEVIEW PUBLISHING COMPANY
SHORT HILLS, NEW JERSEY

Second Printing
October 1998

Library of Congress Catalog Card Number: 98-66426
ISBN 0-9618562-4-6

Cover Art by Fahy & Co.

Printed by Offset Paperback Mfrs., Inc.
Dallas, Pennsylvania

Lakeview Publishing Company
P. O. Box 521
Short Hills, New Jersey 07078

CONTENTS

CHARTS

FOREWORD

I first became acquainted with Dr. A. Gary Shilling when I was a young partner and research director at Goldman, Sachs & Co. I have followed his work closely now for nearly 30 years. He was the first economist to forecast the demise of inflation. His conclusions in *Is Inflation Ending? Are You Ready?*, published by McGraw-Hill in the spring of 1983, were prescient indeed. At that time few investors were prepared for what was to transpire. People's investments, businesses, and personal lives were geared to inflation lasting forever.

Surprising as it may seem now, long-term financial assets were anything but the assets of choice. Long-term interest rates were in double digits and price-earnings ratios were half current levels. Bonds were still being viewed by many as "certificates of confiscation," and common stocks were just recovering after more than a decade of poor performance.

Were you to have followed Shilling's advice in the early 1980s, you would have been a full participant in the 15-year bull market in both bonds and stocks that ensued, and at this writing is still underway.

Recently, Dr. Shilling has become concerned about the increasing likelihood of a worldwide deflation. As he points out in this, his latest book, the 1997 meltdown in Asia or a prospective tightening by the Federal Reserve will be the likely triggers. Still, he is not predicting another 1930s. He points out that the United States is strongly positioned and that there is good deflation as well as bad deflation. What he is troubled by are investors' inflated profit expectations, the current level of the stock market, and what could be a very difficult transition period.

Dr. Shilling writes with clarity, perspective, and insight. Whether you agree or disagree with his conclusions, his analysis, as usual, deserves careful consideration.

Bruce J. McCowan
Former Chairman of McCowan Associates, Inc.

About the Author

Dr. A. Gary Shilling is president of A. Gary Shilling & Company, Inc., economic consultants and investment advisors, managing individual and institutional accounts. The firm also publishes *INSIGHT*, a monthly report of economic forecasts and investment strategy, and Dr. Shilling advises Thematic Investment Partners and Thematic Futures Fund, investment partnerships oriented toward economic, financial, and political themes.

A regular columnist for *Forbes* magazine, he has been twice ranked as Wall Street's top economist by *Institutional Investor* magazine's poll of financial institutions , and *Futures* magazine ranked him the country's number one Commodity Trading Advisor in 1993. Although Dr. Shilling does not yet manage any mutual funds, CNBC anchor Bill Griffeth was so impressed with his investment approach that he profiled him along with 19 well-known mutual fund managers in his 1995 book, *The Mutual Fund Masters*.

Dr. Shilling is well known for his forecasting record. In the spring of 1969 he was among the few who correctly saw that a recession would start late in the year. In 1973 he stood almost alone in forecasting that the world was entering a massive inventory building spree to be followed by the first major worldwide recession since the 1930s. In the late 1970s, when most thought that raging inflation would last forever, he was the first to predict that the changing political mood of the country would lead to an end of severe inflation, as well as to potentially serious financial and economic readjustment problems.

His first book, co-authored with Kiril Sokoloff, was published by McGraw-Hill in the spring of 1983 and entitled *Is Inflation Ending? Are You Ready?* In it, the authors answered the first question in the title with a resounding yes. But to the second they said, no, you're not ready. Your investments, your business, and your personal life are geared to inflation lasting forever, not disinflation. Your portfolio is crammed full of tangible assets like coins, antiques, and real estate—the great inflation hedges of the 1965-80 era of accelerating prices, but assets that would suffer as inflation rates fell. At the same time, you own far too few financial assets, especially stocks and bonds— disastrous investments in periods of high inflation, but great winners in disinflation.

Inflation, however, was so deeply ingrained in everyone's thinking that the initial signs of its exit were ignored. The book's reviewers basically dismissed the authors' ideas. But by the mid 1980s, their forecast of inflation's demise began to look credible. In a delayed victory of sorts, David Warsh of the *Boston Globe* essentially reviewed the book in that newspaper's March 13, 1986, edition, and Bruce Ramsey did the same for the April 2, 1986, issue of the *Seattle Post-Intelligencer* in an article entitled "A preposterous economic prediction that came true."

By then inflation rates not only had fallen considerably, but stocks and bonds were thriving while tangibles were in trouble. Dr. Shilling was convinced that more of the same lay ahead because the world of shortages seemed to be over and a world of surpluses was in prospect. His second book, *The World Has Definitely Changed—New Economic Forces and Their Implications for the Next Decade* (Lakeview Press, 1986) , spelled out this thesis.

The 1987 stock market crash raised the possibility that deflation and not just low inflation might be in the cards, and his third book, *After the Crash, Recession or Depression?* (Lakeview Economic Services, 1988), explored this idea. Despite the title, he wasn't specifically forecasting deflation, but came closer to doing so when he, assisted by Anne D. Willard, created "The Deflation Game" in 1989. It's a Monopoly-like board game that is biased toward winning with financial asset holdings and losing with tangibles.

Dr. Shilling is widely recognized as the world's oldest living disinflationist, since his forecast of low inflation is over 20 years old and his suggestion of possible deflation has been around for about a decade.

He received his A.B. degree in physics, magna cum laude, from Amherst College where he was also elected to Phi Beta Kappa and Sigma Xi. He earned his M.A. and Ph.D. in economics at Stanford University. Before establishing his own firm in 1978, Dr. Shilling was Senior Vice President and Chief Economist of White, Weld & Co., Inc. Earlier he set up the Economics Department at Merrill Lynch, Pierce, Fenner & Smith at age 29 and served as the firm's first chief economist. Prior to Merrill Lynch, he was with Standard Oil Co. (N.J.) where he was in charge of U.S. and Canadian economic analysis and forecasting.

In addition to writing for *Forbes*, Dr. Shilling is a columnist for Standard & Poor's *CreditWeek* and a member of *The Nihon Keizai Shimbun* (Japan Economic Journal) Board of Economists. He appears frequently on business radio and television shows.

Dr. Shilling is on the Board of Directors of National Life of Vermont, the Heartland Group of mutual funds, the American Productivity and Quality Center, Palm Harbor Homes, the Episcopal Evangelism Foundation of which he is Chairman; an Advisory Director of Austin Trust Company; a Trustee and the Treasurer of the General Theological Seminary (Episcopal); and a Chairman of the New Jersey State Revenue Forecasting Advisory Commission. He is also an avid beekeeper.

For more information about economic consulting and investment advisory services of A. Gary Shilling & Co. and Dr. Shilling's monthly newsletter, INSIGHT, contact the firm at 500 Morris Avenue, Springfield, New Jersey 07081-1020, telephone 973-467-0070, FAX 973-467-4073, E-mail shil@ix.netcom.com.

ACKNOWLEDGMENTS

In some ways, writing this book was easy. We've been forecasting the demise of serious inflation for over 20 years and considering the possibility of deflation for about a decade. Consequently, with the aid of our past reports, speeches, and discussions, it was possible to compose this volume in about three months and finish it in early 1998.

At the same time, pulling all of this background information together in useful form was difficult. Earlier reports were often out of date or not focused, as is this book, on deflation. Furthermore, writing our normal eight- to twelve-page report which will be in clients' hands in a few days is far different from writing a book. I had to remind myself constantly that this work is meant to be timely for much longer, and that data and issues that are critical today may be irrelevant or superceded before the printer's ink is dry.

Furthermore, I can't expect you to read a book of this length in one sitting, so it seemed necessary to repeat the essence of a particular point when it is needed later in a different context. For example, the lousy US productivity growth of the 1970s is important to business restructuring (Chapter 5), to the lack of real consumer income growth (Chapter 17), to the outlook for productivity growth (Chapter 24), and to the investment implications of deflation (Chapter 27). I hope that I've succeeded in reminding you of an issue in its subsequent uses and not in boring you with repetition.

Regardless, my task was lightened by the wealth of excellent research and clear thinking of many good friends and professional colleagues. Special thanks go to Ed Hyman of the ISI Group, the nation's absolute best at preparing and interpreting graphs of almost everything in the economic and financial spheres; to Marc Faber whose *Gloom, Boom & Doom Reports* provide some of the most insightful analyses of economic, financial, and political conditions, past and present; and to Kiril Sokoloff of 13D Research, co-author of my first book and another long range and serious thinker about major trends. I am also deeply indebted to Jim Bianco of Bianco Research for his excellent long-term data and analysis of US stock and bond markets; to Steve Leuthold of The Leuthold Group, who always impresses me with his ability to prove with hard numbers many of the ideas I can only conceptualize; to Dennis Gartman of *The Gartman Letter*, who has an uncanny ability to see through the facade of political maneuvers and financial markets and who is one of the few conservatives I know who reads the *Chinese People's Daily* regularly; and to Ed Moos, whose memory and records of past fixed-income market prices and Federal Reserve actions never cease to amaze me.

With the brains and expertise of these gentlemen and my shameless willingness to borrow their ideas and data, this book is a far better work than it would be otherwise. Nevertheless, the blame for misinterpreting and otherwise screwing up their concepts is mine alone.

Furthermore, I thank my colleagues at A. Gary Shilling & Co., past and present, for their considerable help in preparing this book. Tony Riley, our former Research Director, wrote several of the reports excerpted here. Kelly Hinkle put together many of the basic charts before moving on to a job in New York City.

Among our current staff, Russ Nuzzo and Peter Sargen, although relatively new in economic research, were very helpful with data sources and charts. Sean Martin was extremely effective at gathering and analyzing security market data. Chris Saviano, Joe Marsh, and Mike Webb also pitched in to provide special research and analysis. Bruce McCowan, an Advisory Director of A. Gary Shilling & Co., read this book carefully in draft form and provided many thoughtful comments. I also thank Carolyn Sebastian of Fahy & Co. for her excellent art work for this book's cover.

Finally, my very special thanks go to Jeannie Diamandas and Sally Whitney. Jeannie, my personal assistant, did a masterful job of not only deciphering my nearly illegible handwriting and turning it into passable prose, but also in pointing out my many inconsistencies. Furthermore, she was essential in setting deadlines and pointing out to all of us the consequences of not sticking to them. Sally, our editor and desk top publisher, was superb at drafting a number of chapters, editing the rest, and convincing me to throw out tons of irrelevant material that's only claim to fame was the fact that I wrote it. Sally is also responsible for the wonderful layout of this book. Her never flagging upbeat approach and enthusiasm kept us all going strong even during the most trying moments in the project's life. Without the consistent top quality of Jeannie's and Sally's work, this book would never have made it to the printer.

A.G.S.

INTRODUCTION

WHY I'M WRITING THIS BOOK

Why write a book about deflation? More important, why should I ask
you to take the time to read it? After all, what's new about deflation—the
chronic and widespread decline in prices? Isn't it just an extension of the
unwinding of inflation—disinflation, as it's called?

Inflation Is Over

Inflation rates have been falling since the early 1980s (Chart I-1), and
today, inflation is essentially over. US producer prices have been falling since
the beginning of 1997 (Chart I-2) and consumer prices, after subtracting the
widely-accepted 1+% overstatement, are about unchanged (Chart I-3). As
shown in Chart I-4, a number of consumer sectors reported price declines in
1997—including such services as airline fares, interstate phone calls, and public
transportation, even though services tend to be more inflationary than goods.
Other countries have also seen the demise of inflation recently. Note China
(Chart I-5) as well as Australia and Canada (Chart I-6).

Still, the question remains, if inflation rates continue to fall into negative numbers, is there any difference from ongoing disinflation? If not, why
write a book on deflation? I'm doing so for four reasons.

Deflation Is Likely

First, I believe that deflation is not just possible but highly likely. The
forces that are pushing the world into deflation are noted in Chart I-7 and
spelled out in Chapters 1-18. The first 13 of these 14 forces are already in

place. The last, the conversion of US consumers from three decades of borrowing and spending to many years of savings, will be initiated by a major bear market in US stocks which destroys a considerable part of the portfolio

CHART I-1

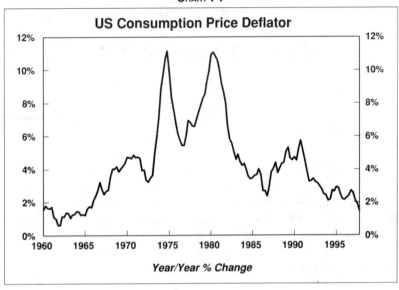

CHART I-2

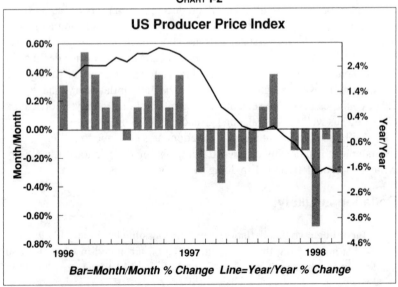

appreciation that many Americans have been using as a substitute for saving in the last decade. This stock sell off, in turn, may be touched off by disappointing US corporate profits, especially if the Asian meltdown proves as significant as I believe it will, or by a Federal Reserve-induced recession if the American economy continues to boom and to tighten labor markets. Either way, global and chronic deflation will follow.

Few Expect Deflation

Second, few expect deflation, so a book on the subject may be useful. Investors don't. In early 1998, 30-year Treasury bonds are yielding about 6%, but if overall price declines of 1% to 2% per year are in store, the inflation-adjusted or real return would be 7% or 8%, far above the 2% to 3% range of the earlier postwar era (Chart I-8). Federal Reserve Chairman Alan Greenspan doesn't think deflation is likely. In the summer of 1997 he said "there are none of the characteristics in the economic structure which lead us to conclude we are moving in a direction of deflation." More recently, in a January 3, 1998, speech he said that the chances of declines in goods and services prices are "not..a significant near-term risk."

Nor does economic titan Milton Friedman expect generally declining prices. In December 1998 he said, "but longer term, inflation is headed up and not down...Some time within the next 10 to 12 years we'll have a period

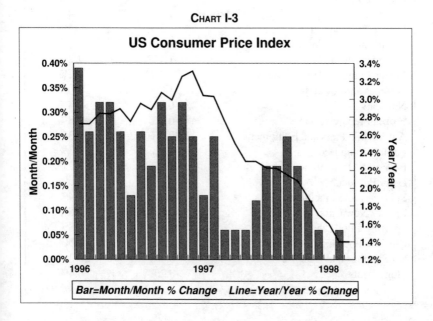

CHART I-3

US Consumer Price Index

Bar=Month/Month % Change   Line=Year/Year % Change

CHART I-4

US CONSUMER PRICE CHANGES		
	DEC. 1996- DEC. 1997	AVERAGE ANNUAL % CHANGE PAST 3 YEARS
Information Processing Equipment	-12.1%	-10.5%
Gasoline	-6.1%	4.9%
Used Cars	-5.0%	3.9%
Airline Fares	-4.8%	2.3%
Telephone, interstate toll calls	-4.3%	3.1%
TV's	-4.3%	-3.6%
Appliances, including electronic equipment	-3.9%	-2.3%
Video and audio products	-3.8%	-2.7%
Energy	-3.4%	3.2%
Automobile Finance Charges	-3.1%	7.7%
Public Transportation	-3.0%	2.7%
Stoves, ovens, dishwashers, and air conditioners	-2.4%	-0.3%
Carbonated Drinks	-1.6%	0.7%
Durables	-1.5%	1.8%
Housefurnishings	-1.4%	0.2%
Electricity	-1.3%	1.4%
Private Transportation	-1.2%	3.3%
Lawn equipment, power tools, and hardware	-1.1%	1.2%
Meats, Poultry, Fish, and Eggs	-1.1%	3.1%
Watches and Jewelry	-1.0%	0.0%
New cars	-0.9%	2.4%
Frozen Prepared Food	-0.9%	1.8%
Automobile Parts and Equipment	-0.9%	0.3%
Furniture and Bedding	-0.7%	2.3%
Beer and Ale at Home	-0.5%	1.2%
Dairy Products	-0.5%	4.6%
Sport Vehicles, including bikes	-0.5%	1.4%
Luxury New Cars	-0.5%	2.5%
Sporting Goods and Equipment	-0.4%	0.8%
Club Memberships	-0.4%	0.3%
Pet Supplies and Expense	-0.4%	3.3%
Men's Pants	-0.2%	0.4%

Source: Bureau of Labor Statistics

CHART I-5

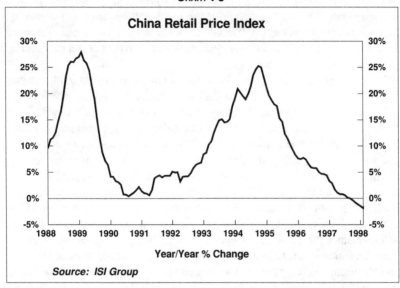

China Retail Price Index

Year/Year % Change

Source: ISI Group

of much higher inflation." He may be right on that last statement, and let's hope that you and I are still around then to see. Most business people and investors, however, seem to consider about five years, not 10 or more, to be their long-term time horizon, and I expect deflation to reign for at least that long.

Even business people right on the firing line don't expect much to fall out of the Asian crisis. In December 1997, six months into the Asian collapse, a National Association of Manufacturers survey of 20 top corporate executives found that half expected only marginal effects on their exports. Most were sticking with their robust capital spending plans for 1998, and four-fifths looked for higher profits. Small business members of the National Federation of Independent Businesses late in 1997 expected record earnings, record job openings, and record capital spending in 1998.

Deflation Is Different

The third reason for this book is that deflation is different from disinflation—declining but still positive rates of overall price change. In the 1970s we saw the self-feeding cycle of inflationary expectations. Businesses and consumers bought ahead of need to beat expected price increases. That increase in demand strained supplies and pushed up prices. Suspicions were confirmed, so buying ahead of need intensified, leading to more of the same.

Deflation will be exactly the opposite. If it is widespread and chronic, people will anticipate it by waiting to buy. Piled up inventories and excess capacity to make goods and services will result, so producers will cut prices to unload. Suspicions will be confirmed, so buyers will wait even further in a reinforcing cycle.

To many, the mere word "deflation" conjures up the financial collapse of the 1930s. As covered in Chapter 20, however, deflation is the norm at this point in the 50- to 60-year Kondratieff wave, and usually occurs without a 1930s-style financial collapse which severely depressed incomes and demand. Indeed, we expect the coming deflation to resemble much more that of the late 1800s or the 1920s, when declining prices resulted from technological advances and vast increases in supply. With technology and capital now free to move around the globe in search of the most cost effective locations, the West is exporting the Industrial Revolution to the developing countries and is importing the resulting low-cost output. It looks like good deflation, not bad deflation since the financial crisis will probably remain confined to Asia.

Deflation also differs from inflation of any magnitude because in deflation, declining interest rates do not stimulate demand and precede good times and a bull stock market. Capacity is so ample that little can induce investment in more of it, and consumers are more influenced by expectations of lower prices than lower borrowing costs.

CHART I-6

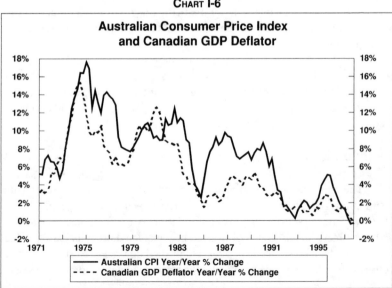

Australian Consumer Price Index and Canadian GDP Deflator

Australian CPI Year/Year % Change
Canadian GDP Deflator Year/Year % Change

With good deflation, corporate profits will rise, but more slowly than in recent years. Like bad deflation, however, the good variety enhances the chances of trade wars.

Chapter 27 outlines our 13-point investment strategy for a deflationary era and the transition to it. High quality bonds will be winners. US stocks overall will do reasonably well once deflation sets in, but will probably be beaten up in the transition to it. You'll also learn in that chapter how deflation separates the technological sheep from the goats. With people saving more

CHART I-7

DEFLATIONARY FORCES

1. End of Cold War led to global cuts in defense spending.

2. Major country government spending and deficits are shrinking.

3. Central banks continue to fight the last war—inflation.

4. G-7 retirements will lead to reduced benefits and slower growth in incomes and spending.

5. Restructuring continues in English-speaking lands and will spread.

6. Technology cuts costs and promotes productivity.

7. Information via the Internet increases competition.

8. Mass distribution to consumers reduces costs and prices.

9. Ongoing deregulation cuts prices.

10. Global sourcing of goods and services curtails costs.

11. The spreading of market economies increases global supply.

12. The dollar will continue to strengthen.

13. Asian financial and economic problems will intensify global glut and reduce worldwide prices.

14. US consumers will switch from borrowing and spending to saving.

and waiting for lower prices to buy goods and services that don't change their form or function much over time, many consumer discretionary spending sectors will be losers. In sharp contrast, buyers will continue to rush to purchases where rapid innovation leads to significant new products, dramatically lower prices, and technological advances that make old models obsolete.

Chapter 28 explores an 18-point strategy for business people who want to survive, indeed thrive, in deflation. The elements range from ruthless cost cutting to emphasizing proprietary products to sharing company risks with employees. Finally, Chapter 29 provides a five-item list of do's and don'ts for consumers in deflation. Hint: save more and make sure you're worth more to your boss than he's paying you. These last three chapters also provide summary tables of investment, business, and personal winners and losers.

Early Warning Signs

The fourth reason for writing this book is that the early warning signs of deflation are abundant. Sensitive industrial commodity prices have fallen sharply, as shown by the Journal of Commerce Commodity Price Index (Chart I-9) and the Goldman Sachs Commodity Nearby Index (Chart I-10). Note that both started to fall well before the Asian crisis commenced in mid 1997.

CHART I-8

Real US Long Term Treasury Bond Yields

Deflated by the Consumer Price Index

The nonprofit sector of the economy is the furthest from the market place, and therefore the last to reflect economic changes. This is especially true of the most prestigious American universities, which can charge almost

CHART I-9

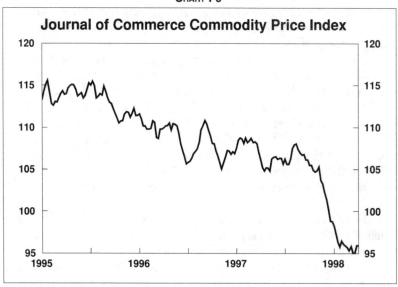

Journal of Commerce Commodity Price Index

CHART I-10

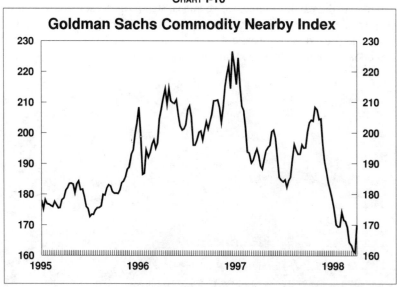

Goldman Sachs Commodity Nearby Index

any tuition they choose. The wealthy will pay the full amount for the privilege of their kids' attending those institutions, and then those universities use part of that money to subsidize poor students to maintain their student body balances. So, the sky's the limit on tuition levels, and double-digit increases have persisted throughout the disinflation of the last 15 years. Yet, Princeton, Yale, and Stanford all recently announced relatively tiny tuition increases. Yale's will increase 2.9% and Stanford's 3.5%. (Thank goodness, since my daughter, Jenny, is only in her first year at Stanford's Business School.)

Finally, deflation must certainly be approaching, since New York City recently cut the costs of subway and bus rides by offering 11 ride fare cards for the price of 10. New York has been run for many decades for the benefit of welfare recipients and public employees with little concern for cost control or efficiency. For 35 years, I've observed that virtually every change booth in the subway system contains two people, one to sell tokens and the other to talk to the person selling tokens. When New York City does anything to reduce riders' trips to the change booths and therefore possibly, but only possibly, reduce the number of token sellers and the watchers, deflation must be at hand.

Move on to Chapter 1 to learn why the end of the Cold War is removing inflation's most significant support, but before you do, I'd like to point out a feature of this book that may assist you in reading it.

Years ago, I learned that most nonfiction books aren't read past the first chapter. So, the obvious advice to authors is, summarize it in the first chapter or forget it! We've done exactly that in this Introduction, but to encourage you to read the whole volume, we've gone a step further—summarizing it in chapter titles, so the Table of Contents provides an excellent overview. This technique proved very successful in maintaining reader interest in our last two books. I hope it does so in this one as well.

CHAPTER 1

THE END OF THE COLD WAR LED TO GLOBAL CUTS IN DEFENSE SPENDING

In late 1975, as the US economy was beginning to recover from the worst recession since the 1930s, we first said that inflation was on the way out, even though prices were still accelerating. Our analysis showed that in this country the history of serious inflation is the history of big government spending, usually in shooting wars but in the Cold War and the War on Poverty as well. We noted that in the 1749-1974 years, wholesale prices rose 1.4% per year on average, but about 12% in the war years while declining 1.3% per year in peacetime.

The *Chicago Sun Times* in its November 13, 1975 edition used our graph of long-run inflation and added a cartoon—American soldiers, marching through the nation's wars (Chart 1-1)—in an article headlined "Maverick Economist Deflates Inflation." The newspaper went on to quote my reasoning for a smaller share of the economic pie going to government.

Voter attitudes have changed. The long liberal swing that began in 1933 ended with the Vietnam War. People now don't trust the government's ability to run much of anything, whether it's foreign policy after the Vietnam War, the political process after Watergate, or the economy after the two recent recessions.

Furthermore, after near runaway inflation, voters seem willing to live with much higher unemployment if that is the price of lower inflation. We stress the attitudes of voters, not politicians, since the latter do want to be re-elected.

CHART 1-1

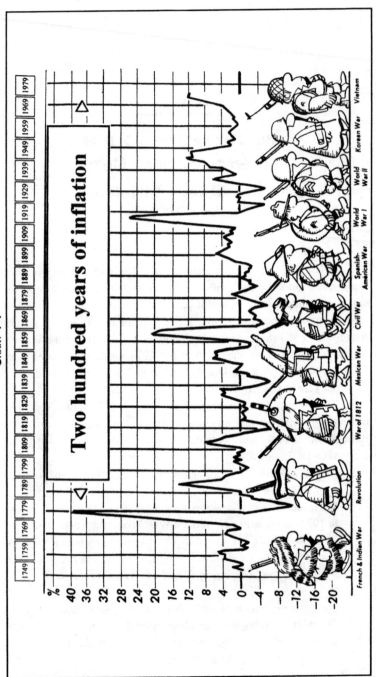

Two hundred years of inflation

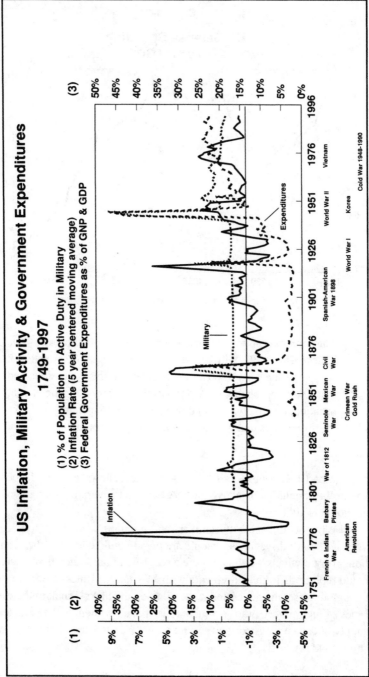

CHART 1-2

US Inflation, Military Activity & Government Expenditures
1749-1997

(1) % of Population on Active Duty in Military
(2) Inflation Rate (5 year centered moving average)
(3) Federal Government Expenditures as % of GNP & GDP

CHART 1-3

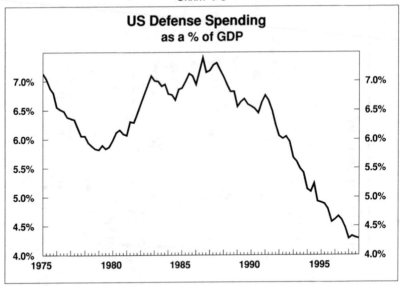

The country is now entering a period of lower inflation rates—we believe 2% or 3% will be the norm—and of stable growth not seen since the early 1960s. Few believe that this is possible, and that's why it probably is. As long as the country is worried about inflation, it is likely to hold down government spending and take other measures that will keep inflationary forces in check.

Chart 1-2 brings Chart 1-1 up to date and shows, as well, the percentage of the population on active military duty and government's share of total economic activity.

Why this linkage between wars and inflation? Quite simply, because you and I don't drive tanks. People are paid to build them, but they can't be bought by civilians—although defensive driving advocates may wish they could replace their banged-up cars with M-1 tanks. Unless taxes are raised enough to offset the government spending on the tanks—seldom the case in times of big military outlays—income is created without a comparable new supply of consumer goods and services. So, overall demand exceeds overall supply and prices rise.

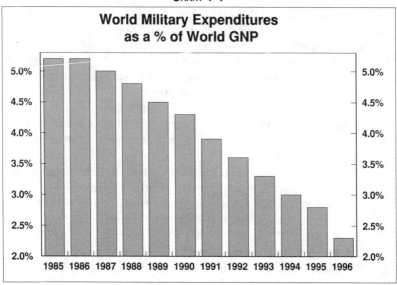

CHART 1-4

The Cold War Is Over

The Cold War, of course, ended in the late 1980s and, as a result, US defense spending is falling in real dollar terms and even more rapidly as a percentage of GDP (Chart 1-3). Furthermore, this is a global phenomenon, as shown in Chart 1-4. In effect, one of the prime causes, if not *the* cause, of inflation is being removed.

In addition, while military spending cuts after hot wars remove inflationary excess demand, the unwinding of the Cold War goes even further. It's actually deflationary since it reduces demand even more. To see why, contrast the post-World War II and post-Cold War experiences.

In World War II, General Motors stopped making cars in order to use its assembly lines to build tanks and other military vehicles. The workers were paid about the same amount as before, but there were no cars to buy. After the war, those factories were converted back to auto production. In fact, during the war GM said it would be making cars within six months of peace, and it beat that time table. Tanks were no longer being produced when the war ended, but assembly line workers went back to making cars immediately, so incomes were again matched by an equal supply of civilian goods and services.

In contrast, the Cold War spawned whole industries that were not converted from civilian production but built from scratch. Nuclear warheads and the rockets and nuclear-powered submarines needed to deliver them have no civilian counterparts. And they are very expensive since, trade-for-trade, defense industry employees in the Cold War earned about 50% more than their civilian counterparts. When this hardware is no longer built, the production facilities are essentially dismantled and employees terminated. There are no civilian products they switch back to building. Sure, some rockets have civilian uses, but they use a much different technology than those that were aimed at the former Soviet Union. Supersonic jet fighters are a different breed in cost and design from Boeing 777s.

The unwinding of Cold War spending has been gradual enough to prevent big nationwide unemployment problems, much less a recession. Nevertheless, the lack of conversion to civilian goods production by many defense industries means that the end of the East-West confrontation is actually deflationary.

Defense spending is the most volatile component of government spending and the most inflationary, but others are significant. As we'll see in Chapter 2, they, too, are moving in deflationary ways.

CHAPTER 2

MAJOR COUNTRY GOVERNMENT SPENDING AND DEFICITS ARE SHRINKING

It's easy to over-complicate things, especially inflation. Fundamentally, overall prices rise when demand exceeds supply, and the reverse in deflation. Any sector of the economy could create excess demand by spending more than its revenues, and then use the resulting inflation to shift the economic pie in its favor. In fact, however, government is the only sector that has the financial credibility to outspend its revenue by enough and for long enough to create serious inflation.

As a result, as goes government spending, so goes inflation. This is primarily due to defense spending, as shown in Chapter 1, but nondefense spending is also important. Although not shown in Chart 1-2, state and local government expenditures add to the federal government's share as do government sponsored entities like Fannie Mae, TVA, rural electrification, government guaranteed loans, and many, many others.

Defense spending is highly inflationary since incomes are paid to military personnel and to civilian defense workers but no goods or services are produced that they can buy. Nevertheless, nondefense spending is also inflationary, especially when it produces things that nobody wants or uses, like many pork barrel projects. Building public housing will satisfy political patronage demands, but provides little value if located in areas of such high crime that it is soon abandoned.

Government Efficiency?

Furthermore, there is no bottom line incentive for efficiency in government spending. Quite the opposite, there is every incentive for inefficiency so more resources can be employed and bigger empires built by government managers. Indeed, the term, government efficiency, ranks with airline food, congressional ethics, military intelligence, postal service, tax simplification, vegetarian vampires, beloved mothers-in-law, and other oxymorons. If you don't agree, just take a trip to your local post office. When you observe its workings, you know you're experiencing a technological excursion into the 19th century. Obviously, the more of the economy that is involved in the inefficient government sector, the higher the inflation.

In addition, government spending surges, defense or nondefense, are even more inflationary if they result in big deficits, since government then creates more income than is removed by tax increases, regardless of whether purchasable goods and services result from the outlays. Spending leaps and large deficits almost always go together, of course, since governments seldom raise taxes enough to pay for hot wars, cold wars, wars on poverty, or other costly exercises. Unless the economy is in a deep recession with excess supplies of unemployed but employable people and equipment, demand rises at a time that supply is constrained by capacity. Prices go up.

And inflation works to government's benefit in a reinforcing cycle by inflating taxable incomes. Rising nominal personal incomes move individuals into higher tax brackets. Inflation also creates taxable but artificial profits through increases in the value of inventories and under depreciation of corporate assets. Chart 2-1 shows the clear correlation between federal deficit and inflation.

Furthermore, the bigger the government and the more involvement in the economy, the more likely that there will be inflation by fiat, a term we coined in 1977. This refers to all the ways in which with the stroke of a pen, Congress, the Administration and the regulators can push up prices. Obvious examples include dairy and other farm price supports, sugar tariffs and import quotas, the minimum wage, and Social Security taxes.

Why Was Big Government Tolerated?

Most Americans detest inflation, and the link between government spending and rising prices isn't all that complicated. Why, then, have voters tolerated the rise in the federal government's share of the economy from a few percentage points up until the 1930s (excluding shooting wars) to almost 20% today? To a great extent it's probably inertia carried over from the days when voters saw government as a positive force in their lives, starting with the New Deal in the 1930s.

Whether the New Deal, which touched off this stratospheric climb in government involvement in the economy, can be credited with getting the nation out of the depression is highly debatable. The return to full employment was probably more closely related to the rise in military spending in

CHART 2-1

US Inflation Rate and the Federal Deficit as a % of GDP
1900-1997

PPI Year/Year % Change   - - - - Deficit

5 Year Moving Average

Europe, the rebuilding of the military structure in this country and finally, World War II. Nevertheless, the inclination then was to give credit to the New Deal for the economic revival because the two moved in parallel.

Then the US entered World War II, a popular war from which she clearly emerged as the leader of the free world. This nation was the only major country not in ashes after the war, and was the last bastion against communism in the Cold War period. After the war, the nation entered decades of substantial economic growth. It was also a period of growing government involvement, and the two continued to be associated with each other in the eyes of many.

Excesses, Excesses

Almost any trend that humans create tends to get overdone, however, and confidence in government was no exception. Recall the excesses. By the 1960s, administration economists actually thought they were so adept at controlling the economy by monetary and fiscal means that they could prevent not only major recessions but minor dips as well—the "fine-tuning" philosophy. In fact, those economists were so sure they could eliminate the business cycle that they changed the title of the Commerce Department's monthly, *Business Cycle Developments,* to *Business Conditions Digest.* Those clever folks kept the same acronym.

Furthermore, many in and out of the Administration in the mid-1960s believed that with just a little more government spending, all the social problems of the nation could be solved. Hence the Great Society programs. Finally, many saw the government as so omnipotent that it could afford to fight a land war in Asia and pursue massive domestic spending programs simultaneously—the "guns and butter" concept.

We can easily look back now at how absurd this confidence in government was—confidence that had all the earmarks of a trend peak. And a peak it was, soon to be followed by the aftermath, an era when everything seemed to go wrong. Frustration over Vietnam and the disappointment in Great Society programs that failed to live up to expectations. Tremendous excess demand created by spending on both that sired serious inflation here and abroad, and eventually, the massive global inventory-building spree that resulted in the 1973-1975 recession—the most severe in this country since the 1930s and the first of global significance since World War II.

Even the CIA and Watergate problems were probably part of this reaction phase. They marked, perhaps, the end of the feeling that Washington was omnipotent and above the law. The net result of the "morning after" was a rapid swing of the pendulum away from the extreme of idealistic trust in government solutions to virtually all problems and toward disillusionment and serious questioning of the government's basic role.

Changed Attitudes about Unemployment And Government Programs

Voters also turned on the government because their attitudes about unemployment and inflation changed markedly, beginning in the late 1960s. Earlier, a majority of the population had vivid memories of the depression and its peak 25% unemployment rate, while few people had seen significant inflation. Consequently, unemployment was consistently ranked as the country's number one economic problem in the polls. By the late 1960s, however, the depression-scarred constituted a much smaller percentage of the population and everyone had begun to witness inflation of frightening proportions. Not surprisingly, the polls began to show inflation as the top-rated national economic concern. Furthermore, people started to relate inflation to government spending and deficits.

The Voters Speak

Politicians, as usual, were slow to realize the depth and extent of the electorate's changed mood that began in the late 1960s. Constituents' grumbling over government deficits and inflation after the late 1960s did not seem nearly as loud or clear to most politicians as the distinct melodic tones of the many well-organized special-interest groups. Moreover, increasing government spending and proliferating programs and agencies proved to be an excellent way to build power bases in Washington while maintaining a compassionate concern for the poor and the unemployed.

But finally, the politicians began to see the footprints on the voter ceiling. One early manifestation was the Steiger amendment reducing taxes on capital gains in 1978. President Carter had proposed a capital gains tax *increase* but wound up signing and, of course, taking credit for, a *cut*. The first big voter revolt against big government size and taxes, however, was Proposition 13 in California in June 1978, which put a ceiling on property taxes at 1% of market value. Similar measures soon followed in other states.

The final proof, of course, was the 1980 election. Not only was a conservative president elected, but on the basis of voting records as opposed to party affiliation, so were conservative majorities in both houses of Congress as well. Seen in this light, the conservative sweep in 1980 was not a fluke or a reaction to Carter's ineptness, but the culmination of a shift that had begun over a decade before. And, as of 1994, Republicans are in control of both Houses of Congress, and that body came very close to passing a balanced budget amendment to the Constitution.

It seems clear, then, that the long liberal swing that began in 1932 in reaction to the Great Depression has ended. Even President Clinton, with all of his liberal instincts, says that the era of big government is over. My liberal friends no longer call themselves liberals, but moderates, and those new moderates may be putting the final nail in the liberal coffin by joining in the trashing of their former idol, John F. Kennedy. His philandering has been known for years. I remember my wife's reading about it a decade ago in a book by Jackie's former maid. But now even normally liberal public television is trotting out his sexual exploits and questioning their effects on his performance as President.

If history is any guide, this shift in attitude toward more reliance on markets and the private sector to allocate the nation's resources and away from government involvement which is so inflationary will last for some time.

Washington Responds

On balance, then, it's not surprising that Washington has become zealous about reducing the federal deficit and curtailing spending and employment, and there have been results. Nondefense spending's share of GDP is falling (Chart 2-2). Congress and the Administration stumbled all over each

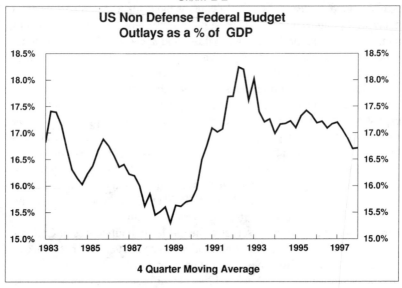

CHART 2-2

**US Non Defense Federal Budget
Outlays as a % of GDP**

4 Quarter Moving Average

other in the summer of 1997 to pass a bi-partisan balanced budget bill. Of course, they had to act fast before the deficit died of natural causes—declining military spending and soaring taxes spawned by the booming economy, the roaring stock market and capital gains explosion, and two tax hikes in the early 1990s. Washington climbed aboard the speeding freight train but naturally took credit for getting it moving.

The federal deficit, much to the amazement of many, is now moving into surplus. This really isn't amazing, however. It simply demonstrates the tremendous revenue generating power of the federal government. All that has ever been needed to eliminate the budget deficit in the postwar era is to restrain federal spending while letting revenues run.

The Federal Government Was the Last to Know

Although Washington finally got the clue from voters, it was the last American political body to know. After the federal government was thoroughly discredited by Vietnam, Watergate, and Great Society programs that didn't work, government initiatives quite naturally shifted to state and local governments. As noted, Proposition 13 in California in 1978 started the ball rolling. Then followed state and local reforms that have since moved to the federal level, such as requiring able-bodied welfare recipients to work in return for benefits, limitations on welfare payments to unmarried women who continue to produce children, term limits for elected officials, and pressure for a balanced budget amendment.

America Is Not Alone

At the same time that America's attitude toward government was changing in the 1980s, Britain, under Prime Minister Margaret Thatcher, made an even more radical shift from near socialism to capitalism. The labor unions were brought under control, many government programs dismantled, and scores of state-owned companies were sold. These actions led to a substantial fall in nominal government spending growth in the 1990s (Chart 2-3). Recognizing the change in voter attitudes, the British Labor Party, under Tony Blair, realized that it had to shift to the right to get elected, and the new Labor government is out conservativing the conservatives. Prime Minister Blair recently proposed tax cuts for business profits and capital gains and measures to encourage the unemployed to leave welfare and enter the workforce.

Canada considers herself a kinder and gentler US—a combination of Anglo-Saxon capitalism and Continental European social concern. Yet Canada has joined the parade recently as fiscal responsibility spreads from the western provinces east to Ontario, where the People's Republic of Ontario government was replaced by the free enterprise, privatization-oriented Harris pro-

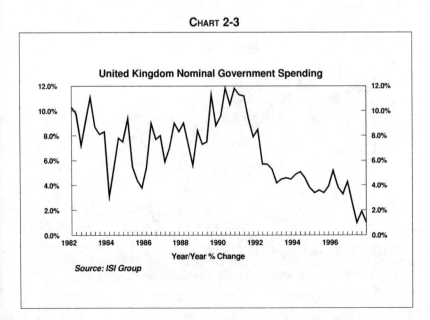

CHART 2-3

United Kingdom Nominal Government Spending

Year/Year % Change

Source: ISI Group

vincial administration. Federal budget outlays are falling (Chart 2-4) and the government's budget calls for balance or even surpluses in fiscal 1998, 1999, and 2000. New Zealand and Australia, too far away and too small economically to receive proper attention, have done bang-up jobs in eliminating government subsidies and spending.

Those Continentals

English-speaking countries, then, are rushing to cut government involvement in the economy. The more socialist Continental Europeans are starting to move in the same direction, but primarily for a different reason. Despite double digit unemployment, European governments have squeezed their deficits in order to meet the Maastricht Agreement maximum, 3% of GDP, that is required to get the common currency, the Euro, started in 1999 (Chart 2-5).

Germany raised interest rates in 1997 and retreated from a tax cut plan, despite falling employment (Chart 2-6). Indeed, she is raising her value added tax this year. The big jump in the Italian unemployment rate (Chart 2-7) has not curtailed budget restraint, and traditional fiscally-loose Spain has slashed government spending growth to almost zero (Chart 2-8), even in nominal terms.

CHART 2-4

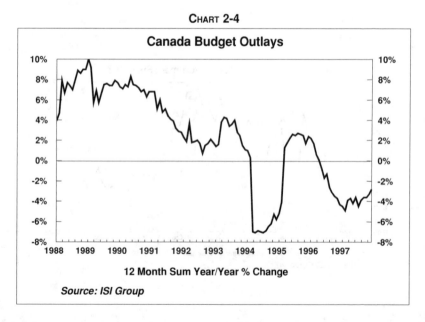

Canada Budget Outlays

12 Month Sum Year/Year % Change

Source: ISI Group

CHART 2-5

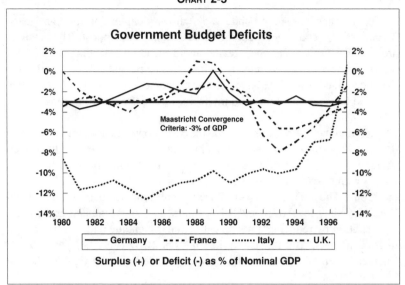

Government Budget Deficits

Maastricht Convergence
Criteria: -3% of GDP

Germany —— France - - - Italy ······· U.K. –·–·

Surplus (+) or Deficit (-) as % of Nominal GDP

CHART 2-6

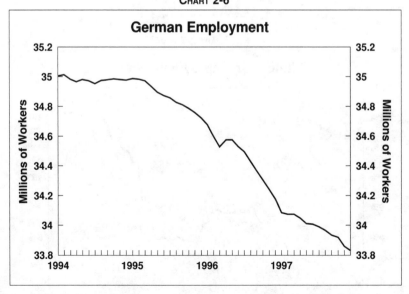

German Employment

The Inscrutable Japanese

Japan has been mired under a deflationary depression for eight years. To get out of it, consumer spending could certainly use a boost. The Japanese are legendary savers and their zeal to avoid spending is leaping (Chart 2-9). Yet, the government is so unhappy with its rising budget deficit (Chart 2-10) that it instituted several measures to raise consumer taxes in April 1997. When you read Chapter 15, you'll find my feeble attempts to scrutinize the inscrutable Japanese.

Without question, wars provide the easiest opportunity for governments to expand their influence and shares of the economic pies. And in the last 60 years, we've seen lots of wars. The war against low incomes that started in the US with the New Deal in the 1930s and ended with the War on Poverty in the 1960s. The hot wars—World War II, Korea, and Vietnam—and the Cold War. Now they're all over, and led by voters, major governments are promoting deflation by reducing government deficits, spending and involvement in their economies. But this is the first of a one-two punch. As you'll see in Chapter 3, central banks are also encouraging deflation by fighting the last war—inflation.

CHART 2-7

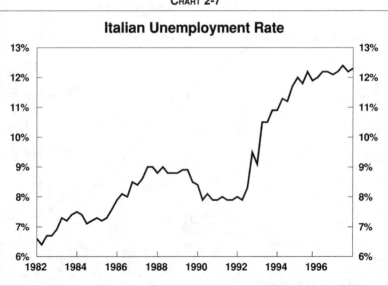

CHART 2-8

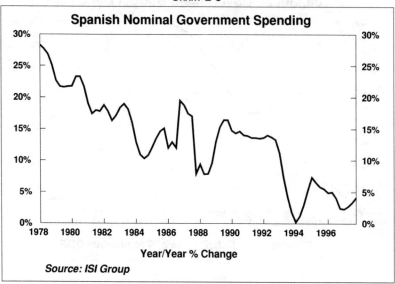

CHART 2-9

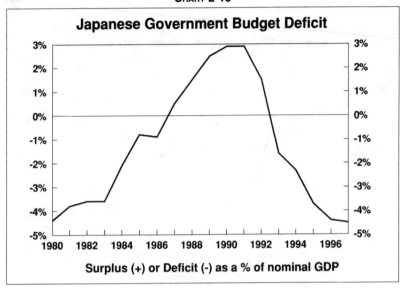

CHART 2-10

Japanese Government Budget Deficit

Surplus (+) or Deficit (-) as a % of nominal GDP

Chapter 3

Central Banks Continue To Fight the Last War— Inflation

I argued in Chapters 1 and 2 that government spending is the root of all, or at least most, inflation. What about money?

I certainly agree that the supply of money has a lot to do with the levels of economic activity, at least in nominal terms, and with inflation. Indeed, the correlation between inflation and the money supply is close (Chart 3-1). The relationship goes back much further, as can be seen from UK consumer prices since 1264 when, as you will no doubt recall, King Henry II was reigning

CHART 3-1

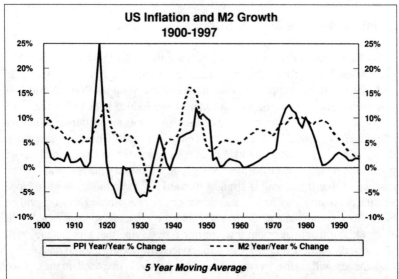

US Inflation and M2 Growth
1900-1997

——— PPI Year/Year % Change   - - - - M2 Year/Year % Change

5 Year Moving Average

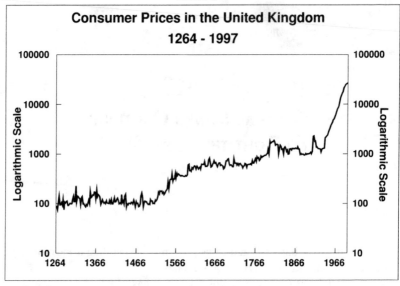

Consumer prices back then, by the way, were
measured by the costs of wheat, one of the few things that many people didn't
produce themselves but bought in the market.

Inflation and the Money Supply

Notice that prices were virtually flat until about 1500, but then in 150
years leaped eight fold. The reason is simple. Money at the time was gold
and silver, and the supply of both mushroomed when the New World was
discovered and its trove of precious metals was hauled back to Europe.

The monetarists, of course, believe that inflation is a purely monetary
phenomenon. Even Fed Chairman Greenspan, probably not counted among
them, said in early 1998 that like inflation, a persistent deflation in prices of
goods and services "necessarily is, at its root, a monetary phenomenon." The
essence of their reasoning is straight forward. If more money is introduced
into the economy, it will get spent and the prices of goods and services will be
bid up to accommodate it. Similarly, if money is withdrawn, prices will fall.

Others would augment that argument by saying that more money will
also stimulate production of goods and services by pushing interest rates down.
Less money will do the reverse by increasing interest rates and, in the case of

deflation, by destroying productive capacity by spawning bankruptcies. Other issues cloud the simple money theory. For example, what is money? Obviously it's no longer gold and silver coins. It isn't even just paper money and checking accounts.

Monetary Policy and Political Reality

The monetary theory, then, isn't as clear-cut as it may appear on the surface. But let's put aside its complications and return to its simple form, because my purpose isn't to discredit it but to show that even if the money supply is the immediate cause of inflation or deflation, it isn't the prime mover as monetarists believe.

Technically, the Federal Reserve, and increasingly other central banks as well, are politically independent. The Fed Chairman is appointed for four years, but he and other board members all have 14-year terms—enough to outlast any President and most members of Congress. The 12 Federal Reserve District Bank presidents, also involved in monetary policy, are appointed by their own boards and are even further removed from political influence. Nevertheless, the Fed pays close attention to the political leanings of Congress and the Administration.

Senior Federal Reserve officers have put it to me this way: The Supreme Court exists because the Constitution says there shall be a Supreme Court. On the other hand, the Fed exists because in 1913 Congress passed, and the President signed, the Federal Reserve Act. What Congress and President giveth, Congress and President can taketh away. For example, a bill could be passed tomorrow that would transfer all the monetary policymaking functions to the Treasury, leaving the Fed to simply count coins and bills.

In the postwar era through the 1970s, the nation's orientation was to accommodate government expansion and promote low unemployment with little concern about inflation. Small wonder, then, that the Fed not only supplied ample credit to help finance federal deficits and increased private transactions demand, but also didn't hesitate to stimulate the economy whenever it showed signs of slipping.

This notion that the Fed is de facto subordinate to the prevailing political sentiments, despite its de jure independence, is the point that monetarists miss. They see growth in money supply as the primary and perhaps only cause of inflation. If additional credit isn't available to fund rising government spending and deficits, they reason, somebody else's spending will simply be curtailed. The net result will be no increase in money demand.

True, but in a practical sense, not very useful. I'd rather focus on the prime mover, government spending, than the intermediate mechanism, the

CHART 3-3

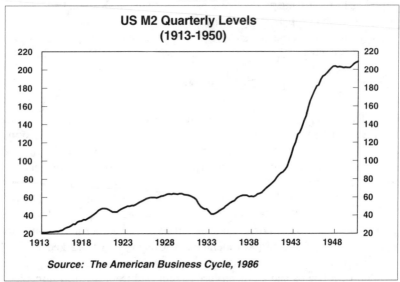

**US M2 Quarterly Levels
(1913-1950)**

Source: The American Business Cycle, 1986

money supply. Otherwise, one might reach the incredulous conclusion that the inflationary bulge in the money supply in the early 1940s (Chart 3-3) was the result of irresponsible credit managers. Of course, World War II was then in progress and the federal government didn't increase taxes enough to pay for its increased spending. That left it up to the Fed, along with Treasury borrowing, to fill the gap. If the Fed had stuck to slow growth in credit, the jump in interest rates needed to get consumers and business to save the additional required amount would probably have pushed rates to politically unacceptable levels, reminiscent of the recent astronomical interest rate spikes in Asia.

The Fed and the Depression

The same reasoning largely exonerates the Fed from a lot of the blame placed on it by the monetarists for that one-third fall in the money supply in the early 1930s. At the time, most businessmen and politicians believed that the depression-inspired leap in the federal deficit was destroying confidence and deepening the collapse. In fact, taxes were raised in 1932 as an offset. John Maynard Keynes did not publish until 1936 his famous book, *The General Theory of Employment, Interest, and Money*, that advocated government deficit spending as the depression's cure. In the early 1930s, a Fed-led flood of money was not acceptable, either politically or in terms of the then-current economic theory.

Besides, the economy, and therefore demand for money, was collapsing faster in the early 1930s than anyone realized as bankruptcies and layoffs spread. Banks were so shell shocked that they did not want to make loans. The monetary authorities would have needed to dump money, literally, out of airplanes all over the countryside to keep the money supply from contracting, and airplanes weren't too reliable back then.

Return to Chart 3-2 with the idea that government spending and deficits are the normal roots of inflation. Note that UK prices were flat from 1650 to 1750 but then again jumped when the struggle for world domination between the French and the British—really the *first* world war—heated up, and rose even faster during the Napoleonic Wars of the 1790s and early 1800s. Of course, World War I made its mark on inflation in the UK, as did World War II and the Cold War. Also, the huge government spending required by Britain's now defunct postwar experiment with socialism was highly inflationary. As a Shakespeare fan, though, I'm disappointed that some of the early shooting, or rather stabbing, wars had little impact on English consumer prices. Maybe

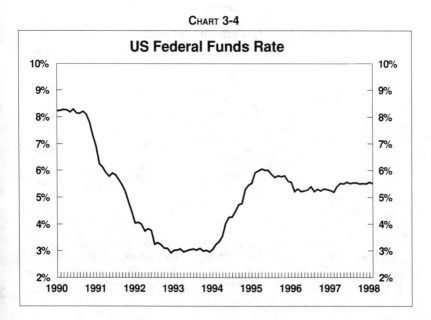

CHART 3-4

the Bard exaggerated a bit the significance of the War of the Roses (1455-1485).

Different Today

As the political mode of the country has changed, so has the policy orientation of the Fed. Since the late 1970s, the Fed has been determined to eliminate inflation, and with considerable backing from Congress, successive Republican and Democrat administrations, and the public. The only problem now, however, is that the credit authorities are still fighting the last war, inflation, and not the next, deflation.

This was certainly the case in early 1994 when the Fed mounted a pre-emptive strike against inflation, ultimately raising the federal funds rate that it controls from 3% to 6% (Chart 3-4). At the time, we thought the Fed was sitting with us in the audience watching the disinflation play unfold on stage. As it turned out, the credit authority was on stage center as one of the principal actors to insure not only the end of inflation, but possibly deflation.

Note that after backing off somewhat in 1995, the Fed raised interest rates again in early 1997, even though inflation rates were falling. It's quite likely that the only thing that staved off further tightening in late 1997 was the

CHART 3-5

CHART 3-6

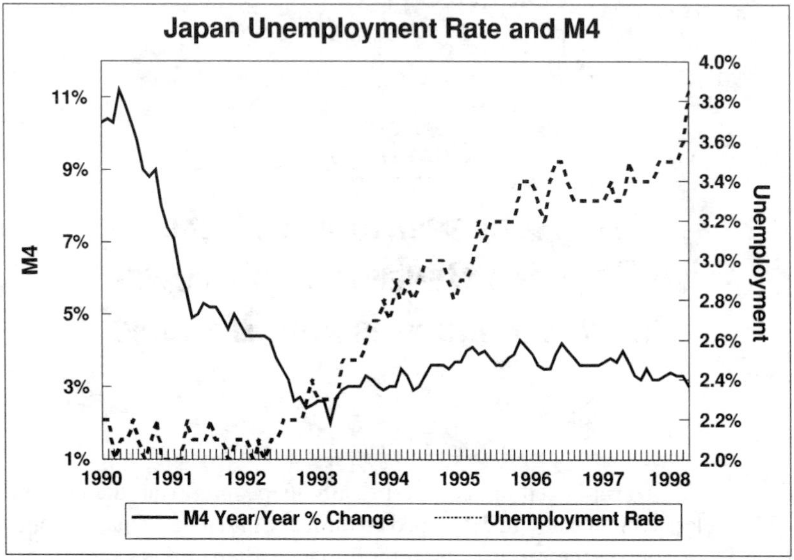

Japan Unemployment Rate and M4

Legend: M4 Year/Year % Change · · · · · · Unemployment Rate

collapse in Asia. On October 29, 1997, Fed Chairman Greenspan said, "It is inflation, not deflation...which serves as the major threat to this expansion."

They're All in the Same Boat

Developed countries' central banks comprise what is probably the world's most exclusive club. And like good club members, they all essentially think and act alike—all are more worried about inflation than deflation. The Bank of England, made independent by the new Labor Government in 1997, lost no time in raising interest rates repeatedly despite no evidence of a surge in inflation. The German Bundesbank also raised rates late last year as the unemployment rate continued to push further into double digits and inflation stayed below 2% (Chart 3-5). Other Continental central banks echoed the Bundesbank's actions promptly with equal disregard to huge unemployment rates. Even the Bank of Japan is doing little to spur money supply growth amid Japan's ongoing deflationary depression and leaping unemployment (Chart 3-6).

Major country governments and central banks are aiding deflation, but so too are the demographics of those countries, as you'll see in Chapter 4.

CHAPTER 4

G-7 RETIREMENTS WILL LEAD TO REDUCED BENEFITS AND SLOWER GROWTH IN INCOMES AND SPENDING

The world is getting older, especially its people. And the process will accelerate, noticeably in developed countries (Chart 4-1). This phenomenon is, of course, the result of high birth rates earlier in this century and extemely low rates more recently. The US postwar baby boom is well known but its importance is magnified by the low birth rates that followed (Chart 4-2). The aging issue is even bigger in Europe and Japan than in the US (Chart

CHART 4-1

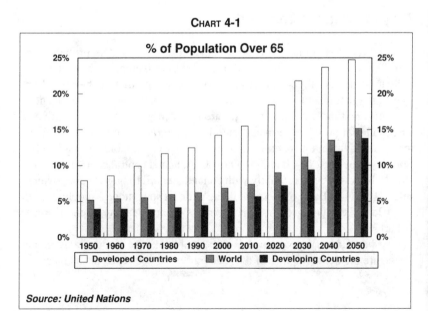

Source: United Nations

4-3). Japan is producing so few people that if current trends continue, her population will actual shrink in time. Similarly, in the European Union, women now give birth to 1.4 babies in their lifetimes, on average, far short of the 2.1 needed to maintain the current population. At this rate, the EU population will decline more than 50% in two generations.

CHART 4-2

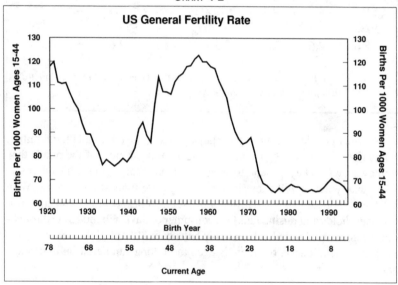

CHART 4-3

POPULATION OVER 65 YEARS OLD			
	1950	**2000**	**2050**
US	8.3%	12.4%	21.2%
Japan	4.9%	16.5%	30.4%
Europe	8.2%	14.6%	25.8%
Asia	4.1%	5.8%	15.9%
Africa	3.2%	3.2%	7.9%
Latin America	3.7%	5.4%	16.7%

Source: United Nations Population Prospects

CHART 4-4

THE RATIO OF WORKING-AGE TO RETIREMENT-AGE POPULATIONS							
YEAR	CANADA	FRANCE	GERMANY	ITALY	JAPAN	UK	US
1960	7.7	5.3	6.3	7.5	10.5	5.6	6.5
1990	5.9	4.7	4.5	4.7	5.8	4.3	5.3
2010	4.7	4.1	2.8	3.9	3.4	4.5	5.3
2030	3.5	3.3	3	3.4	3	3.9	4.9
2040	2.6	2.6	2.1	2.4	2.6	3	3.1

Source: The Federal Reserve Bank Of St. Louis; Organization for Economic Cooperation and Development

Older people, of course, have largely raised and educated their families, bought and furnished their houses and accumulated most of the goods they will ever own. They do tend to spend more on medical and some other services than younger folks, but in general, they are modest consumers. With relatively more of them, and fewer of the younger big spenders who are forming households and raising families, consumer outlays will moderate throughout the developed world, which today buys over 80% of global output. This is clearly deflationary, but there is even more long-run deflation in this age shift.

Too Many Retirees

In future years, there will be fewer people still working for every retiree (Chart 4-4). In the US, the number drops from 5.3 in 1990 to 3.1 in 2040, but in Canada it plummets from 5.9 to 2.6 and in Japan from 5.8 to 2.6. In the 1996-2006 decade, the labor force in the 45-54 and 55-64 age brackets will still be growing rapidly (Chart 4-5), as the postwar babies enter their peak earning years, but notice that the 25-34 and 35-44 groups decline in number. This means trouble ahead since America and most other developed countries' government retirement plans are not savings accounts, but pay-as-you-go schemes. They amount to income transfer mechanisms with money moved from those still working to retirees. This worked just great for the US Social Security system from its inception in the late 1930s (the Supreme Court upheld it the day before I was born on May 25, 1937) up until today. Employment expanded rapidly, more and more workers became covered by Social

Security and therefore were paying into the trust fund, and wages taxed by the system leaped, while retirees drawing Social Security benefits have been relatively few.

But economic activity and wages will grow more slowly in the years ahead as restructuring continues in the US and intensifies in other developed countries, as deflation slows spending while people wait for lower prices, and as US consumers switch from big borrowing and spending to big saving (See Chapter 18).

CHART 4-5

US LABOR FORCE
YEAR/YEAR % CHANGE

	1976-1986	1986-1996	1996-2006
Total	22.5%	13.7%	11.1%
16-19	-12.5%	-1.5%	14.3%
20-24	8.1%	-13.4%	15.8%
25-34	42.9%	-2.2%	-8.8%
35-44	57.3%	34.2%	-3.0%
45-54	4.5%	48.8%	33.2%
55-64	4.1%	2.1%	54.4%
65 & up	4.0%	27.2%	10.3%

% OF LABOR FORCE

	1976	1986	1996	2006
Total	100.0%	100.0%	100.0%	100.0%
16-19	9.4%	6.7%	5.8%	6.0%
20-24	14.9%	13.1%	10.0%	10.4%
25-34	25.2%	29.4%	25.3%	20.7%
35-44	18.0%	23.1%	27.3%	23.8%
45-54	17.7%	15.1%	19.7%	23.6%
55-64	11.9%	10.1%	9.1%	12.6%
65 & up	3.0%	2.6%	2.9%	2.8%

Source: Bureau of Labor Statistics

More important, the burden that retiree benefits under present policies would put on those still working in future years is simply not politically acceptable. By 2020, 25 million more Americans will be getting Social Security checks as the postwar babies retire, at an additional cost of $232 billion in real terms. If they also receive today's level of Medicare benefits, the annual deficit of both programs will run $1.7 trillion. And bear in mind that deflation will increase the real cost of these benefits.

To cover these costs, the current payroll tax of 15% would have to roughly triple by 2040. Add in federal, state and local taxes, and the majority of American personal incomes would be paid to governments. Chart 4-6 shows that in 1989 a retired American man aged 70 could expect net benefits from the government over his lifetime of $50,000 on a present value basis. In other words, adjusted for the time value of money, he'll get more than he puts in. In contrast, the 25-year-old will make net payments of $220,000 under the current plan.

Unfunded pension liabilities are huge, notably in Italy, Germany, Japan and especially in France where they run 100% of current GDP (Chart 4-7). To put it another way, unless present policies change, the gap between government pension payments and contributions will be gigantic in the US and even bigger in Germany and Japan (Chart 4-8). It stands to reason that

CHART **4-6**

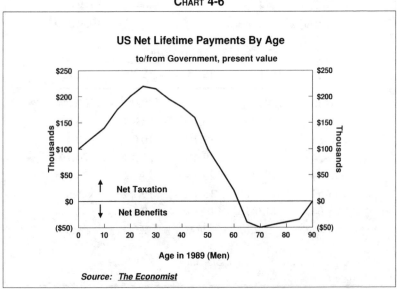

Source: *The Economist*

those working in coming decades will not be willing to see major chunks of their income transferred to the old folks, even if those retirees include their own parents. In the solutions to this problem lie many deflationary forces.

CHART 4-7

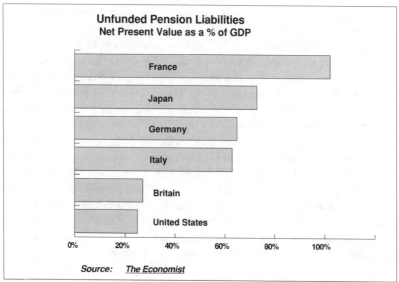

Unfunded Pension Liabilities
Net Present Value as a % of GDP

Source: The Economist

CHART 4-8

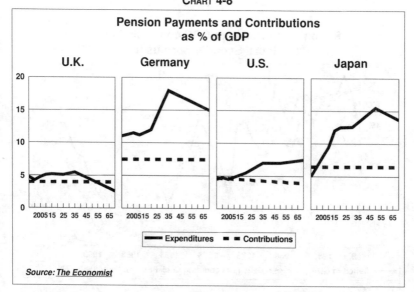

Pension Payments and Contributions
as % of GDP

Source: The Economist

Drive a 1998 Car in 2020?

In the US, most observers want the nation to embark on a massive saving campaign. The federal budget should be balanced and even run a surplus,
they urge. President Clinton asked that any budget surpluses be devoted to
the Social Security system. Indeed, some in Congress are pointing out that the
federal budget really isn't as close to balance as it appears. Note in Chart 4-9
that the Social Security trust funds are still net collectors of money while the
postwar babies are in their big earning years. Many want to encourage saving
by taxing only consumption, and to enact mandatory individual savings accounts, much as in Chile and Singapore. The idea is that by both the government and individuals saving now, the funds will be available to finance the
retirement of the postwar babies.

More saving means less spending, which is deflationary, as would be
federal surpluses, but the problem isn't that simple. What works for the individual doesn't always work for the whole nation. Economists call this the
fallacy of composition. When one person or a small group retires and stops
producing goods and services but keeps consuming, its effect on total supply
and demand is insignificant. Not so for the huge group of people born between 1946 and 1964. When they retire, they will collectively be consuming
large amounts of currently-produced goods and services which they will no

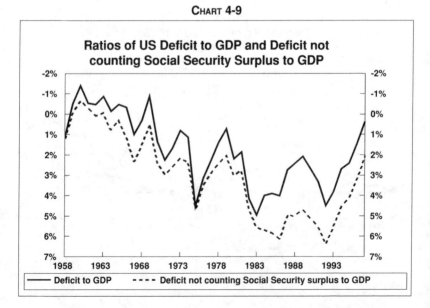

CHART **4-9**

Ratios of US Deficit to GDP and Deficit not counting Social Security Surplus to GDP

Deficit to GDP   - - - - Deficit not counting Social Security surplus to GDP

longer be involved in making. Where will those goods and services come from?

Saving today, by foregoing current consumption, doesn't directly solve the problem since you can't move currently-produced goods and services through time. Services, by definition, are consumed as produced. It's impossible to shift an airline flight people forego today to one in the postwar babies' retirement years. You can't really shift goods through time either. A car that's built but not sold today could be mothballed, but who, except antique car buffs, would want to drive a 1998 model in 2020?

Consequently, even if the postwar babies saved like people do in Singapore, where the national saving rate exceeds 50%, and shoved it all into, say stocks, pushing the Dow Jones Industrial Average to 10 zillion by 2020, they still could end up chewing gum for breakfast. Why? When they stop working, the supply of goods and services would fall. In retirement, they might spend less on themselves and in supporting their kids, and they might have lots of greenbacks as they liquidated their stocks—assuming their collective liquidation didn't kill the stock market. Nevertheless there would not be enough goods and services to go around. The value of their assets would then be inflated away as excess dollars chased a reduced supply of products.

Retire Later with Less

There are other proposals to deal with the feared retirement cost explosion. Raising the retirement age is one, and it probably will be enacted eventually because people now live much longer than when the standard was set at 65 years old. Of course, the resulting increase in the labor supply would be deflationary. Another is to force retirees into HMOs to contain Medicare costs, and this, too, is likely and deflationary.

Another widely-voiced suggestion is to sharply reduce the Social Security benefits for those who make over, say, $40,000 a year when they retire. This, I believe, could lead to big trouble. A critical part of the American Dream is that we will all retire rich. But few employed people today believe they will receive any Social Security retirement benefits, and an income test would make them absolutely sure they wouldn't. Consequently, the little remaining popular support for the Social Security system would collapse.

Foreign Help

Another partial solution would be to open the borders to young, productive immigrants, whose income could be taxed to support the postwar babies in retirement. Attitudes that have surfaced in California—a bellwether for trends—suggest, however, that concern about foreigners' stealing natives' jobs and swelling the welfare roles will intervene (see Chapter 25).

It's also possible to rely on foreigners to provide the goods and services that the postwar baby retirees will consume. The Japanese will basically follow this route. They have been saving heavily for decades and investing abroad, so they can pay for the imports needed to support their retirees by liquidating their foreign assets. Unfortunately, this country's huge trade and current account deficits in recent years have required big imports of capital, so America is now a net debtor nation. These deficits are likely to fade (see Chapter 12) but will probably not turn into a big enough collective surplus to supply the postwar babies when they retire.

Both Sides Give In

To keep supply and demand in balance when the postwar babies retire, they will need to receive less than current Social Security programs provide, while those then working will have to be taxed more to transfer a bigger part of what they produce to the retirees. The net effect will be less spending on both sides. Any remaining gap will be filled by the excess capacity that deflation will bring, and by the further increases in capacity that more savings and rising productivity will spawn in the meanwhile (see Chapter 24). Consequently, when the postwar babies retire, those still working will be able to produce enough to provide themselves with an acceptable living standard and still furnish the retirees with adequate goods and services.

Similarly, retirement bulges in other developed countries, with the exception of Japan, will require deflation-enhancing restraints on the purchasing power of those still working as well as retirees, who will also be required to work longer before drawing benefits. At the same time, more muted spending by both retirees and those still working in North America and Europe will curtail demand for imports from developing countries, another deflationary force.

Admittedly, these demographic issues in developed countries and their deflationary effects will take decades to play out. Restructuring, however, is a here-and-now force for deflation, as you'll learn in Chapter 5.

CHAPTER 5

RESTRUCTURING CONTINUES IN ENGLISH-SPEAKING LANDS AND WILL SPREAD

After World War II, America faced no meaningful foreign competition. The other major countries were prostrate. Indeed, the US economy grew in part by helping Europe and Japan to rebuild. At home, expansion was strong due to pent-up demand. Consumer spending had been curtailed in the 1930s depression years by lack of income and during World War II when everything went to the military. Ditto for residential and non-residential construction. All this catch-up spending was financed by the gigantic liquidity accumulated during World War II when civilian goods were unavailable and people and businesses were essentially forced to save. In this environment, economic activity and real wages and salaries rose rapidly and with little competitive constraints, either domestic or foreign.

Europe and Japan Catch Up

By the mid-1960s, Europe and Japan had caught up with the US, but this was largely unnoticed since the nation's attention and economic activity were diverted by the Vietnam War and Great Society programs. Then came the inflation of the late 1960s and 1970s, which disrupted the US economy even further. It transferred corporate profits to foreign producers of commodities, like oil, that were soaring in price. It also transferred earnings to government, which taxed what were purely inflationary gains—inventory profits and under-depreciation, as mentioned in Chapter 2.

The inflation of that era also hid the growing global competition from American businessmen, many of whom looked at their corporate earnings in nominal terms and missed the pounding they were taking during that decade in real dollars. Most felt duty bound to keep their employees at least abreast of inflation with no idea that their profits were falling far behind. Stock investors, however, were not fooled. The real S&P 500 index (Chart 5-1) fell 62% while inflation raged between December 1968 and July 1982.

At the same time, the productivity growth needed to offset inflation and remain globally competitive was low in the 1970s (Chart 5-2). The postwar babies and older women were entering the workforce as untrained raw recruits. Work ethic declined along with the general collapse in respect for authority and traditional values. Rampant inflation diverted attention as well. Why bother with productive work and investments when there were fortunes to be made speculating in soaring real estate?

The Rude Awakening

The fading of inflation in the early 1980s, however, left American business naked as the proverbial jaybird and exposed not only to strong competition from Europe and Japan but also the fierce onslaught of newly- industrialized countries like Taiwan, South Korea, Hong Kong and Singapore. Imports leaped and many segments of American manufacturing faced virtual extinction.

Fortunately, the response of US producers was to restructure, cut costs and promote productivity, but the process took time to develop. I recall that in the midst of the double-dip recession of the early 1980s, many of our in-

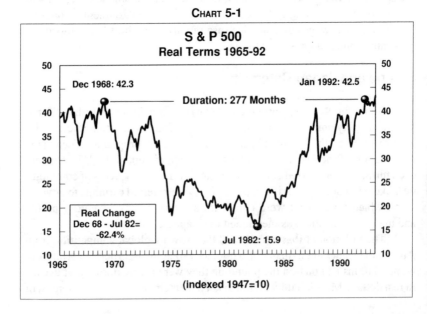

CHART 5-1

S & P 500
Real Terms 1965-92

Dec 1968: 42.3

Jan 1992: 42.5

Duration: 277 Months

Real Change
Dec 68 - Jul 82=
-62.4%

Jul 1982: 15.9

(indexed 1947=10)

CHART 5-2

US POSTWAR PRODUCTIVITY GROWTH			
	TOTAL	MANUFACTURING	SERVICES
1948-73	2.8%	2.5%	2.9%
1973-82	0.7%	2.1%	0.2%
1982-90	1.3%	2.8%	1.0%
1990-97	1.2%	3.2%	0.7%

dustrial consulting clients initially did what they always had done in reaction to recessions. They cut travel, entertainment and advertising—temporary cost cuts that could be reversed rapidly. Several division managers told me that if they did any more substantial and permanent retrenching in recessions, then they would have barely signed the last severance checks before the downturn was over and it was time to rehire.

Substantial Action

As competition persisted into economic recovery, however, it became apparent that much more restructuring was needed. Layers of management were eliminated and then, to make sure they didn't reappear, organization charts were redrawn without all those previous boxes that have a tendency to get refilled. Employees were given more responsibility—and more respect. I recall vividly being told by senior officers of a client that they provided $500 in paint to the employees so they could repaint their rather drab lunchroom on a Saturday, and how amazed those managers were at the resulting improvement in morale.

The restructuring process has only gained momentum in the last 15 years. Part-time and temporary workers (Chart 5-3) are now routinely used to improve efficiency, since they often work only during peak demand periods and usually don't receive fringe benefits. Less and less of labor compensation is fixed as more and more is in the form of bonuses, pay for performance, stock options, etc. (Chart 5-4). It's noteworthy that a leaping portion of retirement funds are 401(k) plans. These have largely replaced defined benefit plans which obligate the employers to fixed pension payments regardless of profitability. Instead, it's largely up to the employee to satisfactorily invest the 401k contributions that he and the employer make year by year. I like this idea, as you'll see in Chapter 28.

The other big fringe outlay, medical costs, have been attacked ruthlessly. In 1997, 85% of employed Americans were enrolled in some variety of managed-care plan compared with 52% four years earlier, saving employ-

CHART 5-3

**US Temporary Employment
as a % of Total Employment**

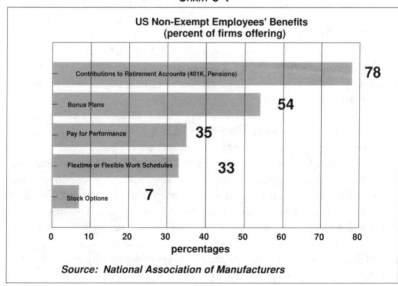

CHART 5-4

**US Non-Exempt Employees' Benefits
(percent of firms offering)**

Contributions to Retirement Accounts (401K, Pensions) — 78
Bonus Plans — 54
Pay for Performance — 35
Flextime or Flexible Work Schedules — 33
Stock Options — 7

percentages

Source: National Association of Manufacturers

ers $40 to $356 per year, according to a recent Mercer/Foster Higgins survey. This shift held medical cost increases to 0.2% in 1997 for managed care plans compared to 3% to 4% in traditional fee-for-service arrangements. Early retirees receiving medical coverage fell to 38% from 40% in 1996, and more were in managed care, 48% in 1997 compared to 30% a year earlier. Some firms charge smokers $500 per year extra for health coverage.

And Even More

Outsourcing is another major component of restructuring with production moving not only to foreign locations, like Mexican border plants or *maquiladoras*, but also to lower cost US locations, and from unionized to non-unionized shops (See Chapter 10). The power of unions has been steadily eroding for 40 years (Chart 5-5). Their appeal has dropped as non-union compensation today often equals or exceeds that paid under union contracts. Also the growth in the economy has been largely in industries like finance, retail trade, and services that are not susceptible to unionization, while employment in heavily-unionized sectors such as mining, manufacturing, construction, and transportation has dropped (Chart 5-6). In fact, without public employee unionization in recent decades, the percentage of the labor force in

CHART 5-5

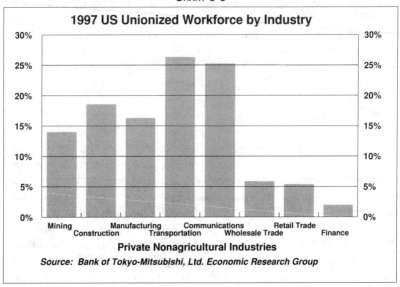

CHART 5-6

1997 US Unionized Workforce by Industry

Private Nonagricultural Industries

Source: Bank of Tokyo-Mitsubishi, Ltd. Economic Research Group

unions would be much lower. Weak unions make it easier to move work to non-union shops and this, in turn, reduces the number of union members and their power.

Another technique for cutting labor compensation, which for American corporations in aggregate is about two-thirds of total costs, is to encourage the retirement of older workers whose pay has crept up over time to levels that exceed their value added. They are rewarded for taking early retirement or otherwise bought out and replaced with younger, cheaper employees—or even themselves, hired back on a lower paid part-time basis. Even after a decade of serious restructuring and in the face of drum-tight labor markets, layoffs continue and have been picking up since last spring (Chart 5-7).

Manufacturing, Then Services

Service industries ranging from health care to retail trade to banking were largely oblivious to the productivity zeal of manufacturers in the 1980s since many faced little direct foreign competition. But pressed, in part by customers who were confronted with the onslaught from abroad, this huge sector, where three-quarters of us work, has joined the ongoing parade. Restructuring and layoffs there are only starting. The undershooting of service productivity growth relative to trend shown in Chart 5-8 means that 15 million more people were hired cumulatively in the 1970s and 1980s to do the

work than would have been the case, had the trend prevailed. The process of
shedding them is underway, but will take many more years.

CHART 5-7

Total US Employee Layoffs

12 Month Average

Source: ISI Group

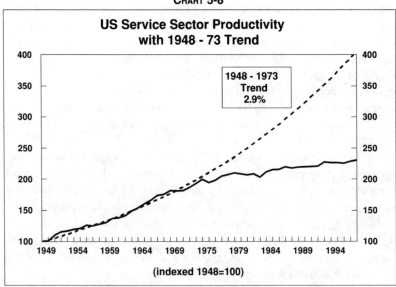

CHART 5-8

**US Service Sector Productivity
with 1948 - 73 Trend**

1948 - 1973
Trend
2.9%

(indexed 1948=100)

As in manufacturing jobs, many service jobs are now being exported. American companies employ Indian and even Bulgarian software engineers who work via satellite at a fraction of the salaries of their US counterparts (see Chapter 10). Visa Card does its credit card processing in Ireland, where skilled labor is cheaper and their next day is still nighttime in the US, so the work is back here by the next business day.

A Permanent Approach

Restructuring has come a long way since the temporary measures I saw implemented in the early 1980s. It has even moved beyond the next phase, which was, in effect, a huge but ad hoc project in the eyes of corporate management. We Americans love well-defined projects that we can rally to take on, complete and then move on. Unlike the Japanese and other Orientals, we don't enjoy never-ending battles.

Maybe that's why we're so unsuccessful at controlling our weight. It's the battle you never win, at least as long as you're breathing. It's also probably why World War II was a hugely popular war. The bad guys were clearly identified, we geared up and beat them and then demobilized—much too soon, as we learned when the Soviets took over Eastern Europe. Vietnam, of course, was the reverse, and we hated it. No clearly defined bad guy. No well defined goals. No end in sight.

When American business got serious about restructuring in the mid 1980s, many of our consulting clients assumed they'd finish the project in a few years. After we reorganize and cut out excess management, outsource, and install just-in-time inventory control, we'll be down to the bits and pieces, they thought. But by the late 1980s they began to realize two things. First, they'd barely scratched the surface of what could be done. Second, the process would never end. Foreign and domestic competition as well as technological changes would keep their business climates in constant turmoil. The need for major cost cutting and productivity enhancement would continue indefinitely.

Not surprisingly, restructuring has been institutionalized in the management training process, both informal and formal, and in business school curricula. And, it can only intensify in deflation. As an example, in recent years, overpaid employees' compensation has been reduced to correct size in real terms by holding pay flat and letting inflation take its course. Not so in deflation when even flat nominal compensation rates produce real cost increases. The result will be more layoffs and more careful compensation administration to begin with.

The Anglo-Saxon Advantage

You learned in Chapters 2 and 3 that other major countries have pursued the same deflationary fiscal and monetary policies as the US in recent years. The same can be said of restructuring, even though the US and the English-speaking countries have commanding leads. When former Prime Minister Thatcher tamed the British labor unions in the 1980s, the door opened for immense restructuring of business, given the near-socialist starting point at the time when many key industries were owned by the government. Voter-inspired changes in government policies also paved the way for privatization and business restructuring in New Zealand, Australia, and, more recently, Canada.

Restructuring has lagged on the Continent of Europe because of the long and cherished history of the social safety nets. German worker welfare programs were enacted over a century ago by Bismarck as he sought to fend off the socialists. These programs, which insured workers against accidents, sickness, and old age, became the models throughout Europe.

France, Italy and other Western European countries also deliberately put primary emphasis on splitting the economic pie more equally, even though many of their leaders realize that in so doing they will not see the pie grow as rapidly as under the Anglo-Saxon approach. Oskar Lafontaine, chairman of the opposition Social Democratic Party in Germany recently said, "The goal of a company shouldn't be to increase the value of its stock. The goal of a company is to assume social responsibility for its employees and social responsibility for all of society." Gerhard Schroeder, the SDP's candidate for Chancellor of Germany next fall said recently, "We will not throw the tested German model overboard only because of a few ideologues."

It Goes Back to the Industrial Revolution

Continental Europe and Japan have responded to the changing external environment more slowly than their English-speaking rivals because of historically different business cultures that reflect the differences in their industrial revolutions. In the UK and the US (New England to be precise), the first industrial nations, it was a gradual, drawn-out affair, very much market-driven and encompassing the efforts of a host of small companies. There was no pressure to reach a particular level of industrialization—indeed to industrialize at all—simply because there was no precedent.

Later industrializers, however, knew they were behind the UK and the US, and equally conscious that unless they too industrialized quickly, they would become second- or third-rate European powers, or in the case of Japan, just another primary-product-producing defacto colony of the leaders. The late industrializers were unwilling to wait for individual entrepreneurs to respond to market opportunities on a piecemeal basis, slowly accumulating their own capital in the process.

In Continental Europe in the mid- and late-nineteenth century, the industrialization process was driven by investment banks, that gathered scarce capital and channeled it to specific industries often with government direction and help. That lay the foundations for the close relationships among government, banks, and industry that is a characteristic of much of European capitalism—but is largely absent in the earlier and more gradually industrialized UK and US. Japan felt the same pressures to industrialize and followed a similar model. In Europe, these sponsored industries quickly became too big and too important to the government's prestige to be allowed to fail. Even today, the French economic landscape is littered with a slew of money-losing, government-owned industries.

The Corporate Legacy Is Clear

The UK and the US may have been the first to industrialize because the UK has the least repressive class structure in Europe, and the US had little at all. Therefore, entrepreneurs had the opportunity to enjoy the fruits of their labors, relatively free of government interference.

CHART 5-9

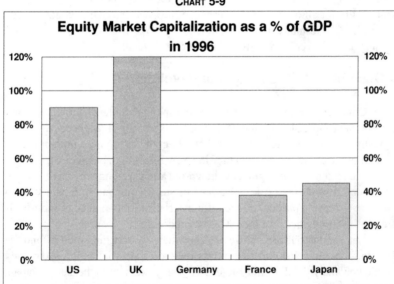

Also, the best and the brightest were not preempted by government service. Even today, entrepreneurs and small business startups, regardless of their prowess, are given second-class status on the Continent. The highest ranking graduates of the leading French universities tend to enter the government, not business. In Japan, the top grads of Tokyo University, formerly Tokyo Imperial University and far and away the most prestigious in that country, head straight for the all powerful Ministry of Finance.

In any event, the legacies of these varying modes of industrialization reinforce themselves and can be seen in the different patterns of company ownership. In the English-speaking model, a much higher share of business financing has been raised on stock markets, and there are far more exchange-listed companies. Chart 5-9 shows that the ratio of equity market capitalization to GDP in 1996 was 90% in the US and 120% in the UK, but less than 40% in the countries of Continental Europe and not that much more in Japan. Continental countries' financing has been traditionally channeled by the banks to large firms. With less well developed equity markets, smaller firms have tended to borrow or rely on internal financing.

A World Bank study revealed that in the US, total bank loans equal 50% of GDP compared with 170% in Germany and 150% in Japan. In contrast, the bond markets, like the equity markets, are much more developed in English-speaking countries. Outstanding US bonds equal 110% of GDP, but only 90% in Germany and 75% in Japan.

And even within the sphere of listed companies, there is a marked difference between the US and UK, on the one hand, and Continental Europe and Japan, on the other. Chart 5-10 shows that in the US and the UK, individuals or their direct proxies—mutual and pension funds and insurance companies—own virtually all the equities that are not held by foreigners. In contrast, in Germany and France such holdings account for only about one-third of equity outstanding and just over 40% in Japan. Corporations and banks through cross-holdings together own over half of the outstanding equity in France and Germany and 44% in Japan.

So the US and the UK Restructured First

These differences in company ownership and business culture explain the different degrees of vigor with which the various countries have pursued efficiency-enhancing measures. The banks and government holding companies that are the dominant owners of Continental and Japanese listed companies are known for working closely with those managements and focusing on the long term. Unlike in the US and the UK, managers there are not slaves to their quarterly earnings reports. But it is easy to see how such collegial relationships can slide into cozy unwritten agreements not to rock the boat and,

CHART 5-10

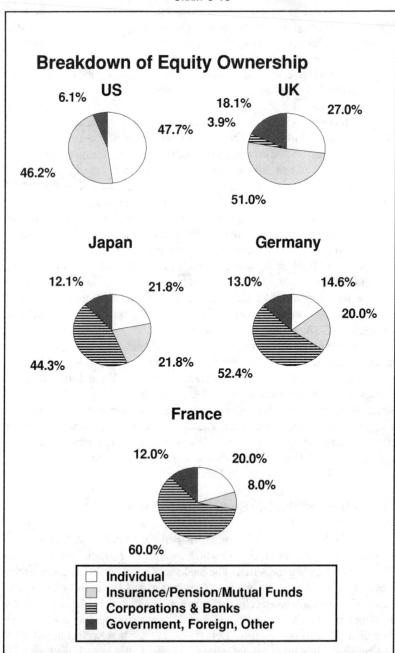

Breakdown of Equity Ownership

US
6.1%
47.7%
46.2%

UK
18.1%
3.9%
27.0%
51.0%

Japan
12.1%
21.8%
44.3%
21.8%

Germany
13.0%
14.6%
20.0%
52.4%

France
12.0%
20.0%
8.0%
60.0%

☐ Individual
☐ Insurance/Pension/Mutual Funds
☰ Corporations & Banks
■ Government, Foreign, Other

consequently, become stultifying obstacles to necessary but painful change. This danger is particulary acute today, when the rapid transformations in the technology and working practices of competitors require immediate and radical responses as the gales of Schumpeter's "creative destruction" rage.

Japan loves such accommodative business relationships, perhaps because that nation only left feudalism 150 years ago. When American occupation forces broke up the large, vertically integrated conglomerates, or *zaibatsu*, after World War II, the Japanese promptly replaced them with *keiretsu*, in which cross holdings of equities replaced formal corporate ties. South Korea's *chaebols*, large family controlled conglomerates, have similar cross equity holdings and similarly, the banks work with the government to distribute the nation's high levels of saving among them. These relationships may be comfortable, but history shows that they miss-allocate capital.

In contrast, UK and US managers face the reality that bad performance will translate virtually instantaneously into tumbling share prices. If such under performance persists, they will either be thrown out or confronted with job-threatening hostile takeover bids.

No Choice

Still the Continental countries know that they must restructure, except possibly for France where the socialist government plans to cut the work week from 39 hours to 35 hours with no reduction in pay. European joint monetary policy, activated when eleven countries initiate a common currency next year, may be tighter than at present in order keep the Euro from being a weak currency. Fiscal policies will also remain tight if the Continental countries live up to their commitments to government deficits of no more than 3% of GDP (Chart 2-5). Consequently, their domestic economies will probably remain subdued and exports will be their sole means of growth.

Indeed exports, which run 25% to 30% of GDP on the Continent, have accounted for around 100% of economic growth of late (Chart 5-11). And exports are vulnerable not only because of their exposure to Asia, as you'll see in Chapter 16, but also because of excessive labor costs. Chart 5-12 reveals that productivity is much lower on the Continent than in the US. In 1996, the value added per hour worked in Germany was only 82.1% of the US level, and after accounting for longer vacations and other factors that reduce German working hours, it dropped to 62.7%

Of course, lower productivity can be offset with lower compensation to hold down the ratio of the two, unit labor costs, but Chart 5-13 shows the reverse to be true. Only the UK has compensation low enough to offset her low productivity. With German pay, including fringes, 80% higher than US level, unit labor costs in manufacturing in Germany have been running almost three times those in this country.

Furthermore, Chart 5-14 shows that unit labor cost performance measured in dollars does indeed inversely correlate well with export prowess between 1990 and 1995. The change in dollar-denominated unit labor costs is on the horizontal axis. On the vertical axis is an OECD measure of relative

CHART 5-11

THE IMPORTANCE OF EXPORTS
1995-IV TO 1997-IV

	REAL GDP GROWTH (ANNUAL RATE)	REAL EXPORT GROWTH / REAL GDP GROWTH	REAL EXPORTS / REAL GDP
Germany	2.2%	80.6%	30.6%
France	2.7%	112.7%	33.3%
Italy	1.3%	133.1%	26.8%
UK	2.8%	73.4%	31.4%
Japan	1.6%	67.0%	13.9%
US	3.5%	32.2%	10.4%
Canada	3.1%	83.3%	38.0%

CHART 5-12

RELATIVE PRODUCTIVITY LEVELS IN MANUFACTURING (1996)

US=100	VALUE ADDED PER HOUR WORKED	VALUE ADDED PER EMPLOYEE
US	100.0	100.0
Japan	73.7	76.3
Germany	82.1	62.7
France	84.3	69.4
UK	67.4	58.2
Canada	68.1	66.5

Source: OECD Working Paper 169 and BLS

export performance, calculated as the percentage increase in the volume of a country's exports less the percentage increase in the growth of its export markets (analogous to a measure of market share growth). The US had the best

CHART 5-13

CHART 5-14

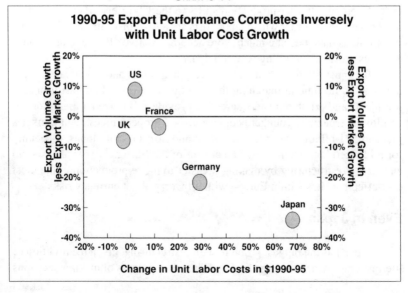

CHART 5-15

German Real Average Hourly Earnings

3 Month Average Year/Year % Change

Source: ISI Group

export performance; Germany and Japan with the worst unit labor cost performance also had by far the worst export performance.

Recently, Germany had begun to show serious interest in restructuring, as high German costs have taken their toll on employment (Chart 2-6). In order to prevent further production shifts to the US or elsewhere, including across the Czech border where labor costs are a fraction of those in Germany, labor unions have become much more accommodative. Real average hourly earnings are actually falling (Chart 5-15).

Italy just lifted her ban on temporary help firms and American companies wasted no time in marching through the open door. Late last year, EU presidents and prime ministers agreed to provide specialized training for unemployed, especially younger people, and the European Investment Bank has pledged $11 billion a year for education and infrastructure loans, especially for mid-sized high-tech firms. The advent of the Euro next year also should encourage restructuring by making it easier to move production to the most cost-effective sites within Europe without worry about currency risks.

Even in Japan

Japan has the biggest problem with restructuring, given the tradition of lifetime employment in large firms and her slow process of making decisions by consensus. As a result, she is even further behind the European Continent in the process. Nevertheless, some movement is starting, especially in financial services.

Lingering financial fallout from the breaking of the 1980s bubble economy is being augmented by new economic and financial difficulties generated elsewhere in Asia. Still, the Japanese government, aided and abetted to be sure by intense pressure from foreign investors and governments, seems committed to proceed with the "Big Bang" deregulation of financial markets, despite some recent backsliding (see Chapter 15). Stock brokerage commissions are being decontrolled. Accounting standards and capital requirements are scheduled to rise to Western standards. And not only will banks be able to own brokers and other financial services, but foreigners will be permitted to buy Japanese firms.

By cutting costs and promoting productivity growth, restructuring is clearly deflationary, not only directly but by pressuring foreign and domestic competitors to follow suit. Cost cutting is manifest. The productivity fruits of restructuring are not as apparent in government statistics, but are probably understated, as explored in Chapter 24. Meanwhile, you'll see in Chapter 6 how restructuring utilizes and encourages another great deflationary force—technological advances.

Chapter 6

Technology Cuts Costs And Promotes Productivity

Americans love high tech and relish the idea of cutting-edge, *avant garde*, thoroughly modern advances. Whether the rise of high tech is the result of its popularity or the cause, expenditures in this area have risen from 0.2% of GDP in the first quarter of 1959 to 6.5% in the fourth quarter of 1997. As a result, graphically (Chart 6-1) it looks like high tech spending has exploded while GDP has hardly grown. This measure, undoubtedly,

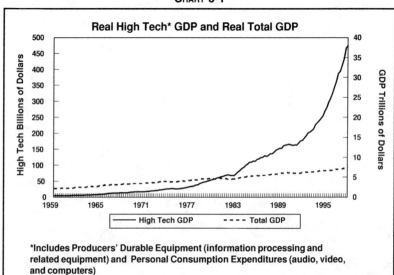

Chart 6-1

Real High Tech* GDP and Real Total GDP

*Includes Producers' Durable Equipment (information processing and related equipment) and Personal Consumption Expenditures (audio, video, and computers)

understates the size and growth of high tech, since it doesn't include such things as semiconductors in cars, watches, and washing machines or gene-spliced seeds, and tons of software that isn't, like hardware, counted as business investment. The Commerce Department estimates that computers and telecommunications have accounted for one-fourth of American economic growth in the past five years.

A big but not the only force behind this current growth is computers and computer-related products. Who'd have thought when computers first came on the scene several decades ago—when there were only a few in government and university research labs, and they took up whole rooms and only ran a matter of seconds before blowing out some of their thousands of vacuum tubes—that today they would be the size of a notebook with many times the computing power.

Americans are probably also enamored with today's high tech since much of it is highly visible—it's sitting on their desks in PC form. In fact, many think today's high tech is history's first. Little do they realize that it's just the latest development in an evolutionary chain that goes back to the beginning of the American Industrial Revolution after the Civil War (See Chapters 20 and 21). A PC may keep your check books and calendar straight, allow you to trade stocks on line, and help you keep in touch with the kids via e-mail, but that's peanuts compared with the transformations that occurred over a hundred years ago in industries like steel, chemicals, paper, and textiles. Think about the glass blowers you've seen in historical exhibits, taking 10 or 15 minutes to blow a bottle. And then think of the bottle machines that replaced them, spewing out glassware faster than they could be counted. And think about the productivity advances when horse-drawn reapers replaced men with scythes, or when cars replaced horses, for that matter. In telecommunications, measure the recent dazzling developments against the revolution of the telegraph, first developed by portrait painter Samuel F. B. Morse in 1838. Once they strung the wires across the continent, it wiped out the pony express, virtually overnight.

I'm always interested in the continual stream of sage comments about how this or that technological breakthrough is more significant than the Industrial Revolution. Those commentators need a tour down history's lane. Until we're capable of cheap inter-planetary movement of goods and people, the Industrial Revolution will, in my view, stand miles taller than all of its offspring.

High Tech Enhances Productivity

This historical perspective, however, doesn't detract from the contribution of today's high-tech to cost cutting and productivity enhancement. Legions of executives, of course, now compose their own correspondence and many of their reports by themselves on computers. Add voice mail to that and you eliminate the cost of a lot of secretaries and receptionists. There are also those employees who, with computers and modems, can do their jobs at home, thus saving themselves the cost of commuting and their employers the cost of office space. The International Telecommuting Association estimates that 11.1 million people were telecommuters in 1997, triple the 1990 number. And what about the entrepreneur who wants to start his own business? The computer lets him be his own accountant, inventory manager, marketing manager, researcher and developer, all in one. For restructuring-oriented CEOs and efficiency-conscious self-employed business people, computers are a boon to lowering costs and increasing productivity. Similarly, telecommunication advances have eliminated the need for lots of business travel and have made it possible to manage global operations much more efficiently.

Cost-cutting and productivity-enhancing characteristics are also dominant in telecommunications, semiconductors, biotechnology, and other high tech areas. Semiconductor-laden pocket calculators are now so cheap and prevalent that some school systems don't even insist that students memorize multiplication tables. In contrast, when I was in high school and college in the Dark Age 1950s, we not only did so, but took a lot more time to gain proficiency with slide rules. Of course, this story of how tough we used to have it never impressed my kids. "What's a slide rule, Daddy?" was their usual reply.

Lower High Tech Prices

Besides improving the productivity of its users, high tech hardware and software are doing so with rapidly falling prices. Last year, Intel reduced prices on its 166 megahertz Pentium/MMX chips by two-thirds. DRAMS, low-end semiconductor chips that provide memory for computers, dropped in price from around $20 a megabit in late 1995 to $2 in 1998. The prices of computers have also been dropping. Notice in Chart 6-2 that all the price changes are negative, and they range from 4% to 25% annual declines. In just the past year, as component and manufacturing costs have fallen, prices on home computers have dropped from the $1,200 to $2,300 range to the $700 to $1,400 zone. With new chip technology, $400 machines are on the horizon.

Consumers took to the cheaper PCs like my honey bees to their queen. Last year 45% of the nation's households owned PCs, a leap from 40% in 1996. Some analysts expect the penetration rate to exceed 50% within several years because of the sub-$1,000 machines. In their first year, the cheaper computers skyrocketed to account for about 40% of the market for retail PCs in the US. The next step, already anticipated, will be a gradual expansion of

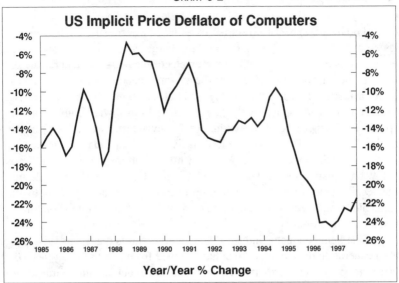

Chart 6-2

US Implicit Price Deflator of Computers

Year/Year % Change

these computers into the corporate market. Many feared that the sub $1,000 PC would replace sales of higher-priced machines while not attracting new buyers, but a survey at the end of last year found that most cheap PCs were sold to first-time buyers. Total unit shipments in the US jumped 21% in 1997, and continued to sell well in 1998 with a 16% rise in the first quarter.

Today each of us carries a load of semiconductors around because the products they're embedded in are so cheap. Inexpensive quartz watches keep better time than the finest Swiss mechanical watch. Anyone who pays more than $50 for a watch today is paying for eyewash. I'm wearing an old mechanical Omega Seamaster that cost many times that, but only because my brother, Bruce, got it for me in Europe 40 years ago. Think of its price in today's dollars.

Twenty years ago, few cars had anything electronic in them, including clocks, which never worked—at least none of mine did. Maybe you were luckier. Now vehicles are overflowing with chips that govern engine ignition, run clocks, automatically time head lights after you leave the car, adjust brakes, etc., The growth in auto electronics will mushroom. Soon you'll be able to replace your car radio with a PC, complete with voice recognition so you can retrieve e-mail and make cell phone calls with both hands on the wheel. Global positioning equipment is in the trial stage.

A Gas Gauge Gripe

I do have one beef with auto electronics, however. I drive a 10-year-old Lincoln Town Car that our kids call "the barge" and whose advanced age embarrasses my wife. Anyway, it has an electronic message center, state-of-the-art when it was built. It records the average speed, miles to a preset destination, elapsed miles, fuel economy, and miles to empty, but in the last case, inaccurately. Ever notice that your gas gauge drops toward empty with the speed of light once it reaches one-quarter full, even faster when there's no gas station for miles? That's because it's attached to a float that drops as the tank empties, and the tank's walls taper in toward the bottom. Once the gas drops below one-quarter, the float drops much faster per gallon used. Well, despite the deceiving accuracy of my digital miles-to-empty readout, it's run by the same old float. I've coasted into more than one gas station, running on fumes, and sweating profusely.

The Semiconductor Industry Association reports that since 1994, new chip generation development time has dropped from two to three years. By 2012 the SIA panel of experts expects producers to put 1.4 billion transistors on a chip the size of your thumb, operating at the speed of 2,700 megahertz. Do those numbers mean anything to you? Not to this former physics major, but comparisons do. Intel's current Pentium II chip has a mere 7.5 million transistors and runs at only 300 megahertz. Also, memory chips in 2012 are slated to hold 275 billion bits of data compared with 16 million today. Let's hope that the quality of the data stored increases proportionally. The investment to produce these advanced chips will be huge, but if history is any guide, so too will be the returns.

Semiconductors and PCs will be far from alone in seeing technological leaps cut prices and open new markets in the deflationary years ahead. Biotechnology is speeding up the development of new pharmaceuticals to the point that some see half of all new FDA-approved drugs coming from biotech firms in five years. I love pork, and we'll probably eat a lot more when genetically-altered pigs fed genetically-altered corn produce nearly fat-free meat. Cotton production promises to expand as costs are cut by genetically rearranged plants that are far less succulent to boll weevils.

Monsanto made a double contribution to expanding soybean production. First the firm developed Roundup, a highly effective herbicide, and then Roundup Ready soybeans that are genetically changed to tolerate the weed killer. The firm expects US farmers to plant 20 million acres of the new soybeans this year, up from 9 million in 1997 (Chart 6-3), and sell more Roundup to go with the increased acreage. Another 10 million acres are planned in Argentina, compared with 3.5 million last year. Monsanto is also

CHART 6-3

TRADITIONAL VERSUS BIOTECH SEED PLANTING
MILLIONS OF ACRES

	1996	1997	1998*
Cotton			
Traditional	12.8	10.6	6.2
Biotech	1.8	3.2	7.0
Soybeans			
Traditional	63.2	61.9	52.0
Biotech	1.0	9.0	20.0
Corn			
Traditional	78.5	74.2	63.8
Biotech	1.0	6.0	17.0

*projected
Source: Furman Selz LLC

touting Roundup Ready corn, as well as corn and cotton that are genetically altered to resist insects. Furthermore, the firm is beginning to combine herbicide and insect resistance in the same corn plant. As a gardener, I don't feel one bit sorry for the weeds or insects—as long as they aren't honey bees.

Despite the fears of the ignorant, genetic engineering doesn't create creatures from the black lagoon. It simply speeds and significantly lowers the costs of what's been done since time in memorium—selective breeding. For example, new cloning techniques for calves will drastically cut the costs of certain human medicines by slashing by two years the time it takes to create a herd of cattle that produces them.

Anything that increases the productivity of its buyer as its own prices fall rapidly normally expands its volume like crazy as it increases its usage in existing markets and opens new ones. The combined effect is to depress economy-wide prices as the high tech sector, with its rapidly declining prices, becomes a rapidly rising share of total economy activity. Chart 6-4 shows how this double whammy is depressing the GDP price deflator. The gap is considerable, and here you're seeing the effects of just computers.

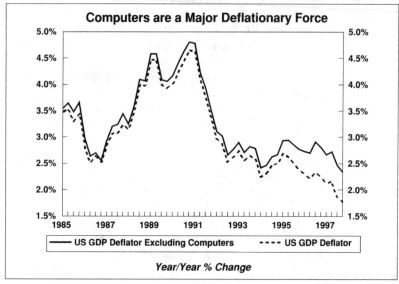

CHART 6-4

Computers are a Major Deflationary Force

US GDP Deflator Excluding Computers   - - - - US GDP Deflator

Year/Year % Change

Radical Transformation

In a 1996 speech, Federal Reserve Chairman Alan Greenspan remarked, "Radical transformations in what we produce in the way of goods and services and how we produce them occur perhaps once or twice in a century at most." Among the examples of revolutionary technology he mentioned were railroads and electric power, and I'd add the post-Civil War Industrial Revolution and autos in the 1920s. Today our radical transformation is coming to us through today's high tech industries, and while they aren't big enough yet to dominate the economy, they still are deflationary (see Chapters 20 and 21).

High Tech Isn't Always the Answer

But before we carry high tech out on our shoulders, singing its praises as the holy grail of productivity enhancement and cost cutting, note a thing or two. Sometimes high tech gives you cost pain but no quality gain, and ultimately it's not just output, but higher quality, more useful, more profitable output that counts.

The wily Rothschilds got early word of Napoleon's defeat at Waterloo via carrier pigeons. They then used that information to make a killing in

British government bonds, which had collapsed following news of Napoleon's earlier escape from Elbe. With today's computers and telecommunications, however, everyone has the Rothschilds' advantage, so no one has it.

The monthly employment numbers, released at 8:30 a.m. Eastern time on the first Friday of the month, are widely followed and can move Treasury bond prices wildly if they differ from expectations. We get them at 8:30 sharp and pay for a lot of hardware and software to do so, but it's all for naught. Everyone else gets the news then, including the boys in the Treasury bond futures pit in Chicago who will beat us to the punch every time. The action may all be over before we can get an order to the pit at 8:31. In fact, instant information can hurt. Quick dissemination of stock prices in the 1987 crash reinforced the collapse and drove stocks down globally as panic set in.

When I first joined the board of directors of a life insurance company about a decade ago, I noticed that every desk had a computer and was told that none existed a decade earlier. I was puzzled. Why, then, did the statistics show that productivity in that industry had actually *fallen* in the previous decade? What were all those computers being used for if not to improve efficiency? I asked the CEO, who told me that a lot of them were employed in designing new insurance policies. But every other company was doing the same thing. Policy buyers didn't benefit much since the new policies were basically variations on the old theme, but the industry competed away the technological advantage of computers. Needless to say, with today's intense competition for the savers' dollars in the financial services industry, those insurance company computers are now put to very productivity-enhancing uses.

Big Econometric Models

Here's another example of where high tech equipment cost a lot but didn't help much. Huge, multi-hundred equation computerized models of the economy were all the rage in the 1960s and early 1970s. They were supposed to quantify the inter-workings of business, government, and consumer activities in all their complexity. For example, the big models were touted to trace through and quantify the effects of a spurt in government outlays on consumer incomes and spending, the resulting increases in industrial capacity utilization and capital spending, and the influence of all these factors on taxes, inflation, and interest rates. These models were supposed to forecast the economy with precision, unsoiled by human judgments and all the biases, hunches, and Kentucky windages of economists. They were expensive in terms of computer and model builder time, but worth it, many believed.

Funny thing, though, they didn't work when they were really needed. None of them picked up the big inventory building spree in the early 1970s and then the collapse into the 1973-75 recession, the worst in the postwar era. To be fair, there's no reason why they should have since their equations were based entirely on postwar data. The last similar cycle occurred right after World War I, and there's no decent data from those years. Only those who realized that the early 1970s events were without precedent in the postwar era, and we were lucky in that regard, got the forecast right.

Furthermore, the econometric boys spent so much time building their models, running them, and adjusting them for past mistakes and nonsensical solutions that they had little time to reflect on the major forces that would drive the economy in the forecast period. There's usually only one or two of them. If you get those right, the rest are just trend projections, and a superior forecast can literally be worked out on the back of an envelope.

Computers and Business Economists

When I started in economic forecasting in the early 1960s, it was routine for each economist to have two research assistants who looked up data in books and government releases and then drew charts by hand. Then it was off to the art department to get the charts prepared for presentations. Each economist also needed a secretary to type reports and retype each draft. At today's prices, two research assistants and a secretary would cost about $120,000, including fringes. Add in about $20,000 for art work and you've got $140,000 in total back-up costs.

Today, one research assistant with a PC and a modem will suffice to download data and draw graphs, and the economist and research assistant can prepare the reports without a secretary. With some help from a desk top publisher, they can turn out finished reports that could only have been done by a professional printer 35 years ago. And at a back-up cost less than half the $140,000 of yesteryear.

I've witnessed, then, tremendous productivity improvements in the business economist business in the last three and a half decades. But how about the quality of the economic forecasts we turn out? I honestly don't believe that we're able to make better forecasts now than 35 years ago. Much more data is available today, but we're drowning in it. The more data you have and the easier it is to manipulate, the less valuable it becomes. Sifting through it and analyzing it can absorb so much time that if you're not careful, you have none left to sit back, reflect, and come up with significant insights to turn information into knowledge, and Frances Bacon wisely said "knowledge is power."

When you're consumed with number crunching, it's also hard to make time to pursue soft data, the anecdotes that can be much more valuable because they're not yet fully understood and exploited. The big model builders aren't the only ones with this problem. And don't forget that in the process of adjusting to rapid technological change, there is a lot of churning and inefficiency as people learn how to use technology that will soon be out of date, and then have to learn its successor and its successor's successor.

While I'm on the subject of how high tech may cut costs but without necessarily improving the quality of output, think about voice mail. How much of the costs that are saved are really just being pushed back on the caller who spends five minutes and several disconnected attempts before getting a real live person on the line? Is it cost effective for a CEO to type a thank you note on his PC rather than tell a crackerjack secretary to compose a letter thanking Bill and his wife for a lovely evening? And is the savings you get by buying things by phone worth the telemarketing calls that always come when you're about to sit down for a nice dinner with your family?

Many current high technologies have developed faster than users' ability to put them into perspective. Let's hope they catch up soon. Still, high tech is a substantial promoter of deflation. So, too, is the Internet, as you'll see in Chapter 7.

Chapter 7

Information via the Internet Increases Competition

Very rarely does a piece of technology come along that can work to benefit both buyers and sellers in the money saving game. Newfangled plows helped farmers raise productivity and lower unit labor costs, but hungry consumers couldn't hit farmers over the head with them to negotiate lower prices for wheat, at least not directly. Today, customers, manufacturers, and retailers are all turning to the Internet to keep more money in their pockets.

Shopping in Your Underwear

For you as a consumer, the Internet offers easy access to information about a product or service, hassle-free comparison shopping, and purchasing in the comfort of your own home. Click on a few icons and you can study sizes, varieties, features, and availability of almost any product you want. You can also examine the range and extent of services, so if one seller doesn't offer exactly what you need, you can go on to the next. You can even shop for a new home without setting a foot outside your own. Real estate brokers now feature pictures and descriptions of every room in houses on the market, so if the bathroom's too small or you don't like the arrangement of the kitchen, you never have to bother to actually see it. Some programs even allow you to redecorate your prospective new house by virtual images.

At Home on the Net

Let's say you find a house you like on the net in Atlanta, but you're also considering a job offer from a company in San Francisco. No problem. The many on-line real-estate directories that are springing up around the Web feature listings in most major US cities, and, surprisingly, in a lot of small ones. The most comprehensive directory of the National Association of Realtors includes more than a million listings. Some listings include maps showing the house's proximity to schools, shopping, banks, and other services. A few provide calculators that let you compare mortgages, the cost of living and salaries in different cities, as well as typical moving expenses and insurance premiums. With a little work, you could find the lowest priced house and the lowest mortgage rate in a city with the lowest cost of living.   You can even by-pass realtors and their fees completely by perusing lists of houses for sale by the owners only.

Information Is Your Best Weapon

Think what the lowdown about dealers' costs can do for you in the automobile showroom, where negotiating is the norm. To check this out, we sent our man-under-cover to a dealer showroom after a session on the Internet. The car he chose was the 1998 Honda Accord DX. *Kelley Blue Book* online showed the dealer's cost for that car totaled $14,445 and suggested retail price was $16,295.   Our man approached a salesman at a typical Honda dealership, offered cash for the Accord DX, and asked for the best price. "Well, because I like you, and it's getting close to Christmas, I can let it go for around $16,395," he replied. After some standard negotiating, the salesman dropped the price to $15,685. Then our man brought out his big gun—the *Blue Book* report printed from the Internet. In his words, "The guy looked at me, then the piece of paper, then dead in my eyes, and said, '$14,945, no lower.'"   The Internet info saved him $740.

But, you may be saying, *Kelley Blue Book* has been around in hard copy for a long time.   Yet, how many people actually consult it?   The point is the consumer is much more likely to arm himself with the information if he can get it with the click of a mouse instead of a trek to the library or book store.

Comparison Shopping

A vital part of the information available on the Internet is price. In essence, it lowers the cost of comparison shopping to near zero. You can visit an enormous number of retailers in a matter of minutes, with no wear and tear on your automobile or yourself.   And you aren't limited in your comparison shopping by distance. You can search out the lowest prices anywhere on the planet. A recent survey reveals that of the 23% of US households with on-line access, over half have used the Internet to research prices. The Commerce

Department reports that 100 million people logged onto the Internet last year, up from 40 million in 1996. There were 50 Web sites when President Clinton took office. Now, 65,000 are being added every hour.

The automobile-buying arena is a good example of firmly established and growing cyber-shopping. Chrysler was the first auto maker to launch its own Web site in 1995, and since then just about every auto maker has joined it online. General Motors' online service, GMBuyPower, lets consumers compare prices on GM and rival vehicles, search dealer inventories, and get a dealer's best price. If you don't want to take the time to hit the manufacturers' sites, you can one-stop shop at independent services that charge dealers a fee to represent them, market their products and prices, and refer the potential customer directly to the dealer. The customer is charged nothing extra for the service, and the only time he goes to the dealership is to pick up the car and pay for it. Auto-By-Tel, an online service based in California, reported that it had served 1,000,000 customers since it started in 1995 and was handling 100,000 purchase requests a month at the end of 1997.

Insurance Industry Next?

Life insurance is also likely to feel the impact of cyber-shopping. To see firsthand, we created a potential customer—healthy, 31-year-old non-smoking male—and went in search of a very standard policy—$350,000 in convertible and renewable 10-year term life insurance. First, we contacted two insurance agents by phone. One quoted a premium of $323.50 per year. The other was even higher—$337.50. But on the Internet we found four quotes—$234.50, $283.50, $267.50, and $316.00—all below the telephone quotes.

Equally interesting, we thought, was the variation among the Internet quotes. Guess which way the prices will gravitate. Certainly not up. To be sure, most people don't deliberately shop for life insurance. It's sold, not bought, especially the more complicated policies that build up cash value over time by, in effect, combining a term policy with a tax-free savings account. Still, the Internet does offer savings for those seeking straight-forward term insurance, and an increasing number of other insurance products.

What about Actually Buying?

So far the most widespread use of the Internet for shopping has been in gathering information and comparison shopping. What about actually completing sales in the cyber-market place? About 7 million households made on-line purchases during the second half of 1997, compared with 3.2 million in the same 1996 six months. And, some were repeat buyers, purchasing goods and services an average of 1.7 times during that period, compared with 1.0 times in the latter half of 1996. Still, the market is small, in part because many on-line sellers are only offering convenience and aren't giving customers lower prices to match their lower overhead. Pressure to achieve sales volume should change this, however, and there are already important examples.

Amazon.com book sellers have pioneered in that area, and as Charts 7-1 and 7-2 show, the firm's net sales and number of accounts have gone straight up. To see how Amazon's prices compared with those of traditional book stores, we shopped for some of our favorite books there and at a low-cost mass merchandiser (see Chapter 8). On average, Amazon's prices were 20% lower.

Online stock brokerage business has helped force commissions to as low as $7.95 per trade, and that's still profitable for discount brokers. They can make money on the other side of the transaction, offsetting the compression in their margins with increased volume and gains from margin loans and stock lending. And, the online brokers are forcing full-service firms like Merrill Lynch to jump into the Internet pool in order to stay competitive.

Although most of the 120 insurance company Web sites we analyzed offer only customer support, product information, and online policy quotes, 1% offer interactive customer service or online sales. Also, about 1% of all US airline tickets—which amounts to more than 4,000,000 tickets a year—are sold through the Internet. For the airline companies, this bypasses travel

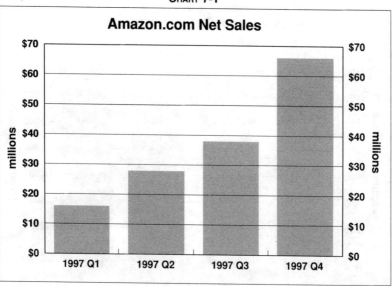

CHART 7-1

Amazon.com Net Sales

agents. Since the early 1990s, airlines have progressively reduced travel-agent commissions, which rank below only labor and fuel as the industry's third highest cost. The Internet alternative to travel agents may have spurred this trend, which is likely to continue. The Commerce Department forecasts Internet bookings in the travel industry to rise to $8 billion by 2000, up from $1 billion in 1997.

Internet in the Seller's Corner

Airlines aren't the only industry using the Internet to cut costs. Back in the auto arena, those same dealers who are having their prices compared by the armchair shoppers are also slashing their advertising costs and sales commissions by selling through the Internet. One dealer pointed out that a full-page advertisement in a Sunday newspaper cost him $3,000, which was as much as the Internet cost him in a month. The same dealer runs his Internet operation with two employees who are paid salaries instead of higher cost commissions, so he can sell at lower prices.

Brickless Banking

The banking industry is also jumping into the Internet with both feet and finding the cost savings invigorating. Everybody understands how elec-

CHART 7-2

tronic transactions are more efficient, but the Internet creates even greater productivity. It typically costs 90 cents to two dollars every time a customer does a transaction with a bank teller. That falls to about 40 cents at an ATM, but costs around a nickel on the Internet. Major banks plan to quadruple their investment in the Internet. Of corporate banks without a Web site in 1997, 65% plan to build one soon, and 42% plan to have advanced sites offering complete interactive corporate banking. The industry predicts that 39% of corporate customers will use some form of Internet banking within three years.

If experience with direct banking using ATMs, direct deposit, etc., is any indication, Internet banking should push expense-to-revenue ratios down considerably. The current average ratio for major US banks is 60%. Direct banking produces ratios in the 35% to 40% range. Projections are that Internet banking could achieve 15% to 20%. Banks have yet to pass this savings on to customers, and in fact, some impose a surcharge for online transactions. Small wonder that only 15% of households with Internet access do electronic banking. Here again, though, zeal on the part of banks to build volume and competitive pressures from the likes of Intuit and Microsoft should force fees lower.

E-Mail And Cheap Data

And don't forget what the Internet and e-mail can do to cut costs by transmitting data quicker and cheaper. In terms of communicating with his parents, our son Geoff, a product manager at Microsoft, doesn't know what a postage stamp looks like, but he's always available by e-mail and even sent us a picture of his new boat. Also, the Internet makes it possible for telecommuters to use much of the technology described in Chapter 6. In 1997, 3.6 million wage-and-salary workers were employed at home, up from 1.9 million in 1991.

Despite what I said in Chapter 6 about being swamped by data these days, I'm delighted with the tremendous scope of information available on the Internet. In our business it saves us countless trips to the library and hours of time spent thumbing through reference books. For example, in writing this book, besides searching for economic and financial data, we used the Internet to find out when Commodore Perry visited Japan (twice, in 1853 when he was rebuffed and in 1854 when he returned with lots more convincing firepower, see Chapter 21), and to do our research on auto and term life insurance policy costs. We also found on the Internet the prices of pressed glass goblets in the 19th century (Chapter 21), the dates of the Irish potato famine (1845-47, mentioned in Chapter 23), the number of days the Hong Kong stock market closed after the 1987 crash (Chapter 27), and the all important SIC codes for manure spreaders that you'll want to learn more about in Chapter 12.

Then there is the global use of the Internet which, along with another great productivity enhancer, FAX machines, has spread information that keeps international competition in line. Commerce on the Internet, barely existent until recently, may exceed $300 billion by 2002, according to the Commerce Department, as more firms go online to cut purchasing costs, oversee branch operations, control inventories, and solicit new business. The Internet also may be speeding economic reforms and deflation-enhancing market liberalization by letting people in closed economies know what's happening in other parts of the world. The Chinese government is concerned enough about the resulting challenges to its control that it has tried to limit Internet access. In this country, stockholders can vote their shares in a growing number of corporate annual meetings.

Are We Ready?

Even if it is cheaper to buy and sell on the Internet, are Americans willing to learn and use a whole new way of doing business, or do we need to wait for the older generation to fade from the scene? Did Great-aunt Bertha ever learn to use the telephone? Even though electric motor-driven machinery offered huge productivity advances by the late 1800s, factories were slow to abandon the overhead power shafts that often ran the length of the building and transmitted power to individual machines by long leather belts. In 1899, only 3% of US manufacturers used individual motor-driven machines. At the beginning of the 1920s, it was a third, but exceeded 50% by 1929. Old habits die hard.

Still, we may be more used to rapid technological changes in our lives today and have developed more technical savvy. In the last four years, the percentage of households owning PCs equipped with modems rose from 12% to 30% and is projected to leap to 47% by the year 2000. Chrysler Corporation's studies show that 70% of new-car buyers have access to a computer, and 45% say they will consult the Internet the next time they buy a car, compared with about 15% who do so now. And auto market researcher J D Power & Associates reported that 16% of new car buyers used the Web for shopping last year, up from 10% in 1996.

As the volume of Internet sales goes up, prices will come down. The same can be said for mass distribution, as discussed in Chapter 8.

CHAPTER 8

MASS DISTRIBUTION TO CONSUMERS REDUCES COSTS AND PRICES

Ever since the Great Atlantic & Pacific Tea Company introduced the idea of chain stores in 1859, the principles of mass marketing have been employed by enterprising US retailers to cut costs and underprice their competitors. The best ideas were adapted and enhanced by the first department stores—Macy's, John Wannamaker, and Marshall Field; the first mail-order houses—Montgomery Ward and Sears; and the most successful early chain store—F. W. Woolworth's.

Today the advantages of volume buying are being exploited to the hilt by such booming mega-retailers as Walmart as well as Office Depot in office supplies; Bed, Bath and Beyond in home furnishings and equipment; Revco and CVS in drugs and sundries; and Borders and Barnes & Noble in books. As you've no doubt seen first hand, the buildings that house these stores cover city blocks, and you feel like you need a road map to get from one end to the other. Or, in my case since I have no sense of direction, I could use a ball of string when I walk through the front door. If you doubt the ability of these giants to sell at lower prices than their smaller competitors, ask the proprietor of any locally owned drug or book store—if you can find one. Most have already fallen by the competitive wayside.

Exhibit 1 — The Auto Industry

One of the best examples of the deflationary effects of expanding mass distribution is the US auto industry. It has a host of complex and deep-rooted problems to start with:

- Costs, especially for labor have risen faster than car buyer incomes for decades.

- Detroit kept monthly auto payments affordable by extending repayments from 35 to 56 months. But many owners let their cars be repossessed when remaining payments exceed the cars' values.

- Detroit then pushed leases, which kept the game going since they require low or no down payments, and the captive auto finance company gets the residual value.

- Expiring leases, however, are depressing used car prices, making them attractive alternatives to new cars, and are also reducing trade-in values for those who own their wheels.

- Greatly improved quality makes cars last much longer, and the stigma of buying a late model used car has faded.

- With better quality and previous excessive buying, the nation's auto fleet is under-aged.

- Cars are big discretionary purchases that will be postponed as consumers shift from borrowing and spending to saving (see Chapter 18).

- Detroit shows little sign of curbing the UAW and labor costs.

- Worldwide capacity is excessive and scheduled to become even more so.

- The strengthening dollar and Asian meltdown will flood the US with Japanese and other imports at lower prices.

Retailing Redone

On top of all these woes, Detroit is also facing a huge blow from the Walmart syndrome, the growing loss of control of its distribution system. About 25% of a vehicle's costs are in distribution—sales, transportation, and advertising. In today's world of retailing efficiency, this is unsustainably large. And it's on its way to being slashed.

Big, no haggle, service-oriented used car superstores, like those run by CarMax Group which is controlled by Circuit City Stores and the Auto Nation USA unit of Republic Industries, are growing. They are also buying new car dealerships and putting together huge chains that sell a wide variety of cars. Among those, Republic Industries had $2.5 billion in 1996 revenues, Hendrick United Auto Group $7.3 billion, and United Auto Group $1.8 billion. In contrast, the average US dealer's sales are about $20 million. These mega dealers will also be easy entry points for foreign producers like Fiat, Peugeot-Citröen and Renault to enter or re-enter the American market without setting up expensive dealer networks. More competition for Detroit.

The Walmart Syndrome

Put all this together and you will end up with cars being sold like refrigerators. Armed with prices and model information supplied by the Internet (See Chapter 7), a customer will walk in the door, view all the competing models side by side, listen to the salesperson explain the features, check the no-haggle prices, and then pick the color and options, arrange the financing and be out the door in an hour. No longer will the customer have to drive from one dealer to another and be accosted by fast-talking salesmen in shiny suits who never seem able to give straight and consistent stories on the cars' specs or prices.

Note carefully, the oncoming retailing method will make cars much more like commodities as many fewer distributors carry a wide variety of competing models. That will increase the power of the retailers and reduce the control of auto manufacturers. I wonder if Detroit knows the implications of its actions when it helps mega-dealers buy up franchises. Those dealers may become like the Walmarts or Home Depots of the world that control such huge volumes that they can dictate price, features and quality to even giant producers like Proctor & Gamble. What does that do to manufacturers' margins? Ever talk to a Walmart supplier? He'll give you an earful of his love-hate relationship.

Fighting Back

Are the auto makers worried about the superstores? They seem to be. Each of the big three is in the beginning stage of creating its own mega dealers. Ford recently tried and failed to consolidate dealerships in Indianapolis and Salt Lake City. General Motors has purchased a large parcel of land close to a busy shopping mall in New Jersey, where it plans to sell all seven of its brands under one roof. It is also working to consolidate dealerships in the San Fernando Valley. Toyota and Honda are attacking the enemy head on. They went so far as to sue Republic Industries in Texas and California to slow its purchase of new dealerships.

If the manufacturers are worried, the small dealerships are terrified. The National Association of Automobile Dealers puts the profit per car sale at

$77. That doesn't leave the average dealer much leeway to afford a fight with Republic Industries and other super stores' economies of scale. Many are simply too inefficient to compete.

Another example of the growing power of mega retailers can be found in magazine distribution. About two and half years ago, major supermarket chain Safeway ended the cozy relationship between magazine wholesalers and retailers by putting its business up for competitive bidding. Other large supermarket and drug store chains followed, and the number of independent distributors dropped from 180 in 1995 to 60 at present. Before the consolidation, retailers paid wholesalers 80% of the magazine's cover price. Now it's in the 70% to 75% range. Since wholesalers still pay publishers 60%, they are being forced to either cut costs, merge, or exit the magazine distribution business.

The Other Extreme

At the other end of the distribution scale, a deflationary force can be seen in women's apparel. If you don't want to go to mega-stores, or even malls, you can buy clothes at home, or at the home of a good friend. In living rooms across the nation, women are gathering to visit with their friends and shop for upscale clothing at the same time. I know about this enterprise first-hand, because my wife is a long-time consultant for New York-based Carlisle Collection. Along with the top-of-the-line dresses, blouses, and slacks, customers are attracted to the ease and intimacy of shopping at the home of the consultant (whom they often know socially), lots of help in choosing and coordinating outfits, and the consultant's reassurance that they won't meet other women in their social circles wearing the same outfit. Heaven forbid!

The only way traditional clothiers, operating in boutiques and malls, can compete with this kind of service and draw customers back is to lower prices. Since home sales of clothes and lingerie more than doubled from 1994 to 1996, according to the Direct Selling Association, they'll need to do a lot of lowering.

Without question, mass distribution cuts costs and is deflationary. So, too, is deregulation, covered in Chapter 9.

Chapter 9

Ongoing Deregulation Cuts Prices

Deregulation is nothing new. It started decades ago in the US. Federal and state resale price-maintenance laws, a carryover from the 1930s and designed to prevent deflation, were among the first to go. They allowed manufacturers to set minimum retail prices on their wares, but were widely circumvented by discounters who sold off-brand as well as different models of well-known products. Deregulation is deflationary. It opens to the bracing winds of competition areas where prices were previously fixed, and, consequently, where producers had limited incentives to cut costs and promote productivity. The electric power industry is a clear case in point. Australia, a pioneer in electricity deregulation, saw prices collapse by 40% and today is home to the lowest electricity prices in the world.

Electricity deregulation bills have already passed in California, Massachusetts, Illinois, Rhode Island, New Hampshire, Montana, New York, Maine, and Pennsylvania. Congress and the Administration have made proposals that would require unrestricted selling of electricity to customers early in the next decade. Originally, consumers in California and New England expected to save 10% on their bills, but when critics denounced deregulation plans as "utility bailouts" that would benefit mainly power companies and their large industrial customers, regulators in several states stepped in to give residential users a larger share of the savings. Note that users like manufacturing plants and office buildings already receive discounts of 25% or more after threatening to build their own power plants or move factories to lower-cost areas.

Residential vs. Industrial

Massachusetts legislators, bombarded by consumer groups, approved a new plan to cut rates at least 15% by 1999 for all power users, big and small.

Illinois Governor Jim Edgar signed a bill granting 15% rate cuts for Commonwealth Edison customers this year and an additional cut of 5% in 2002. New York approved a plan that will eventually cut rates by 7.5% for residential customers of Rochester Gas & Electric Corporation. One way for regulators to foster deeper rate cuts is to reduce the portion of "stranded costs" that utilities are permitted to pass on to customers. These are investments in uneconomic power facilities, especially nuclear power plants, that will become particularly burdensome as competition is introduced and rates fall. Under current deregulation plans, new electricity providers will collect surcharges to pay off at least part of these past investments.

Speeding up the Timetable

One of the electricity innovators, Enron Corporation, is pushing hard for deregulation and is not content to wait while legislatures leisurely formulate their plans. In a move that ultimately opened up the market in Philadelphia years sooner than anticipated, the Houston-based firm offered to cut electricity rates by twice the reduction being proposed by Peco Energy Corporation, the established provider. A veteran of natural gas deregulation in the 1980s, Enron knows what tumbling prices are all about. The corporation expects more than half the US power market will be open to competition within four years and estimates that full deregulation will reduce consumer electricity bills by 30% to 40% or $70-$80 billion a year.

Citizens for a Sound Economy, a Republican think tank, predicts that deregulation will lead to a drop of at least 43% in consumers' electricity bills. That's significant since the electricity industry accounts for roughly 4% of GDP. Also, note that electric power and natural gas are merging into one huge $315 billion industry in which suppliers will deliver to customers whatever energy mix is the most cost effective.

As another example of recent deregulation, or at least more rational regulation, the US Department of Agriculture, pushed by Congress and the courts, is junking its earlier byzantine milk pricing scheme, which proved more a boondoggle for dairy farms far from the efficient Wisconsin center of the industry than a help for consumers. New proposals should encourage more efficient production and, therefore, lower milk costs. And, of course, Congressional action several years ago allows farmers now to plant whatever they like without any acreage restrictions.

Flying High

US truckers were deregulated in 1978, and trucking rates collapsed overnight as the need for empty back hauls disappeared and nonunion carriers mushroomed. The airline industry is deep into deregulation, but it's still going on, especially in the international arena, and depressing prices in the process. The US led the way with the Airline Deregulation Act of 1978. Previously, the Civil Aeronautics Board regulated airlines, controlling the number of airlines, the fares they charged, and the routes which each was allowed to fly. According to a 1996 General Accounting Office report, prices adjusted for inflation dropped by 9% at small community airports, 10% at medium-sized airports, and 5% at large airports between 1979 and 1988 as market forces took over (Chart 9-1).

Furthermore, service increased. In 1995, according to the Department of Transportation, 55% of passengers traveled in city-pair markets served by three or more carriers, up from 28% in 1979. New carriers, such as Southwest Airlines, have concentrated on select routes and achieved lower costs than larger carriers, forcing bigger airlines to follow suit. Overall, the number of flights available from airports serving large communities increased by 68% between 1978 and 1995 (Chart 9-2). And Washington continues to push for free competition. Recently, the Justice Department began investigations to determine whether large airlines are using predatory prices or other means to keep smaller carriers out of the hub airports that the majors dominate, and the Transportation Department has shown similar concern.

CHART 9-1

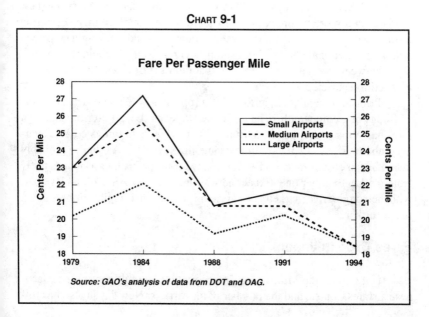

Fare Per Passenger Mile

Source: GAO's analysis of data from DOT and OAG.

CHART 9-2

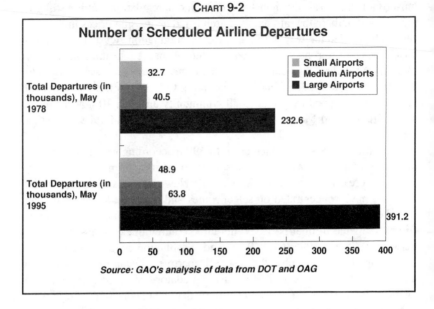

Number of Scheduled Airline Departures

Small Airports
Medium Airports
Large Airports

Total Departures (in thousands), May 1978
- 32.7
- 40.5
- 232.6

Total Departures (in thousands), May 1995
- 48.9
- 63.8
- 391.2

0　50　100　150　200　250　300　350　400

Source: GAO's analysis of data from DOT and OAG

Europe Follows

Full deregulation for European airlines went into effect April 1, 1997. As in the US, lower airfares, new carriers, established carriers' entry into new markets, and more complex pricing should follow. Before then, European airlines were prohibited from operating routes that did not originate or end within their national borders. For example, a French airline couldn't operate a route between two cities in Germany that didn't start or end in France, and competition suffered.

Prior to deregulation, airfares in Europe averaged about twice the cost of flights of a comparable distance in the US, even though French excursion fares had already dropped 25% from 1995 to 1996, and fare decreases averaged about 10% in Germany in the same time period. As you're probably aware, it can cost as much to fly between two European cities as it does to fly from the US to either one. Expect new airlines such as Air UK and Ryanair, with their aggressive marketing and pricing, to assist in bringing airfares down much further.

Fares Drop in Japan

Until 1996, the Ministry of Transportation had full control over Japanese airfares, routes, and the number of air carriers. Now Japan also has followed the US lead and has allowed airlines to start setting their own ticket prices. Provided that the traveler follows guidelines that are similar to those in the US (such as booking in advance and non-refundability), ticket prices have become less expensive. Peak, as well as off-peak, fares have been introduced, too. Before deregulation, a one-way ticket for Japan's most-traveled air corridor cost 23,000 yen. Now, the peak rate for that flight is 25,000 yen, and the off-peak rate is 20,000 yen. But, if one books the flight in advance, and accepts all the conditions, the prices is only 11,200 yen. The Ministry of Transportation has finally allowed additional airlines into the domestic market this year, and they will challenge high-cost carriers like Japan Airlines with lower rates and lower fares.

The international skies are opening as well. US officials have negotiated packs with Europe and Japan to allow more airlines to fly to more cities abroad. Foreign governments have dragged their heals for fear of being swamped by US airlines, but the trend is clear. To date, bilateral packs between the US and 12 European countries allow carriers to sell tickets on each other's flights. Furthermore, as you'll see in Chapter 23, international trade in general continues to be deregulated as tariff and non-tariff barriers fall.

Financial Services Deregulation

One of the hottest areas of deregulation continues to be financial services. It started with US stock commission rates in the early 1970s. Brokers vehemently believed in free enterprise, of course, with one tiny exception: in the setting of their own fees, which were controlled by the NY Stock Exchange and blessed by the SEC. These fees were set to cover the costs of 100-share trades, typical for individual investors who dominated the market until the 1960s. However, the same commission levels spawned unconscionable profits when pension and endowment funds and other institutional investors started buying 10,000-share blocks.

On May Day 1975, however, all restrictions on commissions were removed and competition began to blow the leaves off that famous buttonwood tree under which the New York Stock Exchange was formed in 1792. As shown in Chart 9-3, commission rates in 1975 fell only 2.3%, but by 1978, the cumulative declines reached almost 40%. In one sense, financial institutions were telling brokers that they didn't want to pay for many of those brokers' costs and services.

These sorts of cuts led to the rapid consolidation of the business and the disappearance of many fine, old firms. Gone are such stalwarts as Reynolds, Loeb Rhodes, DuPont, Hornblower, and White Weld (where I worked until Merrill Lynch bought it in 1978), and literally all of the research boutiques that were only viable with high fixed commission rates.

CHART 9-3

**CHANGES IN COMMISSION RATES
FOR US STOCK EXCHANGE TRANSACTIONS
FOLLOWING THE DEREGULATION OF COMMISSIONS ON 5/1/75**

YEAR	CHANGE IN RATES FROM PRECEDING YEAR	CUMULATIVE CHANGE IN RATES FROM 1974
1975	-2.3%	-2.3%
1976	-20.9%	-22.7%
1977	-16.9%	-35.7%
1978	-2.6%	-37.5%

More recently, securities regulations are being eased in a very interesting way, via the Internet. Foreign firms that provide investment information to American investors are generally subject to US registration requirements, but what if that information is posted on the Web? The SEC, probably in recognition that Web sites are impossible to police, has indicated that no registration is likely to be required. In other words, a British mutual fund could provide information to American investors without US registration.

Like airlines and truckers, brokers, banks and insurers have high fixed and low marginal costs, along with the leverage of size—a guaranteed formula for keen competition and consolidation under deregulation, especially in times of weak demand. All have the urge to invade each other's territory and have already begun to do so. With the allowed increase to 25% from 10% of revenues that banks can realize from securities business, Fleet Bank bought Quick & Reilly, and Bankers Trust acquired Alex. Brown. The Travelers Group insurance company was already in the brokerage business with Salomon Smith Barney and now has agreed to merge with Citicorp, thereby combining all three financial services. Brokers long ago entered cash management, and as the Glass-Steagall banking law continues to fade, more mergers and competition will follow among financial institutions. The winners will be the low-cost producers and those that add the most value to their services. Undoubtedly, that's deflationary.

Banks Are Hot

Banks are also benefitting from the Riegle-Neal Interstate Banking and Branching Efficiency Act of 1994 (that's a mouthful!). The final stage of a quarter-century long effort to relax geographical limits on banks, Riegle-Neal enables them to establish branches and buy other banks across the country. In 1975, no state allowed out-of-state bank holding companies to buy in-state banks, and only 14 states permitted statewide branching. Since then regulations have been gradually eased, and those states that were most active in removing geographical limits learned two things:

- Bank efficiency improved greatly once branching restrictions were lifted.

- Loan losses and operating costs fell sharply, and the reduction in the banks' costs was largely passed along to bank borrowers in the form of lower loan rates (Chart 9-4).

Previously, branching restrictions acted as a ceiling on the size of well-managed banks, preventing their expansion and retarding a process of industry evolution in which less efficient firms routinely lose ground to more efficient ones.

Studies show that the expansion of efficient banks promotes growth of state economies as well by routing savings to the most productive users. Efficient banks also tend to provide customers with more information about the profit potential of different businesses and monitor their borrowers to ensure that bank funds are properly used.

Competition Moves into Japan

Telecommunications deregulation in Europe is forcing former state monopolies to restructure or lose out to much more efficient American firms. In Spain, competition doesn't become completely open until 2000. Meanwhile, unlike most European countries which have retained part of the dominate phone companies, the Spanish government sold the last of its Telefonica holdings in 1997.

Financial turmoil and deregulation of the financial services industry in Japan is opening opportunities there for efficient US brokers, banks, and insurers. This clearly pressures Japanese institutions to restructure and cut costs. Merrill Lynch is entering the retail brokerage business in Japan by hiring former employees of Yamaichi Securities and buying attractive branch offices of the defunct firm. Although foreign firms used to be suspect, the Japa-

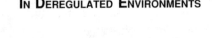

Chart 9-4

Costs and Interest Rates Are Lower In Deregulated Environments

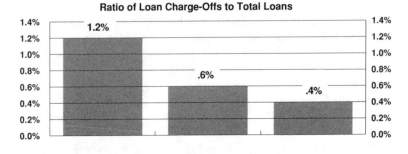

Ratio of Loan Charge-Offs to Total Loans

1.2% .6% .4%

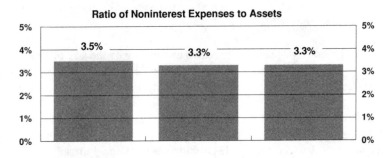

Ratio of Noninterest Expenses to Assets

3.5% 3.3% 3.3%

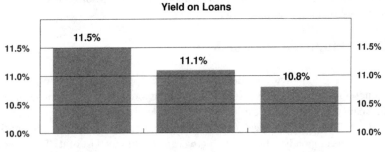

Yield on Loans

11.5% 11.1% 10.8%

| Branching And Interstate Banking Prohibited | Branching Permitted; Interstate Banking Prohibited | Branching And Interstate Banking Permitted |

Note: Chart shows the average level of price and performance measures that would have been observed in the 1978-92 period, had all states been subject to the regulatory regimes listed here. Source: Federal Financial Institutions Examinations Council

nese Ministry of Finance now welcomes competition to help revive Japan's markets.   Already, foreign investment banking firms have emerged as key players in resolving difficult problems such as disposing of bad loans and closing weak financial institutions smoothly. They are among the most active in buying up bank loans to resell as securities. Also, some US banks have seen their retail banking business skyrocket as wealthy Japanese flock to open foreign-currency accounts and pull their deposits from ailing Japanese banks, all at lower costs than were offered by previous clubby Japanese financial institutions.

Opportunities throughout Southeast Asia

As financial collapse has spread through Southeast Asia, so too have opportunities for foreign institutions to enter the markets there and spread their efficiency.   As one of the conditions of IMF bailouts, Indonesia, South Korea, and Thailand are being forced to open up (see Chapter 13). Under her agreement with the IMF, South Korea will lift restrictions on her companies' issuance of bonds, borrowing and equity financing abroad, and on foreign brokers' and banks' business activities in South Korea.

International deregulation goes hand-in-hand with another deflationary force, global sourcing, as you'll see in Chapter 10.

CHAPTER 10

GLOBAL SOURCING OF GOODS AND SERVICES CURTAILS COSTS

In today's world, technology and capital are relatively free to search the globe for the most cost effective sites for the production of goods and services (see Chapter 23). So, as US corporations restructure, they cut costs by moving production facilities out of the United States to take advantage of cheap labor, cheap expertise, cheap real estate, and cheap support services. What might once have been a difficult move is now easier because of the waning strength of US labor unions (Chart 5-5). And not only are corporations manufacturing goods in other countries, particularly developing countries, they're also providing services there and exporting them back to the US—everything from computer programming and airline revenue accounting to processing hospital patients' records and insurance claims, as mentioned in Chapter 5.

Software in India

IBM, Texas Instruments, Apple, Microsoft, and John Deere, for example, are among more than 100 of America's top 500 firms which have found India to be a great place to produce computer software—and that's no accident or surprise. The Indian government created Software Technology Parks of India (STPI) to promote the export of software from the country. An autonomous organization, it set up export complexes equipped with multiple support services in Bangalore, Pune, Bhubaneshwar, Thiruvananthapuram, and other points across the country. Each complex is a 100% export-oriented resource center offering general infrastructural facilities like utility power, ready-to-use build-up space, centralized computing facilities, and high speed data communication facilities. The idea is to make it easy for corporations to come in, gear up quickly without heavy investment, and operate efficiently.

Programmers in India are paid less than a quarter of the American rate. Indian software exports are expected to grow from 3.4% of the worldwide software outsourcing business in 1995 to 6.1% in 1999.

North America's Fastest Growing Region

Closer to home, the border territory of Northern Mexico has attracted many, many US firms with its cheap labor pool, even after considering the much lower productivity levels there. From deep in Mexico's heartland, hundreds of thousands of workers stream northward every year to seek work for wages that are attractive to them but low by US standards. Foreign-owned assembly plants, *maquiladoras*, number close to 1,500 in the border area, a 130-mile wide strip that may be North America's fastest growing region. And investments are not limited to US companies. Sony, Samsung, Matsushita and others have made Tijuana the TV manufacturing capital of the world, turning out 14 million units per year. Sanyo Electric Company recently moved its North American headquarters from New York to San Diego to be next to its factory in Tijuana, where it employs 5,000.

Maquiladora workers earn an average of $5 to $7 a day plus benefits (down from about $9 a day before the peso devaluation). Including rent and administrative expenses, it costs just $4 an hour per worker to run a plant in Tijuana, compared with $18 to $25 in San Diego. These figures aren't lost on corporate management. GM, with 17 auto parts plants operating in Ciudad Juarez, is expanding its division's R&D center there, which serves customers around the world. The number of *maquiladoras*, their employees, and their exports have been on the upswing since 1992 (Chart 10-1) and more of the same is in prospect. Indeed, these facilities may employ close to 1 million people this year.

Among the traditional lands of low labor costs, those in Asia have become even cheaper sites of production in dollar terms than as indicated by the numbers for 1996 shown in Chart 10-2. Despite much lower levels of productivity in these countries, the gap between their unit costs and those in the US has been great enough to attract US industry, and the gap is obviously widening. By 2005, East Asia, including China, is predicted to command 20% of global manufacturing production, while the share of industrial countries continues to erode (Chart 10-3).

Outsourcing at Home

Even within the US, corporations are moving manufacturing and service production out of the expensive Northeast to the South and Midwest, where labor and overhead costs are cheaper. Salomon Brothers, for example, moved its back office to Tampa, Florida, some years back, and Citicorp has its credit card operations in Sioux Falls, South Dakota. In high cost New Jersey, where our firm is located, the manufacturing payroll employment index has dropped almost 40% since 1981, whereas in the US overall the decline has been only about 8% (Chart 10-4). Construction payrolls are down 25% since their 1988 peak in the Garden State, while the national total has rebounded to new highs (Chart 10-5).

Foreign sites for outsourced production were already plentiful before the 1990s, but have gotten even more numerous as political changes abroad have converted command economies to market economies. I'll consider this deflationary force in Chapter 11.

CHART 10-1

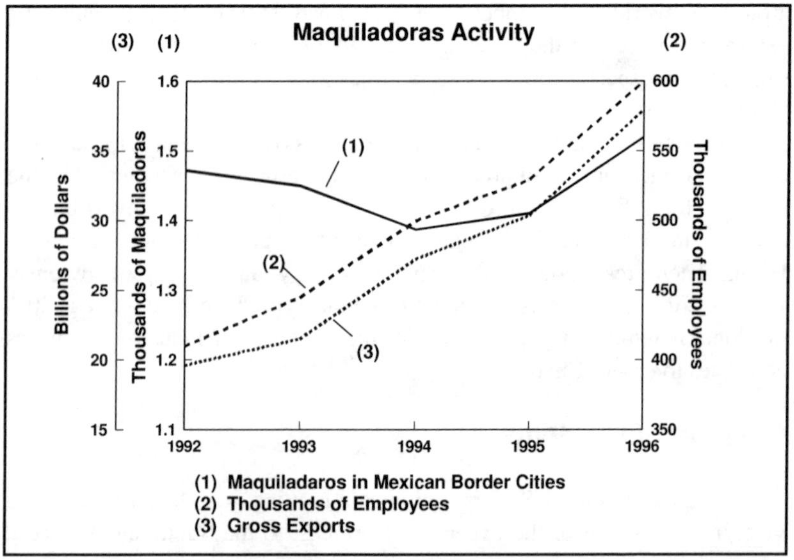
Maquiladoras Activity
(3)
(1)
(2)
40
35
30
25
20
15
1.6
1.5
1.4
1.3
1.2
1.1
600
550
500
450
400
350
Billions of Dollars
Thousands of Maquiladoras
Thousands of Employees
1992
1993
1994
1995
1996
(1)
(2)
(3)
(1) Maquiladaros in Mexican Border Cities
(2) Thousands of Employees
(3) Gross Exports

CHART 10-2

**HOURLY COMPENSATION COSTS FOR PRODUCTION
WORKERS IN MANUFACTURING
PERCENT OF US LEVEL US DOLLAR TERMS**

	1976	1986	1996
US	100	100	100
Canada	102	84	94
Mexico	24	8	8
Japan	47	70	119
Germany	97	101	180
France	68	78	109
Italy	63	79	102
UK	46	58	80
Hong Kong	13	14	29
Singapore	12	17	47
S. Korea	6	10	46
Taiwan	7	13	33
Thailand	5	8	20
Philippines	15	15	20
India	3	3	5
Sri Lanka	3	2	3
China			4
Bangladesh			1

NOTES: 1. Data say nothing about productivity and unit labor costs.
　　　　　2. Germany is West Germany.
　　　　　3. Includes wages, benefits, payroll taxes.

Source: Bureau of Labor Statistics; San Francisco Federal Reserve Bank;
　　　　　AGS & Co. Estimates.

CHART 10-3

THE CHANGING MAP OF WORLD INDUSTRY
REGIONAL SHARES IN GLOBAL MANUFACTURING PRODUCTION

	1970 (%)	1980 (%)	1990 (%)	1995 (%)	2005[1] (%)
Industrialized countries	88.8	82.8	84.2	80.3	71.0
Developing countries	12.0	17.2	15.8	19.7	29.0
East Asia including China	4.2	6.8	7.4	11.1	20.0
Latin America	4.7	6.5	4.6	4.6	4.4
North Africa & West Asia	0.9	1.6	1.8	1.9	2.4
South Asia	1.2	1.3	1.3	1.5	1.7
Sub-Sahara Africa[2]	0.6	0.5	0.3	0.3	0.3

[1]Baseline projection   [2]Excluding South Africa   Source: Unido Database

CHART **10-4**

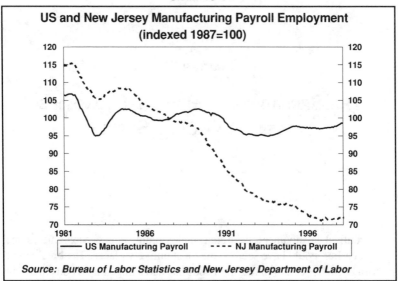

US and New Jersey Manufacturing Payroll Employment (indexed 1987=100)

Source: *Bureau of Labor Statistics and New Jersey Department of Labor*

CHART **10-5**

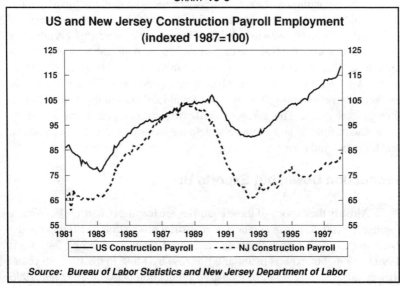

US and New Jersey Construction Payroll Employment (indexed 1987=100)

Source: *Bureau of Labor Statistics and New Jersey Department of Labor*

CHAPTER 11

THE SPREADING OF MARKET ECONOMIES INCREASES GLOBAL SUPPLY

Political developments have created blossoming market economies, some in what earlier would have seemed the most unlikely places. The break up of the former Soviet Union in the late 1980s has had a huge impact on emerging markets, allowing many Eastern European countries to take off as exporters of a variety of products including textiles, petroleum, electronic equipment, and cars. India, haltingly to be sure, is moving toward free markets, pushed by global competition and the demise of her socialist idol, the Soviet Union.

China may still be communist politically, but the old command economy of Mao days is giving way to unbridled, buccaneer capitalism. Recently, in a maneuver that only the Chinese can see as in sync with communism, Beijing announced that the number of government ministries will be slashed from 40 to 29. And, get this, some of the phased-out entities will be converted to free market enterprises that will borrow in capital markets and list their stocks on foreign exchanges. This category is likely to include petroleum and petro-chemicals, fertilizer and chemicals, defense industries, textiles, telephones, and high tech industries.

Production Down, but Exports Up

Already the exports of these countries are leaping (Chart 11-1). What's fascinating is that in many countries, industrial production is shrinking at the same time. In the Czech Republic, industrial production fell by 24% from 1990 to 1996, but exports in dollar terms rose by 146% in the 1991-96 years. Russia suffered a 42% fall in industrial production between 1992 and 1996 while exports jumped 91%, if you can believe Russian numbers. Latvian output dropped 47% in the same years, but that didn't stop exports from exploding by 63%.

Furthermore, the aims of these new market economies fit hand-in-glove with foreign producers looking for cost effective production sites (see Chapter 10), especially in Eastern Europe where levels of education are much higher than in Asian and Latin American developing countries. Some, like Poland, are quite open to foreign capital—and don't forget the most open of all, the former East Germany. Others, such as India, remain suspicious of foreign ownership.

Note that market economies are also being enlarged in countries that were never under communist domination. The privatization of Latin American mines, energy, telecommunications, and railroads are cases in point. So, too, are privatizations in Western Europe, Japan, and Canada. The results are more efficiency and more supply.

Autos and Oil

Automobile industry production is predicted to almost double in Central and Eastern European countries in the next five years, a prime example of how this process will continue. The Economist Intelligence Unit forecasts car output in the region to rise from 1.89 million in 1996 to 3.67 million in 2001. Exports will become increasingly important because local demand is expected to grow by only 40% in the same time period. Belarus, the Czech Republic, Hungary, Poland, Romania, Russia, Slovakia, Slovenia, Ukraine and Yugoslavia are all involved in autos, and Poland, the powerhouse of the Central European vehicle manufacturing sector, is predicted to single-handedly increase output from 439,000 cars in 1996 to 1.09 million in 2001.

From the Czech Republic to Turkmenistan

Next to Poland, which went from communism to capitalism cold turkey, the Czech Republic has been among the most successful of the reforming economies since the fall of communism. When economic growth and the trade balance began to slide over a year ago, the Czech National Bank abandoned its currency peg and allowed the koruna to float. The currency subsequently weakened by about 12% against the dollar and D-mark, and Czech exports began to increase. Exports were also helped by restructurings undertaken in some of the country's export-oriented, mostly foreign-owned companies, such as Skoda Auto AS.

Crude oil is another area in which these new market economies are opening to foreign capital and expertise to promote growth. Crude oil-rich

CHART 11-1

INDUSTRIAL PRODUCTION AND EXPORTS
(EXPORTS IN BILLIONS OF US DOLLARS)

		1990	1991	1992	1993	1994	1995	1996
CHINA	Production	NA	NA	NA	NA	354.5	368.1	400.7
	Exports	NA	74.0	85.0	89.4	115.0	138.1	137.2
INDIA	Production	100.0	101.6	104.5	106.5	116.5	131.3	143.9
	Exports	19.2	18.1	19.6	21.0	23.9	28.5	30.1
HUNGARY	Production	135.9	111.3	100.0	104.0	113.9	119.2	123.3
	Exports	10.4	10.5	10.7	8.7	10.2	11.9	11.9
ESTONIA	Production	NA	NA	NA	100.0	97.8	102.4	108.8
	Exports	NA	NA	NA	0.8	1.3	1.7	1.9
CZECH REP	Production	146.9	114.7	108.1	100.0	100.0	107.1	112.0
	Exports	NA	8.1	8.8	12.5	13.7	20.1	19.9
BULGARIA	Production	100.0	76.6	63.8	56.0	58.7	60.0	58.2
	Exports	4.5	3.7	3.9	3.6	4.1	5.0	4.2

KAZAKHSTAN	Production	100.0	100.6	85.8	71.7	53.3	46.4	NA
	Exports	NA	NA	NA	NA	3.1	4.6	5.7
LATVIA	Production	100.0	97.9	63.8	39.5	35.8	33.4	34.0
	Exports	NA	NA	0.8	1.0	0.9	1.2	1.3
LITHUANIA	Production	NA	126.4	90.3	59.0	41.4	41.8	42.3
	Exports	NA	NA	NA	2.0	1.9	2.4	3.0
POLAND	Production	103.5	87.0	90.5	80.2	90.7	100.0	109.4
	Exports	15.3	15.2	13.3	13.3	16.4	21.2	22.2
ROMANIA	Production	124.4	100.0	77.7	78.4	77.1	85.3	91.5
	Exports	6.8	4.3	4.3	4.4	5.7	7.0	6.9
RUSSIA	Production	218.0	200.5	164.7	131.3	103.4	100.0	96.0
	Exports	NA	NA	42.4	43.2	63.0	78.8	80.9
SLOVAK REP.	Production	145.3	119.8	102.4	92.1	98.5	106.6	109.7
	Exports	NA	3.4	3.7	5.3	6.4	8.0	8.0
SLOVENIA	Production	NA	108.1	93.8	91.2	97.1	99.0	100.0
	Exports	NA	NA	6.7	5.9	6.5	7.7	7.5
UKRAINE	Production	100.0	95.3	87.6	79.5	51.3	46.2	42.9
	Exports	NA	NA	11.3	10.6	9.8	11.6	12.8

countries such as Turkmenistan are bringing in companies from around the globe to help in prospecting, extracting, and pipeline building. Even Russia is opening a bit to foreign assistance in developing oil and gas, one of her few big foreign exchange earners. Vietnam is simultaneously industrializing and increasing exports. China's growth is driven by exports which are about one-fifth of GDP (See Chapter 14).

As these countries continue to send their products out into the world, the question is, who's going to buy them? Without a ready buyer, they'll simply add to the already deflationary global glut, and the US, the buyer of last resort, may be less likely to absorb the world's excess production of goods and services than in recent years (see Chapter 18). This is likely despite the flood of cheap US imports that will be stimulated by the already strong dollar that should continue to rally, as you'll see in Chapter 12.

CHAPTER 12

THE DOLLAR WILL CONTINUE
TO STRENGTHEN

A strong dollar has distinctly deflationary effects on the US. As the buck rises, foreigners can reduce the prices of their exports to America and still receive the same number of yen, D-marks, or baht. This, in turn, encourages US imports, to the detriment of domestic producers of competing goods and services. They are forced to cut prices or risk losing market share and being stuck with excess capacity. In either case, the response of domestic competitors to more imports at lower prices is deflationary.

A Strong Dollar Is Deflationary

A robust greenback depresses domestic production of services as well as goods even though lots of US services lack import competition. It's hard to import a haircut, and with my lack of thatch it's irrelevant, but many services do compete with imports. As discussed in Chapter 10, modern telecommunications have made it possible to import services ranging from financial back office operations to computer software writing. At the same time, some goods imports, such as certain consumer electronics, have few or no domestic competitors. And, products like wall-to-wall carpeting, 25-cubic-foot refrigerators, and king-sized beds are not made outside North America.

Chart 12-1 quantifies the penetration of imports broken down into 23 categories. Some, like tobacco and coal have little import competition. Others, such as industrial machinery, electronic equipment, and leather and leather products (shoes) are dominated by imports. Obviously these are broad categories and a finer breakdown (which isn't readily available) would show greater extremes. Still, most US-produced goods do face foreign competition, in finalized form or in some of their components, and all it takes to

CHART 12-1

IMPORT PENETRATION IN US MARKETS
1996

	US CONSUMPTION ($ BILLIONS)	IMPORTS ($ BILLIONS)	IMPORTS % OF US MARKET
lumber and wood products	46.2	12.2	26.4%
furniture and fixtures	26.7	9.3	34.8%
stone, clay and glass products	36.7	9.1	24.8%
primary metal products	63.9	34.6	54.1%
fabricated metal products	99.1	17.5	17.7%
industrial machinery	159.1	112.9	71.0%
electronic equipment	178.3	114.1	64.0%
motor vehicles and equipment	133.9	65.9	49.2%
food and kindred products	116.5	20.9	17.9%
tobacco products	13.1	0.2	1.5%
textile mill products	26.5	7.2	27.2%
apparel and other textile products	61.6	43.1	70.0%
paper and allied products	57.9	14.8	25.6%
printing and publishing	88.9	3.0	3.4%
chemicals and allied products	142.1	42.8	30.1%
petroleum and coal products	41.7	18.8	45.1%
rubber and misc. plastics	54.5	16.9	31.0%
leather and leather products	17.7	14.2	80.2%
agriculture, forestry and fishing	113.4	19.8	17.5%
metal ores and concentrates	7.1	1.4	19.7%
coal	8.8	0.2	2.3%
petroleum and natural gas	137.7	54.5	39.6%
nonmetallic minerals except fuels	9.9	1.0	10.1%

CHART 12-2

Ratio of US Goods Imported to US Total Goods Consumed

pressure domestic producers is for imports to have 1% of the US market and the potential for much more. For most domestic producers, there are few places to hide from imports, fewer than in the past. Note (Chart 12-2) that as a percentage of goods consumed in the US, imports have risen from 5% in the early 1960s to 20% in the mid 1980s, and close to 30% today.

A booming buck also makes US exports more expensive to our trading partners in their currency terms and thereby discourages them. This slows American production and increases price-depressing excess capacity. Again, deflationary.

Not Quite What It Seems

As in many other economic relationships, however, the dollar's effect on imports and exports isn't a nice straightforward one-to-one affair. When the dollar rises, foreign producers may increase their profit margins in their own currencies by not cutting prices on exports to the US by the same amount. Also, to the extent that those producers import raw materials or semifinished goods from dollar-dominated areas, their costs may not fall as much as their currencies. Chart 12-3 shows the limited correlation between the dollar and US imports, while Chart 12-4 suggests a closer fit between imports and US economic activity. When the US economy is booming, Americans are buying more of everything, including imports.

By the same token, in times of a rising dollar, US firms may shrink their profit margins and cut their costs in order to reduce their dollar selling prices on exports. Otherwise, they would lose foreign sales as their prices in weak-

CHART **12-3**

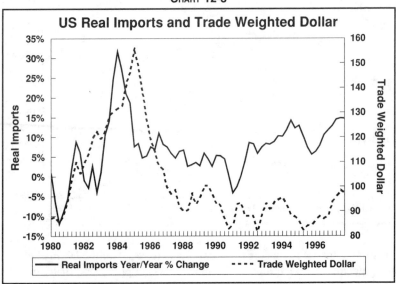

CHART **12-4**

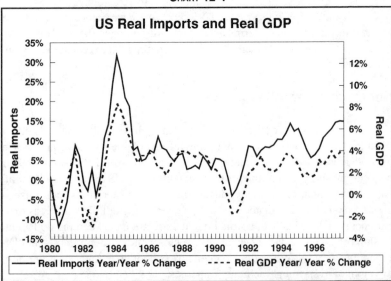

ening currencies rose by the full extent of devaluations. Use of imported materials whose prices fall as the buck climbs can help hold down dollar export prices. Consequently, it's not surprising that the dollar's correlation with US exports is weaker than the relationship between our exports and economic activity in our major trading partners (Charts 12-5 and 12-6). When they're buying more of everything, the US gets its share.

Big and Long Swings

This does not, however, suggest that the dollar's value is unimportant to US production and prices. Detroit auto producers are certainly sensitive to the yen. Furthermore, a long-lasting big rally in the dollar, such as we foresee, will have significant effects.

Note (Chart 12-7) two things about the trade weighted dollar. First, the swings in the buck have been long-term affairs. It was weak from the mid-1960s until 1980, then strong for five years, fell for five years and than flat on balance from 1990 to 1995. Second, the buck's rise since 1995 is small compared with history. We expect continuing strength in the greenback for a number of reasons.

CHART **12-5**

America's Competitive Advantage Is Huge

To begin, through aggressive restructuring America has gained a huge competitive advantage over other major economies. In Chapter 5 you saw the tremendous need for the Continent of Europe and for Japan to restructure and their impediments to doing so. The flip side is that the US is way ahead of the pack. Charts 5-12 and 5-13 revealed starkly the dynamite combination of higher US productivity and lower labor costs. Only the other English-speaking countries, in any sense, rival America.

And America is gaining on major competitors who will have to run very fast just to avoid falling further behind. Chart 12-8 shows that so far in the 1990s, robust productivity growth and restrained labor compensation have kept US unit labor cost increases below those of Germany and close to Japan and France in their national currencies (Column 3). In other words, the US gains in earlier years were not just due to dollar weakness that would be eliminated as the buck climbs. Nevertheless, the weak dollar, on balance, did help, especially against Japan and Germany (Column 5).

This is an extraordinary performance, since US productivity started from a higher level. It's harder for the leader to increase efficiency than for those that begin with a lower base, as the UK, the first nation to industrialize, found out in the second half of the nineteenth century. The leader must constantly come up with genuinely new technology and processes to push out the

CHART 12-6

US Real Exports and Real G-7 Growth

— Real Exports Year/Year % Change
- - - Real G-7 Growth Year/Year % Change

Note: Real Growth Excluding US

productivity frontier; the followers can, with much less risk and expense, simply adapt the leader's innovations.

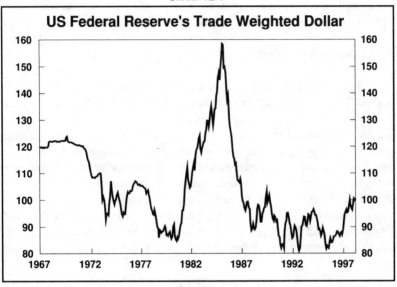

CHART 12-7

US Federal Reserve's Trade Weighted Dollar

CHART 12-8

MAJOR COUNTRY MANUFACTURING PERFORMANCE 1990-1996

	OUTPUT PER HOUR	COMPENSATION PER HOUR (NATIONAL CURRENCY)	UNIT LABOR COST (NATIONAL CURRENCY)	EXCHANGE RATE VS. $	UNIT LABOR COST IN $
US	15%	23%	7%	0%	7%
Japan	20%	23%	3%	33%	37%
France	18%	20%	2%	6%	8%
Germany	17%	38%	18%	7%	27%
UK	19%	38%	16%	-12%	1%

Source: Bureau of Labor Statistics

Continental Europe and Japan Need a Strong Dollar

Competitive strength from restructuring will come slowly in Continental Europe and Japan. Meanwhile, domestic demand is sluggish in all of those lands. Very low interest rates (Charts 12-9 and 12-10) have failed to ignite those economies domestically. Furthermore, as covered in Chapter 2, fiscal policy is tight on the Continent in order to comply with the Maastricht common currency agreement, and in Japan due to hatred of government deficits.

Not Like Brazil...But

This leaves both the Continent and Japan reliant on exports for growth, and as Chart 5-11 shows, exports have accounted for about 100% of the GDP gains on the Continent in the last several years and over 50% in Japan. While waiting for restructuring to make these countries more competitive internationally, their quickest route to more exports is devaluation. Of course, devaluation is never a permanent solution to a noncompetitive economy. If it were, Brazil would be the most successful country in the world. It is, however, a short-term political expedient on the Continent.

And also in Japan, who has perennially used exports as her growth engine (Chart 12-11). Also, soft markets for her goods in Asia have already enhanced her zeal to export to other areas, especially to the US. Furthermore,

CHART 12-9

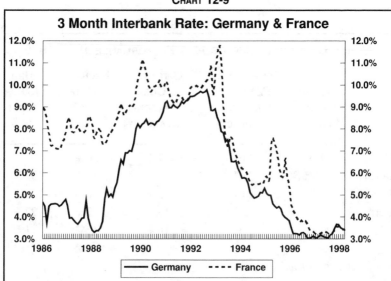

a weaker yen may be necessary for Japan to escape her ongoing deflationary depression in which buyers postpone purchases in anticipation of lower prices. Note (Chart 12-12) the close correlation between manufacturing output prices

CHART **12-10**

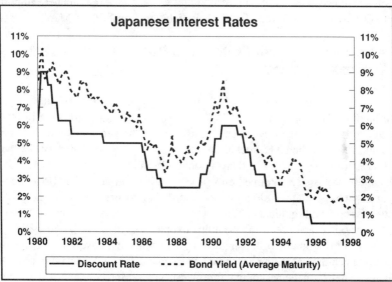

CHART **12-11**

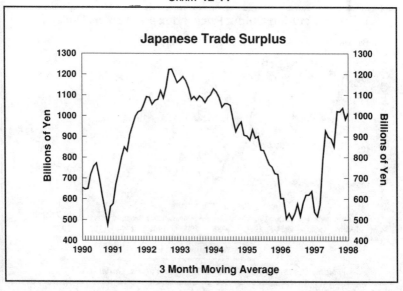

at the factory gate in Japan and the yen. Lower costs of imported raw materials and relentless cost cutting in the face of the stronger yen pushed these prices down in lockstep with the falling dollar against the yen in earlier years. Now, with the Asian crisis, the weakness in other Asian currencies against the yen has replaced the falling buck of earlier years in pushing Japanese import prices down. In 1998, they fell 8.4% in February and 1.2% in March..

The Gentleman Doth Protest Too Much
His Weak Currency

To be sure, Japanese leaders continually protest the weakening yen. Influential Finance Ministry official, Eisuke Sakakibara, said in early November 1996 that the downward "adjustment in the yen looks like it's just about over." By then it had declined from a low of 79 per dollar in April 1995 to 112. But the yen fell further to about 130 in early 1998 (Chart 12-13). Japanese protests seem aimed only at keeping Detroit and other US projectionists at bay, and their strategy appears to be not to arrest the yen's descent, but to keep its fall gradual.

Another factor favoring the dollar over the yen in the deflationary years ahead is the orientation of Japan toward perfection, not innovation. The Japanese are geniuses at taking a standard product and making constant improvements. They took the best of two fine German cars, Mercedes and BMW, and

CHART **12-12**

Note: Declining Yen Curve is Stronger Yen vs. Dollar

made them even better in producing the Lexus. My wife loves her 1990 Lexus, but she's unhappy because she can't find an excuse to buy a new one. Hers still runs beautifully, has no rattles, and is nearly identical with the new models.

But the Japanese are not nearly as good as Americans at creative, new technologies. Hear anything lately about their plans, announced about a decade ago with great fanfare, to bury us with homegrown super computers? Furthermore, their other recent government-directed technological programs have gone awry. Semiconductor memory chips have become commodities, while high-definition TV and artificial intelligence have sold poorly. As you'll learn in Chapter 27, deflation will create even bigger differences than now exist between the old technologies, like autos, and the new, such as computers, software, telecommunications, biotechnology, networks, and others where Americans are enjoying global leadership and explosive growth.

US Current Account Deficit Will Shrink

The dollar should also gain from a declining US dependence on foreigners to finance American domestic investment. The extent to which domestic investment exceeds national savings by consumers, businesses, and government measures that amount of foreign funds needed each year to bridge the gap. If domestic investment exceeds domestic savings, only foreigners can make up the difference.

CHART 12-13

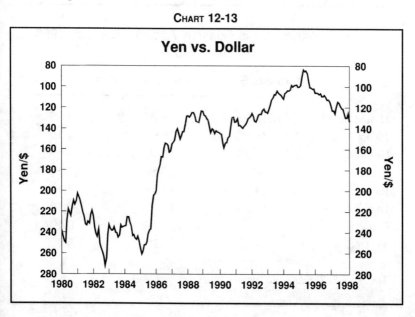

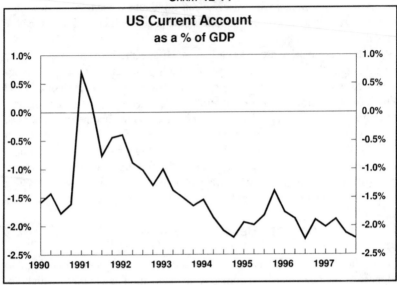

CHART **12-14**

US Current Account
as a % of GDP

CHART **12-15**

SAVING, INVESTMENT, AND CURRENT ACCOUNT BALANCE 1996
(AS % OF GDP)

	NATIONAL SAVING	INVESTMENT	CURRENT ACCOUNT
United States	16.6%	18.7%	-1.9%
Japan	31.3%	29.8%	1.4%
Germany	20.0%	21.0%	-0.6%
France	18.7%	17.5%	1.3%
Italy	20.5%	17.0%	3.4%
United Kingdom	14.6%	14.7%	-0.1%
Canada	17.8%	18.9%	0.5%
Switzerland	27.4%	20.2%	6.9%

Source: OECD Economic Outlook

CHART 12-16

NET EXTERNAL DEBT (-) OR ASSETS (+)
AS A % OF GDP

United States	-15%
Switzerland	130%
Japan	23%
Germany	9%

Statistically, this difference is also the current account deficit, the surplus dollars placed in foreign hands each year because of our broadly-defined trade deficit. These surplus dollars don't necessarily depress the buck's value. Indeed, if foreigners want to invest even more dollars in the US than they gain from our current account deficit, the buck will rise, as has been the case since 1995. It's clear, though, that a smaller current account deficit generally makes the dollar more attractive, and a smaller deficit requires a smaller shortfall of US savings compared to domestic investment.

The US current account deficit continues to be large (Chart 12-14) and will get bigger in the next year or so as imports from Asia and elsewhere flood the country while exports languish. It also contrasts with the surpluses of Japan, Italy, France, and Switzerland (Chart 12-15). Still, the deficit will fall as individuals' saving rises (Chapter 18) and as, in the years ahead, total government, including state and local entities, continues to run a surplus. A smaller current account deficit in time will also aid the buck by pushing down the size of Uncle Sam's external debt in relation to GDP (Chart 12-16) and its servicing costs. Surpluses would obviously speed the decline.

US Exports Are Undercounted

One more reason to be bullish on the buck is, simply put, US exports appear to be greatly undercounted. C. Harvey Monk, Jr., Chief of the Census Bureau's Foreign Trade Division, was quoted in a 1997 *Journal of Commerce* article saying that the US Customs Service is not counting 10% or more of American exports. The problem is particularly acute in services where we dominate the world in the likes of software, entertainment and financial services. Exports in these areas have been exploding. Services were 18% of total exports in 1980 and leaped to 27% in 1997, and would be a much bigger share if fully reported. Says Ed Grose, International Trade Manager for the

Customs Service, "Our reporting of international trade in services may be deficient by 40%."

Why the big export undercount? Largely because government officials don't really care. With no duties on exports, their value isn't important to the Customs Service. They don't even bother counting exports to Canada, our biggest trading partner that takes 22% of the total. Instead, they accept Canada's import numbers as the official US export statistics.

Also, some exports, especially services, are hard to detect, much less measure. My son Geoff, the product manager with Microsoft, told me, "Dad, we now sell our programs on the Internet through outside vendors. You can call one of them, give the vendor your credit card number and they will download the software over the phone." If the buyer is in, say, Germany, what are the odds of that sale being recorded as a US export? Zero.

They Understand Goods, but Not Services

Dennis Gartman, a great friend of mine, recently talked to a former customs official of the Port of Norfolk, and was told that they don't know how to value the computer software copies being loaded onto ships there—but they do know how to weigh physical commodities. So they weigh the floppy disks and the CDs on which the software is recorded and price them as plastic at about 1¼¢ per lb. This is obviously absurd, but it shows clearly that the Customs Service is oriented toward goods, not services—typical of government data collectors.

Services have dominated the American economy for decades and now account for well over half of output, but Washington statisticians are still living in the nineteenth century when manufactured goods were paramount. For example, they produce tremendous detail on manufacturing output, down to the 7-digit SIC code level. Rear discharge manure spreaders, for example, are SIC Code 35233 61, while side discharge models are SIC Code 35233 65. I wonder which way the intervening numbers, 35233 62, 36233 63, and 35233 64, discharge? But try to get much more detail than the 4-digit level for services? Forget it! SIC Code 8734, testing labs, is as fine as it gets, so those testing manure spreaders are in the same boat as those testing semiconductor chips. Hell, they don't even break out economic consultants. We seem to be thrown in with other nondescripts in SIC Code 8748, Business Consulting Services Not Elsewhere Classified.

They Scrutinize Imports

Imports, in contrast, are carefully measured by Customs officials because of the long history of slapping tariffs on them. If you need further proof

CHART 12-17

1996 MERCHANDISE TRADE
(BILLIONS OF US$)

	EXPORTS	IMPORTS	TRADE BALANCES	WORLD TRADE BALANCE IF US EXPORTS PLUS 5%	WORLD TRADE BALANCE IF US EXPORTS PLUS 10%
Industrial countries	3355.1	3350.8	4.3		
US	582.5	770.9	-188.4		
Europe	2072.7	2009.4	63.3		
Japan	443.0	335.9	107.1		
Other	1646.3	1748.6	-102.3		
World	5001.4	5099.4	-98.0	-68.9	-39.7

Source: IMF Direction of Trade Statistics

CHART 12-18

US TRADE IN GOODS & SERVICES AND CURRENT ACCOUNT 1997 IN $ BILLIONS

| | REPORTED | IF EXPORTS UNDERSTATED BY... | | |
		...5%	...10%	...15%
Exports of Goods & Services	932.3	978.9	1025.5	1072.1
Imports of Goods & Services	1046.0	1046.0	1046.0	1046.0
Goods & Services Balance	−113.7	−67.1	−20.5	26.1
Current Account Balance	−166.4	−119.8	−73.2	-26.6

Source: US Department of Commerce

of the careful count of imports but not exports, note that in 1996 imports reported by all countries exceeded their counted exports by $98 billion (Chart 12-17). In reality, of course, the two must be equal since one country's exports are another's imports.

And, the bulk of the difference is probably with the US. We're a lot less concerned about what leaves the country than other nations. Also, we are the world's biggest international trader. We're even more dominant than shown in the table when you consider that most of the exports and imports of Germany, France, the UK, and Italy go to other countries within the European Union. When European countries establish a common currency next year, their trade with each other is no more international than is California's trade with New York.

If 10% of US exports were missed in 1997, the trade deficit would drop from the reported $113.7 billion to only $20.5 billion (Chart 12-18). A 15% undercount would mean an actual surplus of $26.1 billion. Also, as shown, the $166.4 billion current account deficit would drop to $73.2 billion with a 10% export undercount and only $26.6 billion if exports were 15% too low.

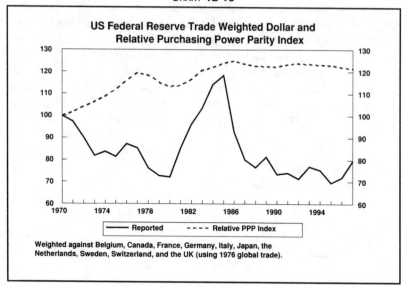

CHART 12-19

US Federal Reserve Trade Weighted Dollar and Relative Purchasing Power Parity Index

Reported — — — Relative PPP Index

Weighted against Belgium, Canada, France, Germany, Italy, Japan, the Netherlands, Sweden, Switzerland, and the UK (using 1976 global trade).

So What?

Does this export undercount mean anything? Aren't the true deficits already understood and fully discounted in currency markets? I don't think so because the facts aren't clear to many. The Customs Service, however, recently implemented its Automated Export System, which should simplify and improve trade data collection vastly. This will aid the greenback by alleviating fears that chronic big deficits are putting too many dollars in foreign hands.

Adjusted for Inflation Differences, the Buck Is Cheap

The dollar is very cheap in terms of what it buys abroad. Chart 12-19 adjusts exchange rates for the differences in inflation between the US and our trading partners. This is the purchasing power parity concept, a glorified version of the Big Mac index that prices a McDonald's hamburger in various countries around the world. I don't get too excited about this concept, however, since the vast majority of international dollar transactions have nothing to do with US imports and exports. They're used to facilitate other countries' trade and much of the globe's vast capital flows. Furthermore, as you'll note, the dollar has been chronically undervalued, assuming that it was in balance in 1960, the initial year in this graph. That's another problem with purchasing power parity—there's no way of knowing when equilibrium existed, if ever. Still, there may be some upward pressure on the dollar from the huge gaps between what the dollar buys in the US and what it buys in other countries. Buy your Big Macs in this country in the meanwhile.

Since 1995, Japan, most of the rest of Asia, and to a lesser extent, Europe, have all deflated in dollar terms. American competitiveness, the needs of the European Continent and Japan for a strong dollar, a shrinking of the current account deficit in time, the understatement of US exports and the cheapness of the inflation-adjusted dollar all argue for an even stronger buck and more deflationary effects on the US. An added reason can be found in Asia, where competitive devaluation and other global deflationary eggs are being hatched, as you'll see in Chapter 13.

Chapter 13

Asian Financial and Economic Problems Will Intensify Global Glut And Reduce Worldwide Prices

Most remember the October 1973 oil embargo as the root cause of the near runaway inflation of that period. It wasn't, but it did focus attention on inflation and was important because of all that had come before. In the late 1960s, the Johnson administration embarked on a massive Great Society spending program while engaging in a very expensive land war in Asia. This "guns and butter" approach strained capacity here and abroad and touched off serious inflation, as noted in Chapter 2.

Then, after disastrous harvests in Russia, the Soviets in the early 1970s surreptitiously bought-up all of the grain in sight. Soon, thereafter, El Niño caused the anchovies to disappear off the coast of Peru. Who cared? European livestock owners did since they used these fish as a principal food for their animals. So they had to buy grain instead and prices soared.

Then the Club of Rome made their famous, now infamous, pronouncement that the shortages were a permanent way of life in their 1972 report, "The Limits to Growth." Small is beautiful, many bellowed. The ghost of the Reverend Malthus stalked the land. By the fall of 1973, the world was beginning to believe that shortages and high inflation were here to stay. The oil embargo and subsequent skyrocketing crude oil prices confirmed growing suspicions. All that preceded the oil embargo gave it an impact that would not otherwise have occurred. Even the imposers of the embargo, the Saudis, were amazed at its effects.

1997 Mirrors 1973

The Asian crisis, starting in the summer of 1997, in many ways is the mirror image of the 1973 oil embargo. The subject this time is deflation and global surpluses, the inverse of the earlier inflation and world-wide shortages. As back then, the way has been paved by all the deflationary forces discussed in Chapters 1 to 12. Without the resulting cumulative deflationary storm, the Asian crisis would not be a major hurricane. No more important in the longer term scheme of things than the mid-1980s Latin American debt crisis or the 1994 collapse in the Mexican peso. But with those previously-laid paving blocks, the Asian meltdown is significant and probably insures global deflation in the years ahead.

Surprise! Surprise!

Another reason that the Asian problems are meaningful is they were so unexpected. After all, the Asia work ethic, dedication to family, willingness to put the community above self and huge savings rates are the envy of the world. This was the Asian miracle and we were about to enter the Pacific century. These were countries that had dutifully followed the successful—at least previously successful—Japanese model. The International Monetary Fund (IMF) in June 1997, just a month before the crisis started, praised Indonesia for "prudent macroeconomic policies, huge investment and savings rates, and reforms to liberalize markets." In May 1997, the IMF lauded Thailand as well as Indonesia as "exceptions to the boom-bust cycle." Well, its's nice to know that I'm not alone in making some lousy forecasts.

Trade Here, Currency Linkage There

The immediate cause of the Asian crisis was the linkage of their currencies to the dollar, even though the bulk of their trade is with Japan and other yen-dominated areas in Asia (Chart 13-1). Some had specific links to the dollar, like Hong Kong's 15-year peg of 7.8 Hong Kong dollars per buck, while others were less formal but still closely tied. This is understandable. The dollar is the world's reserve currency and safe haven. US capital markets are by far the globe's largest, and these countries all need foreign capital to develop. Probably most important, these countries suffered at the hands of the Japanese before and during World War II, and preferred to be tied as closely as possible to a friendlier power who was also their military protector in the Cold War.

These links to the dollar were also very advantageous from 1984 to April 1995 when the dollar slid 65% against the yen. Their currencies all fell about the same against the yen (Chart 13-2), which made them much more competitive against the Japanese in global markets. At the same time, they received large infusions of money from Japan as producers there moved fa-

CHART 13-1

ASIAN TIGERS' TRADE IN 1996

	US	JAPAN	ASIA	OTHER
Thailand	14.7%	22.6%	33.5%	29.3%
Malaysia	17.3%	19.5%	39.8%	23.5%
Philippines	22.9%	21.4%	29.7%	26.0%
Indonesia	13.6%	26.3%	26.9%	33.3%
Taiwan (exports only)*	23.2%	11.8%	50.7%	14.3%
Hong Kong	14.3%	10.2%	55.0%	20.5%
Singapore	17.4%	13.3%	44.0%	25.4%
China	14.8%	20.7%	36.3%	28.2%
S. Korea	19.7%	17.2%	26.4%	36.7%

Source: IMF Direction of Trade Statistics
*Data from Industry of Free China Journal

cilities to those cheaper locales in order to avoid the effects of the soaring yen. This was especially true of the four new tigers (Thailand, Malaysia, Indonesia, and the Philippines), with even lower costs than the original quartet (Chart 13-3).

The dollar linkage removed the exchange rate risks in the eyes of many foreign investors, so money piled in. How could robust economic powerhouses like these Asian lands ever possibly devalue? It also made it very attractive for borrowers in those countries to raise capital funds abroad in dollars. In Indonesia, for example, borrowers had to pay 18% to 20% rates for rupiah but only 9% to 10% for dollars. Even with the rupiah depreciating 4% or 5% per year against the dollar, the choice was clear—as long as devaluation stayed modest.

The Root of the Asian Crisis

But trouble was brewing even as the dollar fell against the yen. Most Asian tigers have followed Japan's lead in economic development philosophy (see Chapters 5 and 15), and that is the root of the Asian problem. Governments did not trust free markets to maximize growth. In part because they

CHART 13-2

CURRENCY CHANGES AGAINST THE JAPANESE YEN

	1984[1] - 4/95[2]	4/95 - 6/97	6/97 - 3/31/98
U.S.	-65%	37%	15.4%
S. Korea	-63%	18%	-25.9%
Taiwan	-42%	25%	-2.2%
Hong Kong	-64%	36%	15.4%
Singapore	-46%	34%	2.6%
Malaysia	-67%	35%	-20.3%
Thailand	-66%	37%	-25.1%
Indonesia	-84%	24%	-68.1%
Philippines	-78%	34%	-18.7%
China	-90%	39%	16.0%

[1] *Year average*
[2] *Dollar's low against the yen*

had little experience with them. In part because they didn't believe they could achieve viable economies of scale in the face of competition from long-established developed countries. In part because of traditional suspicion of foreigners and unrestricted capitalism. In part because of anti-colonialism sentiments. So they turned to government-controlled collection and allocation of scarce resources as a substitute.

Free markets have plenty of faults, but at least through Anglo Saxon eyes, they're in the same position as democracy as described by Winston Churchill. It's the worst form of government ever devised by mankind—except for every other one that's been tried.

In Asia, the result is paternalistic governments headed by semi-dictators who run top-down regimes that hold down wages as well as social welfare spending and environmental outlays. At the same time, chronically high levels of saving (Chart 13-4) and foreign capital funds are largely collected and redistributed through the banks. In Malaysia, bank loans equal 100% of the country's GDP compared to 50% in the US, while bonds outstanding in Thailand and Indonesia are less than 10% of GDP, far less than the 110% level in the US.

CHART 13-3

JAPANESE NEW DIRECT INVESTMENT IN ASIA
JAPANESE FISCAL YEARS (IN BILLIONS OF DOLLARS)

	4 OLD TIGERS *	4 NEW TIGERS **	TOTAL
1988	3.3	2.0	5.2
1989	4.9	2.8	7.7
1990	3.4	3.2	6.6
1991	2.2	3.1	5.3
1992	1.9	3.2	5.1
1993	2.4	2.4	4.8
1994	2.9	3.9	6.8
1995	3.0	3.9	6.9
1996	3.4	4.8	8.3

South Korea, Taiwan, Hong Kong, Singapore are 4 Old Tigers

**Thailand, Malaysia, Indonesia, Philippines are 4 New Tigers*

Then these funds are channeled into selected industries that support national (usually the leader's) domestic ambitions, and export industries like autos, steel, aircraft, electronics, textiles, and shipbuilding. With no guidance from markets, resources are wasted on pet projects, often run by cronies and relatives. Exports are overemphasized to the detriment of the domestic economy with excess capacity in export industries the result. Overconfidence by those involved in these favored industries and dangerously high financial leverage also flow from this system.

Real estate speculation is another hallmark of the suppression of market reality. And, in contrast to free markets, this approach invites graft and corruption while protecting and covering up difficulties. Also, in contrast to Latin America, both domestic and foreign borrowing under the Japanese development model tends to be in the private, not the public, sector. This, too, obscures problems from view. It also makes international financial assistance more difficult because it appears to bail private borrowers and lenders out of their own folly, not help innocent citizens who are victimized by national crises.

CHART 13-4

> ## ASIAN NATIONAL SAVING
> ## AS A % OF GDP 1996
>
> | | |
> |---|---|
> | S. Korea | 32.6% |
> | Hong Kong | 21.1% |
> | Taiwan | 25.1% |
> | Singapore | 50.4% |
> | China | 34.2% |
> | Malaysia | 36.8% |
> | Indonesia | 29.8% |
> | Philippines | 19.8% |
> | Thailand | 33.3% |
> | | |
> | U.S. | 16.6% |
>
> *Source: Asian Development Bank*

Here Comes the Money

The ready availability of foreign money exacerbates many of these problems. Despite its shortcomings, the Japanese model promoted rapid growth in other Asian lands that, along with exchange rate stability, attracted gobs of foreign capital. Notice (Chart 13-5) that the rush of international banks lending to the developing Asian countries continued in the first half of 1997, even as storm clouds grew. In the Philippines, bank loans, significantly fueled by foreign money, leaped 52% in 1996.

In Indonesia, money was destined for projects controlled by President Suharto's six children—electric generating plants in already oversupplied Java, and world class cars—and others like a domestic aircraft industry. By 2001 Malaysia's Petronas Tower, the world's tallest building, will contribute to a doubling of Kuala Lumpur's office space, pushing vacancy rates from 5% to 30%.

When money is readily available and no one believes there is any possibility of loss, it will get spent and spent promptly. Clear evidence of one aspect of over investment is the vast inventories of unsold goods now seen throughout Asia—not only inventories of everything from chicken gizzards

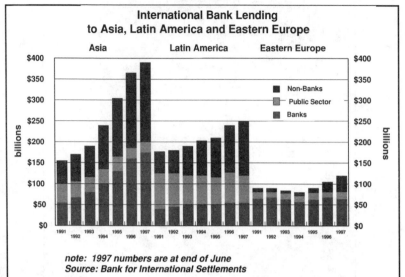

CHART 13-5

**International Bank Lending
to Asia, Latin America and Eastern Europe**

note: 1997 numbers are at end of June
Source: Bank for International Settlements

to steel piled up in warehouses, but inventories of unsold apartments and office buildings.

Furthermore, these excesses were encouraged by the very high financial leverage that is typical of Asian businesses, especially in South Korea. There, companies, on average, borrowed four and a half times their equity capital, literally more than ten times as much as American firms. This, of course, put the pressure on competitors in other countries to follow suit. State-of-the-art China Steel, Taiwan's largest steelmaker, for example, has great difficulty in competing with South Korean steelmakers due to its much lower, 25% debt-to-equity ratio.

Besides their currency weakness against the yen in 1985-95, a big help to the Asian tigers was the strong growth in developed countries' economies, especially in the late 1980s. Even though they are increasingly trading among themselves, those lands still send major shares of their exports to developed lands (Chart 13-6). They can't all take in each other's laundry. When countries like the US and especially Japan experience slower growth as developed countries have in the 1990s, their import growth also slows (Chart 12-4).

Then Came the Morning After

In retrospect, Asia was vulnerable by the mid 1990s, but few, including stock investors, realized it even after the dollar started to rise against the yen

CHART 13-6

1996 ASIAN MERCHANDISE EXPORTS TO G-7 AS % OF TOTAL EXPORTS

	G-7 TOTAL	US	GERMANY	FRANCE	ITALY	UK	CANADA	JAPAN
China	48.2%	17.7%	3.9%	1.3%	1.2%	2.1%	1.6%	20.4%
Hong Kong	39.4%	21.3%	4.2%	1.6%	1.0%	3.3%	1.4%	6.6%
Indonesia	57.2%	16.5%	4.1%	1.9%	1.8%	2.9%	1.0%	29.0%
Malaysia	40.2%	18.2%	3.0%	0.8%	0.8%	3.4%	0.6%	13.4%
Philippines	63.1%	33.9%	4.1%	1.1%	0.5%	4.6%	1.0%	17.9%
Singapore	36.2%	18.4%	3.1%	2.0%	0.4%	3.8%	0.3%	8.2%
S. Korea	37.7%	16.7%	3.6%	0.9%	0.7%	2.5%	0.9%	12.3%
Taiwan	55.7%	30.6%	4.7%	1.8%	1.1%	2.8%	1.8%	12.9%
Thailand	45.1%	18.0%	2.9%	1.8%	1.2%	3.3%	1.1%	16.8%

Source: International Monetary Fund and Industry of Free China

in April 1995. The buck's ascent was firmly established by December 1995, and with major developed countries growing more modestly in the 1990s and slowing Asia's export increases, we advised clients then that slower advances for the Asian tigers lay ahead. Candidly, however, we had no idea of the collapse to commence a year and a half later.

In the meanwhile, the dollar continued to grind ahead against the yen, forcing those currencies tied to the buck to follow suit. As always, economic reality wins out sooner or later. When Thailand couldn't stand the hot water any longer and pulled the plug on its support of the baht on July 2, 1997, not only did a run on that currency ensue promptly (Chart 13-7), but it quickly spread to the Philippines, Malaysia, Indonesia, Hong Kong, South Korea, other Asian lands, and even Brazil.

These currency slides (Chart 13-8) were largely forced by the markets, but the markets only sped-up the inevitable—competitive devaluations. Once one tiger does it, how can others that compete with her resist? Some did resist, notably Hong Kong and Brazil, but at horrible costs. The run on the Hong Kong dollar in October 1997 was met with determined defense. Overnight interest rates skyrocketed to 300% at one point and the government there made it clear that their monetary reserves of almost $100 billion were available to maintain the Hong Kong dollar at 7.8 per US dollar.

CHART 13-7

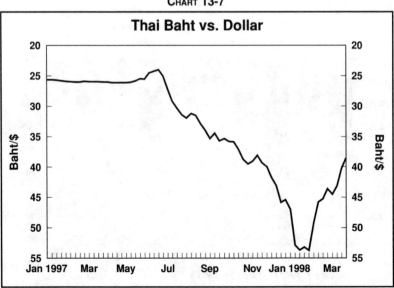

Hong Kong Dollar's Costly Defense

But Hong Kong is one big real estate casino. The currency peg kept interest rates there at US levels but below local inflation rates until the crisis erupted. In effect, real estate speculators were paid to borrow, in real terms. A leap in rates is lethal to real estate, especially in Hong Kong where the government owns most of the undeveloped land and sells it slowly enough to maintain constant shortages and guaranteed price rises—and hence huge speculation. But as high interest costs leaped (Chart 13-9), real estate prices collapsed.

Even still, the devaluations of other Asian currencies in relation to the Hong Kong dollar have pushed her already relatively high real estate costs to new heights in their currency terms. Office rents are about 50% more than in Singapore and five times those in Kuala Lumpur. Tourism has also slipped, not only because of the huge cost of Hong Kong hotel rooms for other Asians but also because the British cache ended with the Chinese takeover.

Hong Kong is primarily a service economy and doesn't have a lot of manufacturing to lose to devaluing neighbors. Still, much of her service business is linked to Chinese manufactured exports which will be hurt as long as China doesn't devalue (See Chapter 14). Meanwhile, the Hong Kong Hang Seng stock index, over half of whose components are property companies and banks that lend heavily to them, nosedived (Chart 13-10). Recession

CHART **13-8**

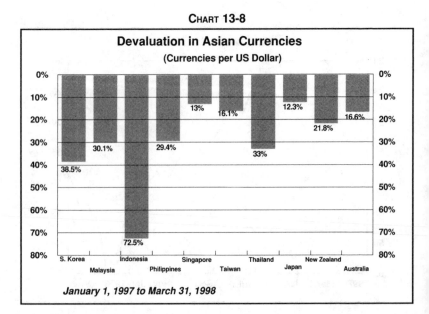

there seems inevitable. Hong Kong will probably join China in devaluing eventually.

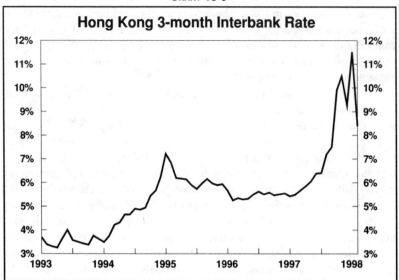

CHART 13-9

Hong Kong 3-month Interbank Rate

CHART 13-10

Hang Seng Stock Market Index

Brazil Fights On

Brazil's currency, the real, was also attacked last fall and for good reason. The real, instituted by President Cardoso in 1994, is pegged to the dollar with a modest 0.6% per month depreciation, and has cut inflation rates from 40% then to under 5% in 1997. The currency was overvalued initially, but the imbalance was supposed to be eliminated by fiscal reforms that would revamp the tax system, fire excess public employees, and rein in the social security system that now pays benefits to some workers in their 40s. Then monetary policy could be eased.

But the Brazilian Congress dragged its heels on fiscal reform and the current account balance dropped to huge negative numbers (Chart 13-11), while the trade deficit jumped from $5.55 billion in 1996 to $8.52 billion last year. In effect, the real has gotten even more overvalued or, conversely, Brazil has lost more international competitiveness. Indeed, wages have risen by 80% in dollar terms since the real plan was initiated, even though unemployment is rising, and unit labor costs have risen almost 40%.. Another problem is the government deficit, now running over 5% of GDP. Also, although privatization will finance part of the current account deficit, unless it falls sharply, heavy reliance on flows from foreign investors will continue.

Brazil, then, was ripe for a bout of the Asian flu, but this perennial "land of the future" fought back to maintain her currency peg. Who can blame Brazil? To devalue would invite a speedy return to the bad old hyper-inflationary days of yesteryear. But the cost of defending the real is huge. Brazil lost $10 billion in hard currency reserves in a flash and the central bank doubled short-term interest rates to a 46% annual rate. In addition, the President proposed, and Congress has largely accepted, draconian fiscal restraints that amount to nearly 3% of GDP. Federal spending will be cut, taxes raised, public utility rates hiked, government real estate sold and revenue sharing with state and local governments slashed.

Interest rates remain in nosebleed altitudes, which have re-attracted some foreign money, but which are also murdering retail sales. In Brazil, 85% of goods are sold on credit, much of which was extended with no down payments to low income consumers. Now high interest rates and shorter loan maturities have jacked up monthly payments on electronics goods by 50%, leaving many Brazilians unable to repay their debts. Government restraint may reduce the current account deficit and save the currency peg, at least for now, but at the cost of an almost certain recession.

Of course, Brazil will be at a distinct disadvantage against competing countries that have devalued. Further, a number of Brazilian financial houses are at risk as super higher interest rates menace their highly-leveraged derivative positions. No wonder Brazilian stocks took a nosedive.

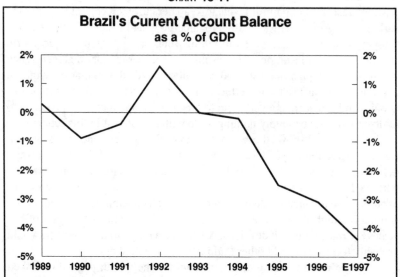

CHART 13-11

Brazil's Current Account Balance
as a % of GDP

Currency Pegs Turn into Financial Sawdust

Hong Kong and Brazil are not alone in facing the choice between recession and devaluation. Since 1992, Finland, Sweden, Norway, the UK, Italy, Spain, Portugal, Mexico, the Czech Republic, Thailand, Indonesia, Malaysia, the Philippines, South Korea, Taiwan, and Vietnam have all thrown in the towel on currency pegs. Ironically, Indonesia, who in part got into trouble because of her linkage of the rupiah to the dollar, recently considered another currency peg. President Suharto, apparently impatient over the lack of quick economic recovery and unwilling to swallow all of the bitter IMF medicine, was attracted to the witch doctor's promise of instant rejuvenation. He showed interest in a currency board but was apparently forced to back down by the IMF, President Clinton, and other Western leaders.

A currency board would link the rupiah completely to a strong currency, probably the dollar, much as in the case of the Hong Kong dollar or the Argentine peso. The government would exchange rupiahs for dollars at a fixed rate. But to work, a currency board requires credibility by foreign and domestic investors, and big enough foreign exchange reserves to withstand attempted runs on the currency.

Indonesia will probably not have either one anytime soon, and the only other alternative under a currency peg to keep money from fleeing is disastrously high interest rates. Even Hong Kong, with her huge reserves, had to push interest rates to painful levels to keep her currency peg intact, as noted earlier. And Argentina was willing to undergo what President Menem called "surgery without anesthesia" by installing a currency board in 1991 to get rid of 2,300% annual inflation. I'm absolutely sure that the fact that a currency board with the rupiah fixed at 5000 per dollar would allow Suharto's children and buddies to at least double the current dollar value of their fortunes of about $2 billion each, convert them to greenbacks, and move the proceeds to Switzerland had absolutely nothing to do with his interest in this scheme.

Chart 13-12 shows those countries that still have currency pegs, at least for now. Argentina's peg has worked, but is precarious. Her current account deficit will run about 5% of GDP this year due to a surge in consumer imports, a 14% decline in export prices in the last two years, and her loss of exports to weak-currency Asian competitors. The unemployment rate in Argentina is a high 14% and real GDP in 1988 will rise at less than half of last year's 8% rates. If Brazil devalues, Argentina, a major trading partner, would probably follow as would other Latin American neighbors.

As we're now seeing clearly throughout the world, pegged or linked currencies can make foreign investors feel safe and, therefore, eager to pour money into developing countries. They also can encourage trade by eliminating exchange risks. But they also allow corruption and miss-allocation of assets to get much further out of hand than would be the case if free foreign exchange markets were available to signal problems. Consequently, defending inappropriate pegged currency rates is very expensive. Letting them go may make the countries involved once again competitive, but the process is extremely disruptive.

Commodity Prices — Down and Up

Inflation is an immediate problem with big devaluations as the costs of imports leap, even if the prices of those imports are falling in dollar terms. For example, cotton and copper, two important and globally traded industrial commodities have both fallen in dollar terms because of rapidly declining domestic demand in Asia and elsewhere. But those declines have been much more than offset by weak Asian currencies (Charts 13-13 and 13-14). This means much higher costs for goods produced for local markets that contain copper and cotton. At the same time, these higher import prices will prevent copper- and cotton-containing exports from reflecting the full extent of Asian currency declines.

Furthermore, the gyrations in commodity prices are not even a zero sum game for developing countries. Since the Chilean peso has only fallen about 9% against the dollar since last October, the price of Chile's principal

CHART 13-12

CHART 13-12

CURRENCY PEGS TODAY

COUNTRY	PEGGED TO	COUNTRY	PEGGED TO
Angola	US Dollar	Hungary	US Dollar 30%,
Argentina	US Dollar		European Currency
Aruba	US Dollar		Unit 70%
Austria	Deutschemark	Iraq	US Dollar
Bahamas	US Dollar	Jordan	US Dollar
Bahrain	US Dollar	Latvia	Special Drawing
Bangladesh	Index		Rights
Barbados	US Dollar	Lesotho	African Rand
Belize	US Dollar	Liberia	US Dollar
Bermuda	US Dollar	Lithuania	US Dollar
Botswana	Index	Macau	Hong Kong Dollar
Brazil	US Dollar	Namibia	African Rand
Cambodia	US Dollar	Nauru	Australian Dollar
Eastern Caribbean	US Dollar	Nepal	Indian Rupee
Cayman Islands	US Dollar	Netherlands Antilles	US Dollar
Central African		Oman	US Dollar
Countries	French Franc	Panama	US Dollar
Chile	Index	Qatar	Special Drawing
China	?		Rights
Cyprus	European Currency	San Marino	Italian Lira
	Unit	Slovakia	US Dollar 40%,
Czech Republic	US Dollar 35%,		Deutschemark 60%
	Deutschemark 65%	Sudan	US Dollar
Djibonti	US Dollar	Swaziland	African Rand
Dominican Republic	US Dollar	Syria	US Dollar
Estonia	Deutschemark	Tunisia	Index
Ethiopia	US Dollar	Vanuatu	Index
Fiji	US Dollar	West African States	French Franc
Haiti	US Dollar	Western Samoa	Index
Hong Kong	US Dollar	Yemen	US Dollar
		Yugoslavia	Deutschemark

export, copper, in peso terms, has declined sharply (Chart 13-15). Chile is in good financial shape with $17 billion in central bank reserves and a $2 billion reserve fund to smooth out copper price fluctuations. But rises in interest rates needed to defend the currency are pinching debt-laden Chilean companies, and her current account deficit is likely to rise from 4.7% of GDP in 1997 to over 6% this year. Also, 30% of Chilean exports go to faltering East Asia, and she, like all Latin American countries, also competes with Asia in exports to developed countries. Lower growth , if not recession, is in the cards in Chile.

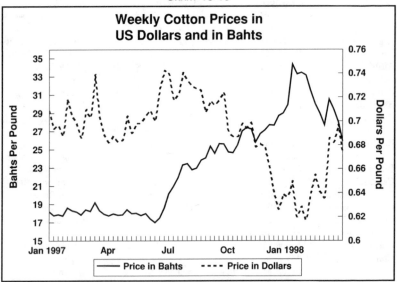

CHART **13-13**

Weekly Cotton Prices in US Dollars and in Bahts

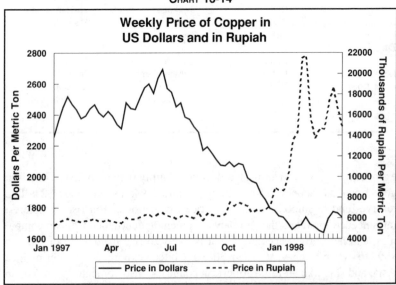

CHART **13-14**

Weekly Price of Copper in US Dollars and in Rupiah

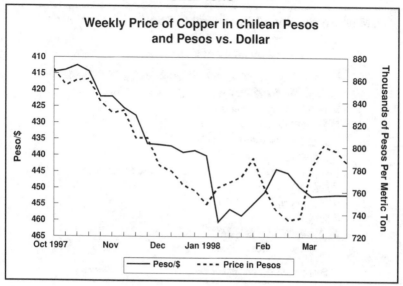

CHART 13-15

Keep Operating Even at a Loss?

Copper production costs have dropped more than 30% since the 1980s, but the plummet in prices has pushed them below break-even levels in some countries. Don't assume that as a result, prices have reached a floor. True, in developed countries, where production is in private hands, producers won't operate at losses, at least not for long. But not so in developing lands where production is usually controlled directly or indirectly by governments. There they will keep operating indefinitely, even at losses, in order to maintain employment and to earn precious foreign exchange. In fact, they will probably increase production and exports as prices fall in order to maintain their foreign exchange receipts. This is not what you call normal economic response to price declines.

Note (Chart 13-16) copper is largely produced in developing countries and even China, a previous importer, is now exporting. Advanced lands, principally Australia, Canada, and the US, only account for 28% of the total. Production, which rose sharply in 1997, is expected to advance another 7% this year, at least twice as fast as demand growth—maybe even faster as desperate producing countries try to offset the effects of lower prices on export earnings with even greater output.

In contrast, 54% of aluminum is produced in developed countries, where production is cut promptly when prices slide. In fact, the recent merger agree-

CHART **13-16**

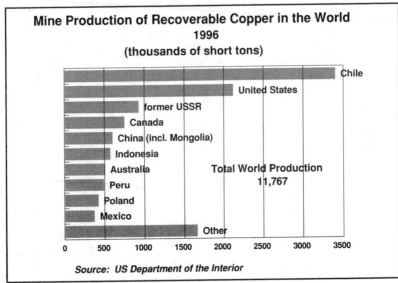

Mine Production of Recoverable Copper in the World
1996
(thousands of short tons)

Total World Production
11,767

Source: *US Department of the Interior*

ment between Aluminum Co. of America, the world's largest aluminum company, and Alumax, the third biggest US producer, is aimed, at least in part, at controlling output. Small wonder that copper prices have fallen much more than aluminum prices as markets anticipate the full effect of the spreading Asian crisis (Chart 13-17).

Crude Oil — Same Scene

The fall in crude oil prices (Chart 13-18) is similarly negative for Latin American oil exporters. In Mexico, petroleum accounts for a third of government tax revenues and 10% of merchandise exports, and the recent price decline has forced budget cuts and reductions in economic growth projections. And Mexico has enough other problems. The 1994 peso collapse made Mexican wages very competitive, but with economic recovery there and currency collapses in Asia, that's no longer true.

Far East countries are already cutting into Mexico's share of the US markets in steel, petrochemicals, electrical components, textiles, and auto parts, among others. About 20% of Mexican exports to the US compete with Asian products. Mexico's $6.5 billion trade surplus in 1996 has evaporated, largely because of surging imports in response to a booming economy and rapid wage growth (Chart 16-2). The government is forecasting a current account deficit of $12 billion this year, up from $7.5 billion in 1997, but this is based on exporting her oil at $12.50 per barrel. Mexican oil was recently selling at $10, however, and in our view, going lower. Big trade deficits again loom,

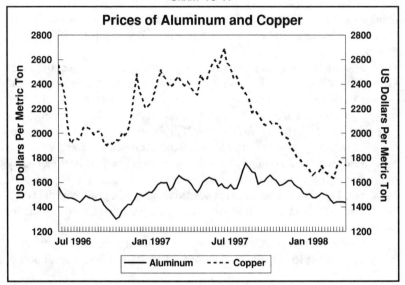

CHART **13-17**

Prices of Aluminum and Copper

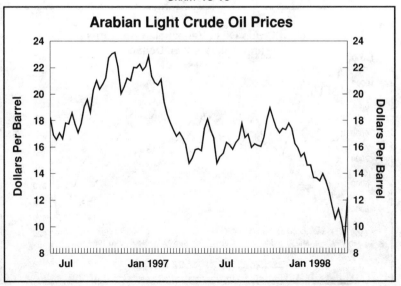

CHART **13-18**

Arabian Light Crude Oil Prices

and perhaps another peso crisis, especially since the Asian currency crisis and the 1994-95 peso collapse (Chart 16-1) are still fresh in people's minds.

Other Latin American countries have big exposure to Asia's problems and suffer from falling crude oil prices. Equador has more than a third of both her merchandise exports and government revenues from oil, and huge foreign debts to service which equal 73% of GDP. Crude oil, not coffee, is now Colombia's leading legal export. In Argentina, oil accounts for 12% of total exports.

Venezuela is the most exposed to oil, which accounts for a third of GDP. The bolivar has fallen against the dollar, but not enough to offset the decline in oil prices in dollars (Chart 13-19). Consequently, she is busily cutting government spending and growth forecasts. At the same time, this perennial cheater on her OPEC quota will probably step up her cheating, despite her recent agreement with Mexico, Saudi Arabia, and other OPEC and non-OPEC exporters to cut production. As with copper, oil is produced by many developing countries, in and out of the Middle East, that rely on it almost entirely for the export earnings needed to service huge foreign debts and pay for imports. And, as with copper, falling oil prices will encourage more production.

Even though US crude oil prices have declined from $21.50 per barrel last fall to below $15 in early 1998, this could mean even bigger drops ahead.

CHART **13-19**

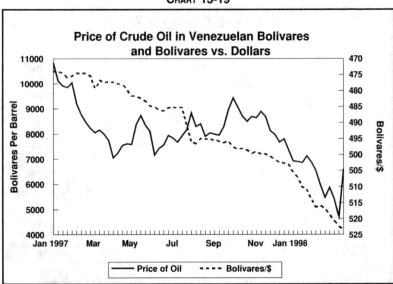

Development and production costs are much lower than when crude oil prices dropped below $10 per barrel in the mid 1980s due to technological advances such as 3D seismic surveys. In the Middle East it costs only about $1 per barrel to get oil out of the ground, and with new technology, the same cost applies to Norwegian oil under the otherwise inhospitable North Sea. OPEC increased its quotas in November 1997 to legitimize Venezuela, Qatar, Nigeria, and other cheaters, but that hasn't held them back and won't in the future. Each dollar decline in oil prices cuts Venezuelan export and tax revenues by $1.7 billion, money she requires to service large foreign and domestic debts. Venezuela is now America's biggest foreign crude oil supplier, in part because she's closer and safer than Middle East oil exporters. Also, interestingly, her proximity reduces floating inventories of oil in transit in tankers, a distinct liability when prices are falling (more on this in Chapter 28).

Indonesia, another big debt-laden oil producer, also has plenty of incentive to step up output. The Saudis are exceeding their new quota. Russia, who also depends heavily on oil for export earnings is planning to raise production and exports. The world's proven oil reserves are up 40% since the mid 1980s with much of it in non-OPEC lands, due in part to developments in new areas like Turkmenistan (Chapter 11) and in part due to new technology. Contrast this with current and impending demand weakness from Asia and elsewhere. The nine Asian tigers accounted for only 7% of oil consumption in 1986 and 13% in 1996, but for 52% of consumption's growth in that decade. It may be time to say bye-bye to OPEC, at least as an effective cartel.

You can easily see the vicious circle in globally-traded commodities. For example, Asia consumes 34% of the world's copper. So, as the Asian economies and their needs for copper collapse, prices nosedive. This, in turn, depresses the export earnings of developing-country producers, who then produce and export more in response, further depressing prices. Meanwhile, Asian currencies have fallen so much that imported commodity prices have risen in local currency terms, making life there even more difficult.

Devastating Inflation

It sounds ridiculous to talk about high current inflation in a book dedicated to deflation, but it is an intermediate step for some countries that have experienced massive devaluations. With the rupiah's collapse, consumers stormed the supermarkets to beat feared price hikes. And why not? From the time that Indonesia became a nation 50 years ago, the rupiah has dropped to less than a millionth of its initial value versus the buck.

The country faces at least a doubling in imported food prices, and will have to import more since domestic harvests are delayed by El Niño-related dry weather. Indonesia imports 100% of her wheat, a third of her sugar and soybeans, and 10% of her rice. Medicines, almost all of which have significant imported raw material components, have become so expensive that many are simply unavailable.

Overall, consumer prices rose 32% in February 1998 from a year ago in Indonesia, and wholesale prices were up 20%. On top of this, the prices of fuel, electricity, soybeans, sugar and wheat flour are still subsidized in Indonesia, but are scheduled to be free in coming months under the IMF agreement. Devaluations will make these countries more competitive, but with distressing temporary domestic inflationary effects.

Debts Get More Expensive

Deflation raises the cost of servicing all of those dollar and other hard currency debts that continued to pile up even in the first half of 1997 as currencies fell (Chart 13-5). The rupiah's collapse against the dollar means that the cost of Indonesia's dollar-denominated debts have more than doubled in rupiah terms. Without IMF bailout funds, that almost eliminates any near-term servicing on the $65 billion owed to Western banks and other lenders by private Indonesian firms. In reality, a de facto moratorium on debt repayment was instituted, although Treasury Secretary Robert Rubin describes it as "a framework for a voluntary private-sector initiative to help address the debt burden of the corporate sector." If this is voluntary, what does mandatory look like?

Adding fat to the fire, credit rating agencies, belatedly, cut the ratings on the sovereign and private debts of South Korea, Indonesia, Thailand, India and many other developing countries, often to junk status. This, of course, makes it even more expensive to borrow since many Western financial institutions aren't permitted to own junk obligations. New borrowing is drying up, and despite the best efforts of the IMF to help, additional debt moratoriums aren't out of the question. Note that in Indonesia, the Philippines, Malaysia, South Korea, and Thailand there was a net capital outflow of $12 billion in 1997, a far cry from the $93 billion net inflow in the salad days of 1996.

Meanwhile, domestic interest rates in countries with weak currencies, jacked up to prevent complete currency collapses, are pushing domestic borrowing costs to prohibitive levels (Chart 13-20). As lenders retrench, many firms are completely cut-off from credit. This has occurred in countries as far from the Pacific Rim as Russia and Latin America, as noted earlier. Scared depositors in Malaysia and elsewhere shifted money from local to foreign banks, thereby further depressing the supply of local capital.

CHART **13-20**

Pac Rim Short Rates

Hong Kong, S. Korea, Indonesia, Malaysia, Philippines, Singapore,
Thailand, Taiwan; Equal Weights

Source: ISI Group

And don't forget that financial institutions in some of the stricken countries were major lenders to others who are also now desperate for funds. South Korean merchant banks, now in many cases in liquidation after being pressed to repay their own borrowing, were major buyers of Russian Treasury bills and Latin American Brady bonds, as well as big lenders to now defunct South Korean firms. Last year's South Korean bad bank loans nearly quadrupled, and those figures are undoubtedly understated.

Inflation Breeds Deflation

Domestic inflation in developing countries is actually deflationary. Remember from Chapter 3 that inflation, at least in a direct sense, is a monetary phenomenon. As lending falls, money is simply not available to pay for the increased costs of imports at previous volumes, and imports fall. So do economic activity and prices. Of course, it isn't just domestic funds that are short. Foreign investors are reluctant to put money into a country whose currency shows no sign of ending its plunge. Real estate projects get canceled as lending evaporates. Even badly needed infrastructure is postponed. Anyone who's spent three hours in a Bangkok traffic jam on a hot day knows the need for more roads as well as sewers. Construction workers are laid off. Incomes fall. Bonuses, very important components of compensation in many Asian lands, are being slashed or eliminated.

The IMF—To the Rescue?

As usual, the IMF is pushing all out for deflation in return for committing almost $120 billion, so far, to Thailand, Indonesia and South Korea. Many of its demands—for more transparent accounting; openness to foreign ownership of financial and nonfinancial firms; canceling wasteful government projects; giving the central bank full autonomy to raise interest rates; restructuring the banks; the end of monopolies and trade restrictions, as well as cronieism, government subsidies and nepotism—make sense.

But IMF insistence on higher taxes and government spending cuts to balance budgets, and high interest rates to attract foreign capital, do nothing but depress economic growth domestically and spread the effects internationally. Already, some of the millions of people from Indonesia, Burma and Bangladesh who are working at low-paid jobs in Thailand and Malaysia are being sent home. In Malaysia, one quarter of the work force is from abroad, and when many of them are returned, social unrest may result in their home countries. Returning workers and the collapsing domestic economy have pushed Indonesian unemployment from 2.5 million in mid-1997 to 8 million in early 1998, or 9% of the labor force. In addition, disguised unemployment—those with less work than is needed to fulfill basic needs—may reach 40 million this year, or 45% of the labor force, according to the Federation of All Indonesian Workers Union.

To meet IMF demands, Thailand has not only hiked interest rates but also is cutting government spending, raising taxes, and planning to run a budget surplus. What will they do when the collapsing economy depresses tax collections? As a result, at least in part, Thailand is skipping the intermediate, local inflationary, stage and going directly to deflation. Despite the baht's collapse, the economy is falling so fast that little inflation is in evidence. Inflation-fueling imports have dried up as salaries fall, even in baht terms, and bonuses, often six months' salary, disappear. Office space rental rates have fallen, as much as 50% for cash payments.

A Tough Row to Hoe

South Korea, another IMF client, has already seen a collapse in industrial production and imports, which were down 68% in February 1998 compared to a year earlier. Auto and gasoline sales have nosedived as people turn to public transportation. Restaurants, too, are under pressure as citizens brown bag it for lunch. South Korea's citizens have donated their gold jewelry to help the nation, and have been asked to donate blood for export. The IMF has eased up a bit on its demand for a South Korean budget surplus, but that's simply facing reality. Budget surpluses are almost impossible in recessions.

CHART 13-21

ASIAN TIGERS REAL GDP ANNUAL GROWTH RATES			
	1975-1980	**1980-1985**	**1985-1990**	**1990-1996**
China	8.4%	10.2%	7.9%	11.9%
Hong Kong	12.0%	5.6%	7.9%	6.4%
Indonesia	8.0%	4.7%	5.6%	9.5%
Malaysia	8.5%	5.1%	6.8%	10.4%
Philippines	4.6%	-1.4%	4.7%	3.3%
Singapore	8.5%	6.2%	8.0%	10.1%
Taiwan	10.6%	6.7%	9.1%	7.8%
Thailand	7.9%	5.4%	9.7%	8.1%
S. Korea	7.5%	8.4%	10.0%	9.0%

Indonesia plans to meet her agreement with the IMF by massive spending cuts and by finding big new sources of revenues. She's more likely to suffer soaring budget deficits and falling employment as recession sets in. Indeed, the government hopes to limit the budget deficit to 3.2% of GDP for the fiscal year ending March 31, 1999, and foresees a 4% decline in economic activity and an inflation rate of 17%. A real GDP decline of 10% to 15% seems more likely, with prices rising 50%.

Economies geared to rapid growth of the sort these nations have seen in the past (Chart 13-21) are ill prepared for rapid slowdowns. Most of their growth goes into exports and capital investment, and, of course, into the hands of those running the country. Consequently, it takes economic growth rates that far exceed Western standards to raise average living standards, especially considering their growing and young populations, hoards of people moving from rural to urban settings in search of better jobs and lives, and, in some cases, sizable immigration.

And rapid slowdowns they have been. In the last five months of 1997, manufacturing production fell 27% in Indonesia. Hong Kong retail sales dropped 36% in the last quarter of the year. Taiwan's industrial production declined 14% in the October 1997-January 1998 period. South Korea suffered a whopping 57% plummet in retail sales in that same period, while industrial production nosedived 29%.

The constraints on buying anything, domestically produced or imported, isn't confined to the middle and lower income classes in Asia. Previous zillionaires are back manning their pushcarts. Recent major art auctions have been busts with bids 25% to 50% below auction house estimates, with many works left unsold. Cognac was the hallmark of the new rich in Asia. In 1989, people there drank less than a third of the world's output, but more than half of it in 1992. And they demanded quality. The Taiwanese, for example, paid three times the average US price. The deflationary depression in Japan first took its toll on big cognac spenders, but the booming rest of Asia stepped into the breach. Now cognac drinking throughout Asia has virtually collapsed.

Political unrest and calls for new leaders are to be expected. In Indonesia, the students and the powerful military are restless. The new South Korean President, Kim, may owe his victory, at least in part, to the crisis there. Furthermore, ethnic problems are, as usual, surfacing in hard times. In Indonesia the ethnic Chinese, 4% of the population but controlling 70% to 80% of the country's wealth, are frequent targets of riots. The indigenous Indonesians hold them responsible for the crisis, and many have moved their families and household goods abroad and prepared to flee themselves.

Financial Effects

In effect, then, Asian devaluations will deflate those economies. So, too, will the attempts of Hong Kong and Brazil to maintain their currency

CHART 13-22

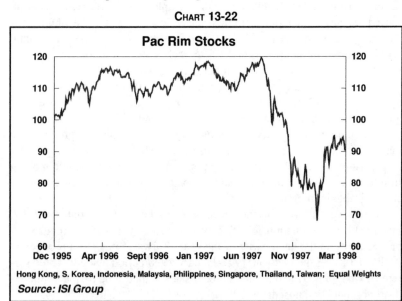

Hong Kong, S. Korea, Indonesia, Malaysia, Philippines, Singapore, Thailand, Taiwan; Equal Weights
Source: ISI Group

CHART **13-23**

	% DROP IN MARKET CAPITALIZATION	RATIO OF DROP IN CAPITALIZATION TO 1996 GDP
Hong Kong	-30.2%	-131.6%
Singapore	-27.4%	-42.2%
Indonesia	-26.2%	-14.3%
Malaysia	-33.2%	-116.4%
South Korea	-38.3%	-10.0%
Taiwan	-9.0%	-13.1%
Philippines	-32.1%	-36.7%
Thailand	-36.0%	-19.4%
China	-16.8%	-2.8%
Japan	-19.4%	-20.2%

Figures are from 1997 peaks of the markets to March 31, 1998

pegs, as you saw earlier. And these downward economic pressures are being augmented by growing financial crises in Asia and elsewhere. Stock market collapses (Chart 13-22) had destroyed huge amounts of wealth, especially in relation to the GDPs of these countries (Chart 13-23). Not surprisingly, local mutual funds, encouraged by governments in recent years to boost local involvement in their stock markets, are being abandoned by investors, and unfortunately, few diversified outside their region. There goes another source of capital.

Previously unreported debts are, as usual in financial crises, coming out of the wood work. The Indonesian government says total external debt is $117 billion but private estimates put it closer to $200 billion. About 50% of loans are nonperforming, far above the 20% level that normally forces banks to recapitalize. It recently came to light that in the last year and half, Thailand's central bank dumped in $25 billion to prop up financial institutions, most of which have now folded. Those countries certainly aren't going to be retiring debt soon, at least not voluntarily. Look at what's been happening to govern-

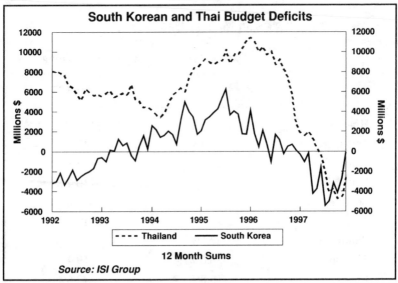

CHART 13-24

ment budget balances in South Korea and Thailand (Chart 13-24). They're collapsing from big surpluses to equally big deficits.

Self-Feeding

And like any financial crisis, this one is feeding on itself. It is becoming clear that a number of Asian banks and companies used financial derivatives to bet heavily against the dollar last year when the Asian crisis commenced. Some even doubled their positions on the basis of government assurances that their currencies would be supported. Indonesian state-owned bank Ekspor Impor, for example, was short the dollar to the tune of $2.23 billion in December 1997. These derivatives are not reported on balance sheets and normally only become visible when the contracts mature.

Huge losses are in prospect unless Asian currencies rebound quickly, and those losses may be shared by the international banks that sold the derivatives. Indeed, JP Morgan took substantial loss provisions late last year for $500 million it's trying to collect on derivative contracts sold to four South Korean financial institutions. I wonder how long it will be before the Boards of those banks will allow any similar transactions in Asia, regardless of the borrowers' reputations. Indeed, a recent Federal Reserve survey shows that banks are tightening their loans in Asia drastically.

Financially-pressed South Korean companies can't issue stock due to weak demand, can't find banks willing to lend, and can't sell real estate and buildings for much of anything because there are so many sellers and few buyers. Not surprising, they and other Asian firms are dumping foreign assets to shore up their balance sheets. With US properties rising in dollar terms, an owner that keeps its books in rupiahs has seen a huge gain on holdings in America.

The Crisis Spreads

What makes the Asian financial crisis so significant is the speed with which it has spread. Soon after Southeast Asian countries devalued last fall, Pakistan followed, citing competitive pressures. Note that Pakistan has $30 billion in foreign debts and a slim $2 billion in foreign exchange reserves. Meanwhile, India's central bank was spending meaningful chunks of its slender foreign exchange reserves, tightening credit and imposing currency restrictions. Those measures slowed, but did not arrest, the rupee's descent (Chart 13-25). Indian exports to troubled Asian lands are suffering as well. South Africa's is now being pushed down by the devaluation in Asian countries that compete with her in global markets.

CHART 13-25

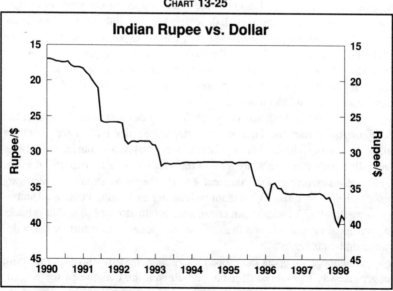

CHART **13-26**

The devaluations spread to the Philippines and the peso's decline there has led to severe belt tightening. Federal workers have been told to cut expenses by 25%. The Asia crisis threw the booming Russian stock market into reverse (Chart 13-26) and interest rates there leaped to keep the ruble from collapsing as foreign investors fled, worried, among other things, about the effect of commodity price weakness on Russia's export earnings. Not to be excluded, share prices in Poland, the Czech Republic, Hungary and elsewhere in Eastern Europe were hard hit. Sure, that region is economically tied to Western Europe, but it also competes in global markets with Asia in auto parts, chemicals and electronics.

The Vietnam dong fell in sympathy with devaluations elsewhere, but not enough to offset the Thai baht's collapse. So rice buyers are switching from Vietnam to Thailand, a big blow to a country where farmers are living basically at subsistence and are 80% of the population. Rice exports, at 4% of GDP, are a key foreign exchange earner. Furthermore, export-oriented garment and shoe factories in Vietnam are closing as demand falls. And smugglers are flooding Vietnam with cheap Thai toothpaste and soap that is backing out local production and draining scarce dollars. Can further dong devaluation be far behind?

Singapore shoppers have been charging across the three-quarter mile long causeway to Malaysia for bargains, given the collapse in the ringgit. This obviously delights Malaysian shopkeepers, but what they gain, their counterparts in Singapore lose. Also, despite the excellent financial conditions of Singapore, the island nation has not been immune from the crisis. It has deepened the effects of the government's mid-1996 anti-real estate speculation measures, and buyers are on the sidelines waiting for still lower real estate prices. Construction is drying up. Foreigners are abandoning the island nation, now that rapid economic growth there is being halved.

Singapore's stocks have fallen with the rest and interest rates have been hiked to protect the currency, which has weakened against the dollar but not nearly as much as her neighbors'. This and the falling economies all around her paint a bleak picture for Singapore's exports, half of which go to Asia. Furthermore, Singapore, where half of all national income is saved, much of it through the compulsory Central Provident Fund, appears to have big shareholdings in Indonesian companies whose prices have collapsed. Banks there have 16% of their total assets in Malaysia, Indonesia, Thailand, South Korea, and the Philippines. Not surprising, six major Singapore banks reported a 30% decline in 1997 earnings from 1996.

Taiwan, another country with little foreign debt and $80 billion in foreign-currency reserves, still has been hurt by her neighbors' problems. Her currency has not slid nearly as much as theirs, so her exports in January and February 1998 are down 10% from the previous year, turning a trade surplus to a deficit. Meanwhile, like Hong Kong, Taiwan has far too many office buildings and factories, fueled by huge domestic borrowing that equals 160% of GDP. Almost 40% of loans outstanding are for real estate investments, and two-thirds of all bank loans are backed by property collateral, twice the ratio of Japanese banks. In the midst of the Asian meltdown, this degree of financial leverage is precarious.

Excess export capacity is simply being shifted from one developing country to another through competitive devaluations. Bad enough, but the situation will be a lot worse if the 500-pound gorilla, China, joins the parade. Will she? And what will be the effect on and responses of Japan? How about the fallout on the financial and economic structures of developed Western countries? I'll address these questions in the next and following chapters.

Chapter 14

China May Well Devalue

In a way, China led the devaluation parade, having cut the yuan 70% against the dollar in 1994 (Chart 14-1) after five previous devaluations in the last 13 years. This wasn't nearly as negative for the other developing Asian countries as the fall in the yen, starting in 1995, since China's economy is less than 15% of Japan's (Chart 14-2). Still, China accounts for a third of the developing Asian country output, and if she follows them in another devalu-

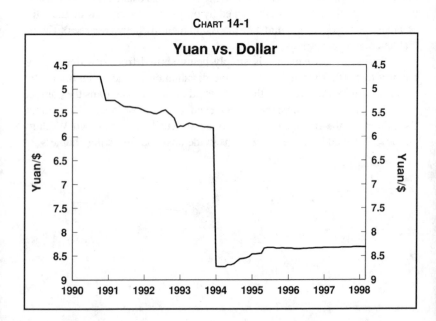

CHART 14-1

ation, they will be forced to respond in a competitive devaluation race for the bottom. She's the 500-pound gorilla. Taiwan, with huge investments in China and big trade ties, could hardly stand still for a cut in the yuan. Nor could the rest of Asia nor Latin America without unacceptable losses of global market shares to China.

We'll Never Do It!

Chinese officials deny that they will devalue, but so, too, did Mexican leaders right up to the very day they cut the peso loose in late 1994. China will probably devalue, but later. A drop in the yuan now would undoubtedly

CHART 14-2

ASIAN SHARES OF WORLD GDP AND MERCHANDISE EXPORTS 1996

	GDP	EXPORTS
China	2.6%	3.0%
S. Korea	1.7%	2.4%
Taiwan	1.0%	1.8%
Indonesia	0.8%	0.7%
Thailand	0.6%	1.3%
Hong Kong	0.5%	3.2%
Malaysia	0.3%	1.5%
Philippines	0.3%	0.7%
Singapore	0.3%	2.2%
Total	8.1%	16.7%
Japan	18.6%	8.7%
Total Asia	26.7%	25.3%

Source: IMF Direction of Trade Statistics and IMF International Financial Statistics

take the Hong Kong dollar with it and destroy that currency's 15-year peg to the dollar at a time that is embarrassingly close to the takeover from Britain.

It can be argued that China has such low labor costs relative to her neighbors (Chart 10-2) that she has no need to catch up with their devaluations. Low labor costs, yes, but low productivity too, so unit costs aren't all that low. Besides, in the low-skilled labor area, China competes with the likes of India, and the rupee has fallen in sympathy with other Asian currencies (Chart 13-25). The Bank of China, the central bank, said the nation will face considerable competitive pressure from neighbors in Asia, especially in textiles, shoes, home appliances, and clothing. The advantage of her 1994 devaluation has now evaporated as the yuan has risen sharply against her competing neighbors' currencies (Chart 14-3). In the December 1997-February 1998 period, Chinese goods exports dropped at a 20% annual rate while imports climbed 12%, narrowing her trade surplus from both sides.

Export Dependent

Exports account for about one-fifth of Chinese GDP, but for the bulk of last year's disappointing 8.8% economic growth, and much of the rest was due to unsustainable inventory building. The domestic economy has been slowed by earlier inflation-fighting monetary and fiscal restraint, but now inflation is non-existent and deflation is setting in (Chart I-5). Consumers,

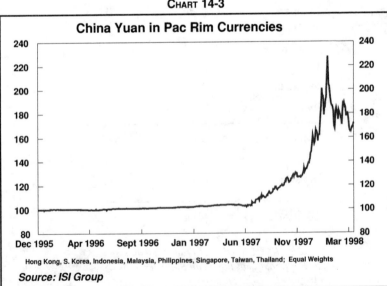

CHART 14-3

China Yuan in Pac Rim Currencies

Hong Kong, S. Korea, Indonesia, Malaysia, Philippines, Singapore, Taiwan, Thailand; Equal Weights

Source: ISI Group

CHART 14-4

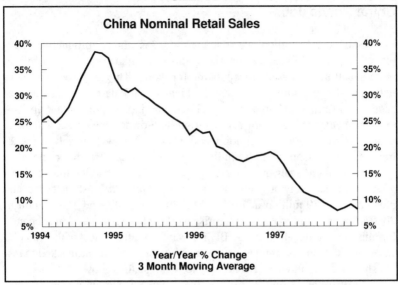

China Nominal Retail Sales

Year/Year % Change
3 Month Moving Average

who routinely save 40% of their after-tax incomes, are subdued, perhaps waiting for even lower prices (Chart 14-4). Interest rates have been cut repeatedly to rekindle the economy, but to no avail. Reserves are piling up in banks as they cower under already huge bad loans and refuse to lend.

About $200 billion or 20% of those loans are nonperforming—five times the banks' equity capital—and 5% or 6% of them are unrecoverable, according to the Bank of China. The banks are essentially broke, but the government owns them and most of the companies they lent to (50% of which are in the red with debt to equity ratios of 200% to 400%), so there's little likelihood of foreclosures. Nevertheless, credit rating agencies are cutting their outlooks on China from stable to negative, and also reducing their ratings on Hong Kong's debt.

Still, China wants to clean up these bad loans, but at the current pace, it will take decades even if the government plan to raise $33 billion for that purpose is successful. Now, you're probably aware that the Chinese take the long-term view. Chairman Mao was once asked his opinion of the French Revolution. "Too soon to tell," he replied. Still China can't wait because of her immense employment problems.

China Needs Jobs

She has 200 million people in coastal areas who are productively employed, about 1 billion in the hinterland who would like to be, and 100 million more squatting in coastal cities looking for work. This last group is potentially socially disruptive. Note that the Tiananmen Square uprising was preceded by a similar unemployment problem, and jobless protests are up 50% in the past year. Furthermore, restructuring state-owned enterprises will make about a third of their 100 million workers surplus, as well as half of the 20 million civil servants, while 15 million people enter the work force annually.

In addition, a new government proposal calls for halving the 8 million government and party officials. The *China People's Daily* estimates the surplus labor at 130 million in 1996, 370 million in 2000, and 450 million in 2010. About 12 million state enterprise workers have been axed in exchange for minimum living allowances. Beijing wants to sell off most of the 100,000 state-owned businesses and merge the rest into 50 government-backed titans, but she needs employment for those who will lose their jobs.

Furthermore, China has about 40% excess capacity in manufacturing. Sure, some of it is in state-owned factories that turn out shoes that nobody wants to buy. Only the guys building warehouses to hold them benefit. Still, the nation has plenty of unutilized and economically useful productive potential. Textile industry capacity utilization is 20%. China produces 30 million TV sets a year, 35% of global production, but can sell only about half at home.

Real estate is also in abundance. Construction continued to leap and support the economy for years after inflation started to fade, but activity was flat in 1997 from 1996 and will probably fall as prices collapse. Vacancy rates in Beijing for Class A space are about 35%, and 70% in Shanghai's new Pudong Financial District. Rent at Beijing's China World Trade Center is now $65 a square meter, down from $110 in 1995. New apartments elsewhere are selling at about one-sixth the original asking price.

Growth Needed Desperately

China needs growth to employ people, to utilize excess capacity, and to restructure, but the outlook is bleak. Foreign direct investment accounts for one-third of China's total investment, or 12% of GDP, but only grew 3% last year when foreign contracts fell about 30% as international money fled Asia. Nearly two-thirds of that investment used to come from Hong Kong, but her highly-leveraged lenders are suffering their own financial problems. So, Hong

CHART 14-5

FOREIGN DIRECT INVESTMENTS IN CHINA
(IN BILLIONS OF DOLLARS)

	1993	1996	FIRST 6 MONTHS 1997	—JAN-JUNE 1997— % CHANGE YEAR EARLIER	% TOTAL
Hong Kong	$73.9	$28.0	$8.8	-51%	38%
US	$6.8	$6.9	$1.7	-63%	7%
Taiwan	$10.0	$5.1	$1.3	-64%	6%
Japan	$3.0	$5.1	$1.2	-61%	5%
Others	$17.8	$28.1	$10.0	-38%	44%
Total	$111.4	$73.3	$22.9	-50%	100%

Sources: Chinese Ministry of Foreign Trade and Economic Cooperation; US-China Business Council

Kong's direct investments in China dropped 51% in the first half of 1997 and accounted for only 38% of the total (Chart 14-5). The numbers in early 1998 are undoubtedly a lot smaller. This drying up of critical foreign investment growth occurs at a time when no government or bank funds are available to replace it. And competition from devalued countries will probably slash Chinese export growth from the 20% forecast for this year. Also, the liquidation of superfluous inventories and a falling trade surplus will be drags on growth. Furthermore, a management think tank in China recently predicted 6% real GDP growth for 1998, far below the government's earlier 9% to 10% projection. Given China's problems, 6% is painfully low, a sure ticket to regional recession and riots. The 50% fall in Chinese stocks (Chart 14-6) illustrates dramatically investors' outlook.

CHART **14-6**

China Shanghai B Shares Index

Exports, Not Imports

Despite a faltering economy, Beijing shows little interest in domestic consumption growth, but rather favors exports to the exclusion of imports. American corporations have learned, painfully, that their investments in China better provide a big component of technology to help China develop domestic production that will then substitute for imports and achieve self-sufficiency. GM recently won the right to build a plant in Shanghai because it was the high bidder in the technology transfer game. In the import arena, capital equipment is vastly preferred over consumer goods. Many American CEOs salivate over the prospect of 1.3 billion Chinese consuming their products. Suppose each one of them drinks just one Coke a year, is the logic. I think it's more realistic to see them as 1.3 billion producers who are concentrating on exports of anything and everything they can sell abroad.

And China is taking steps to make sure consumers spend less of their money on imports or anything else. Beijing is encouraging saving in forms that will not be tucked away in mattresses, but can be channeled into export industries. Starting this year, younger workers must fund their own pensions, unlike their older colleagues. Employers and employees will be required to contribute 20% of company total wages to retirement funds. By emphasizing personal responsibility for retirement, the state, ironically, plans to raise money for state-directed investments.

If you were running China and faced this gloomy outlook, and were philosophically oriented toward self-sufficiency and export-driven growth, what would you do? I'd devalue and take away from our dear friends in Asia, and elsewhere, whatever low-labor cost export business there was available in the world. I bet they reach the same conclusion, sooner or later. Indeed, the Export-Import Bank of China is increasing lending to exporting companies by as much as 60% this year, and the export-tax rebate on textiles has been raised. China is running a $50 billion trade surplus, but even that isn't big enough to provide the necessary domestic stimulus. Watch it get much bigger—much to the consternation of Washington—especially if China devalues.

If China's the 500-pound gorilla in Asia, Japan is the whale. And so far, Japan is a beached whale, part of Asia's problem, and not a leader in its solution. Will this continue? See Chapter 15.

CHAPTER 15

JAPAN IS STILL PART OF THE ASIAN PROBLEM, NOT THE SOLUTION

Honey Bees and Japanese

Honey bees work for the good of their colony with no concern for their own welfare. (They certainly don't work for the benefit of the beekeeper, as my 500+ stings this past season attest.) During the spring and summer, worker bees live an average of 28 days, literally working themselves to death in order to lay in honey and pollen to feed yet-unborn generations over the next winter. Furthermore, worker bees die when they sting, but don't hesitate to do so to protect the hive.

Honey bees are also highly efficient, much more so than the native bees, wasps and hornets, that they have replaced as pollinators ever since they were introduced from the Old World by immigrating Europeans. But with efficiency goes vulnerability. Loss of a hive's single queen can be curtains for the colony without swift action by the beekeeper. Native yellow jackets, in contrast, die off in the fall except for the queens, which hibernate.   If a yellow jacket queen doesn't make it through the winter, she doesn't take 10,000 to 20,000 workers with her, as is often the case with honey bee queens.

Japan, Inc. Lives

The Japanese society and economy resemble a honey bee colony, at least much more closely than do Western countries in which the individual is much more valued. Consider the Japanese willingness to die for the Emperor in World War II, and the structure of the economy since then. Tariff, and more recently, non-tariff barriers to trade are used consistently and effectively to limit imports of consumer goods and services and push up their prices.

CHART 15-1

MANUFACTURING IMPORTS
AS A % OF TOTAL IMPORTS
1985-95

Canada	87.2%
France	78.9%
Germany	79.1%
Italy	73.3%
Japan	58.0%
UK	82.6%
US	84.2%
EU-15	76.5%

Notice (Chart 15-1) that only 58% of Japanese imports are manufactured goods, while all other major countries have at least 73%. In 1985, a government-connected organization prohibited the importation of skis because they hadn't been tested on Japanese snow—which, I guess, is different from snow anywhere else in the world.

At the same time, the prices of competing domestic items are kept high by inefficient distribution systems and sanctioned cartels. As a result, the Japanese have about the same incomes as average Americans but only two-thirds of their spending power.

Since goods and services are expensive, Japanese consumers are encouraged to save, and save they do in legendary fashion—three or four times as much of their after-tax incomes as Americans (Chart 2-9). The cozy relationship among the Japanese government, bureaucracy, and big business that runs the whole system then directs the investment of this low-cost savings away from foreign investments and through the banks into export industries in which Japan can achieve global dominance, as discussed in Chapter 5. This satisfies their "export or die" mentality, all for the greater glory of the land of the rising sun, not the individual Japanese who make it possible. This mercantilism system would have made the 18th century French green with envy—and it has been copied throughout Asia, as noted in Chapter 13.

Despite the lowly position of consumers in Japan, they apparently don't mind. I say "apparently" because each time I visit Japan, I come back realizing that I understand these people and their culture less than I did on the previous visit. But look at the facts. In recent years Japanese governments have been weak and short-lived, ever since the Liberal Democratic Party lost

CHART 15-2

FISCAL POLICY
CONTRIBUTION TO JAPAN GDP GROWTH

FISCAL YEAR	IMPACT OF FISCAL PACKAGES ON GDP	ACTUAL GDP GROWTH
1991	0%	2.9%
1992	1.1%	0.4%
1993	0.8%	0.5%
1994	0.8%	0.7%
1995	1.2%	2.7%
1996	0.4%	3.4%
1997	–1.5%	0.4%

Source: Nomura Research Institute

its four-decade long strangle hold. Many say that the weak governments allow the Ministry of Finance to assert itself, and without question, the powerful bureaucrats there are more concerned with cutting the government deficit than with promoting economic growth and consumer purchasing power.

Little to Show for Fiscal Stimulus

This isn't to say that there has been no fiscal stimulus in Japan, but as Chart 15-2 shows, the five packages of tax-cuts and spending increases introduced in the 1992-96 fiscal years had little effect. In fact, in some of these years, the stimulus exceeded the GDP growth. These packages caused a stimulative shift in Japan's government budget balance from a 3% surplus to a 4½% deficit (see Chart 2-10)—a huge swing of 7½ percentage points. As the money from tax cuts and public works outlays is spent and respent, the multiplier effect is at least double the stimulus effect. The fact that after all this stimulus, the economy remains stagnant shows that the private sector has been very weak . In all likelihood, Japanese are saving more to make up for losses on their stock and real estate holdings, the exact reverse of what's going on in the US (see Chapter 17).

During this time, stocks have deflated by over 50% (Chart 15-3) and some land prices even more (Chart 15-4). As you saw back in Chart 12-12, manufactured goods prices have been deflating since 1990. In these circumstances low, almost zero, interest rates are to no avail (Chart 12-10). In deflation when buyers are waiting for low prices, as they seem to be doing in Japan (Chart 15-5) and capacity is in excess, low interest rates provide little stimu-

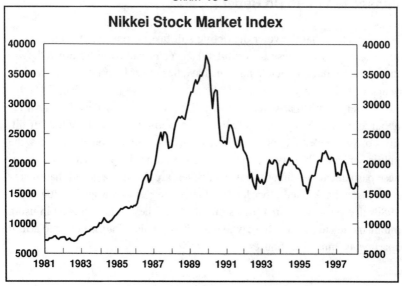

CHART **15-3**

Nikkei Stock Market Index

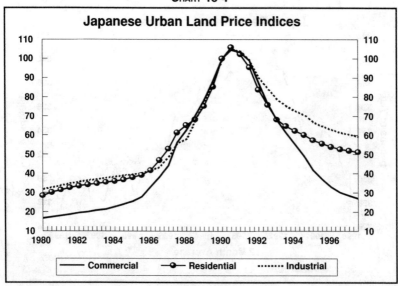

CHART **15-4**

Japanese Urban Land Price Indices

— Commercial   —○— Residential   ········ Industrial

lus (see Chapter 18 for more). Also, unemployment rates that are startlingly high for Japan (Chart 3-6) and the threatened end to lifetime employment guarantees have scared many into restraining their spending further.

Japanese Voters Do Rebel

It is true that the voter districting still favors conservative agricultural interests over urban consumers. Still, urban voters could force reform if they're mad enough, but no notable outcries have been heard, despite the now eight years of deflationary depression in Japan.

And it isn't that voters aren't willing to protest if they feel strongly about an issue. Two years ago when the government spent hundreds of billions of yen in cleaning up the failure of seven *jusen*, or housing lenders, the public screamed bloody murder, even barricading the entrance to the Japanese parliament building to show its displeasure. Voters believed that money from *jusen*, banks, and other lenders fueled the real estate speculation in the 1980s that pushed housing prices out of sight. They had no interest in using public money to bail out those who made it impossible for the public to afford apartments, much less houses.

CHART 15-5

Japan Real Household Spending

Source: ISI Group

Dead 96% of the Time

This honey-bee like support for the nation at the expense of individuals' welfare says a lot about the Japanese character. Individualism is not prized in Japan, as demonstrated by the old expression, the nail that sticks up will be pounded down. This attitude and the national acceptance of ongoing economic malaise also suggest a deep seated fatalism in Japan that is not known in the West.

Some years ago, my wife and I attended a Kabuki play in Tokyo. The theater had a marvelous translation system, complete with individual receivers and ear phones. During the intermission the interpreter traced the history of No and Kabuki plays and other forms of classic Japanese literature. He also noted that a contemporary Japanese scholar had tabulated the plot outcomes of this complete range of literature—all written, by the way, before Japan's disastrous World War II experience. In 96% of the plots, the hero ends up dead. Wow! Even the ancient Greeks had a lot more comedies than that to mix with their famous tragedies.

And, like a honey bee colony, Japan, Inc. can be extremely efficient when all is going well. This was certainly true in the 1980s when Japanese manufacturing exports were so threatening that many Americans thought that they'd soon be either run out of jobs by the Japanese juggernaut or working for them. But like a honey bee colony, Japanese efficiency comes at the cost of limited adaptability to changing circumstances. With their slow, group-wide decision-making process, or *ringi*, the Japanese can be fearsome once they've all agreed on the marching orders, but when the battlefield shifts unexpectedly, they often deteriorate into inaction and chaos as disorder sets in quickly.

Japan in the 1990s Is Like the US in the 1930s

That has happened in the 1990s. Back in March 1988, while the Japanese bubble economy was still expanding rapidly, we published our third book with a chapter titled, "A Depression is More Likely in Japan than in the US." In it, we compared the 1980s in Japan with the Roaring '20s in America, and went on to forecast that the 1990s there would resemble the 1930s here—a decade of depression and slow workout of the previous decade's excesses. We also noted the many structural changes Japan needed to make, like redirecting the engine of growth away from exports and toward consumer spending and infrastructure building, and the elimination of lifetime employment.

Now, you may be thinking, the Japanese are smart people. They are also great imitators. Surely, then, they will learn from the US experience in the 1930s, and, equipped with the modern understanding of economics and finance, they will correct their problems and regain economic health quickly. But for the first eight years of the 1990s they haven't, despite continuing pressure from Washington and elsewhere for structural reform. Like members of a medieval Christian flagellate procession, they seem to enjoy beating themselves with whips. It's hard for me to understand, but remember that 96% of their literary heros end up dead.

The 1936 Parallel . . .

The Japanese seem determined to rerun the US miserable experience in the 1930s, even down to the serious American mistakes of 1936. After the economic collapse ended in 1933, US bank reserves grew rapidly—not due to aggressive Federal Reserve open market action but because of the gold influx from abroad, after the US revalued the yellow metal, and silver purchases by the Treasury, which used them to support Western mining states. The banks, sick of bad loans and fearful of further runs, let their reserves pile up.

By 1936, however, the Fed worried that these reserves would turn into inflation-spawning loans. In the first quarter of 1936, the economy had grown for four years and wholesale prices were up 33% from their trough in 1933's first quarter, although they had regained only about half their fall from the fourth quarter of 1928. The Fed didn't want to halt the economy, but still raised reserve requirements in three stages. Central reserve city banks' required reserves went from 13% to 19 ½% in August 1936, to 22 ¾% in March 1937 and 26% two months later. Meanwhile, the Treasury began to sterilize increases in the gold stock in a coordinated attempt to prevent growth in lendable bank reserves. The banks reacted by cutting lending and selling Treasury securities in order to retain liquidity, so the money supply shrank and interest rates rose.

Furthermore, after the 1936 election, President Roosevelt responded to widespread criticism of the federal deficit, then 5.5% of GNP. Although deficit spending was probably helping the economy on balance, few, including the President, approved of it. He engineered income tax hikes to boost federal revenues, with the top tax rate rising from 63% to 79% in 1936, and spending cuts the next year. The result of both monetary and fiscal stringency was the sharp 1937-38 "Roosevelt depression." The unemployment rate jumped from 14.3% to 19.0% and industrial production nosedived by 33%. That's a lot! In the 1973-75 recession, the worst in the postwar era, industrial production fell *only* 15%.

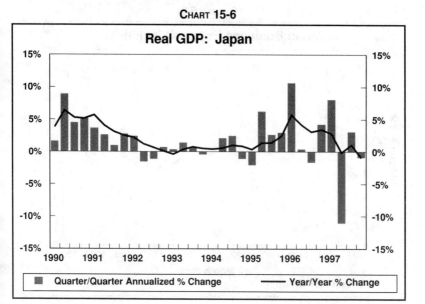

CHART 15-6

Real GDP: Japan

Quarter/Quarter Annualized % Change — Year/Year % Change

. . . Repeats in Japan

Almost on cue, 60 years later the Japanese government decided to tighten fiscal policy to counteract the government deficit, despite the bare beginning of economic recovery in 1995-96 (Chart 15-6). The consumption tax was hiked from 3% to 5% on April 1, 1997, income tax rebates were removed, and the social welfare tax was increased, as mentioned in Chapter 2. Furthermore, earlier public works spending programs were not renewed, resulting in a negative fiscal stimulus effect (Chart 15-2).

Also on cue, economic activity collapsed in the second quarter of 1997 and has remained weak ever since, with real GDP falling 0.9% in 1997. In March 1998, Tokyo department store sales dropped 21% from a year earlier. Business sentiment continues to be depressed, and as Japanese firms react to weak sales by cutting labor and other costs, real disposable income has been falling since the first quarter of 1997. Business failures (Chart 15-7) leaped 64% in the March 31 fiscal year.

Terrible Timing

Renewed business weakness in Japan couldn't come at a more inopportune time, since the government has embarked on the deregulation of finan-

CHART 15-7

cial services, the "Big Bang" program, as noted in Chapter 5. This is coming just when the previous interlocking business relationships and tightly drawn business territories are no longer feasible.

Consequently, even though Japanese authorities said that Hokkaido Takushoko Bank, Japan's 10th largest, was "too big to fail" in 1997, other banks were too weak to take it over in the traditional Japanese fashion. Authorities also said that fourth ranked Yamaichi Securities was "too big to fail," but when that broker's obligations were downgraded to junk status, the main bank in its *keiretsu*, Fuji Bank, declined to help. No government bailout materialized either, and the firm folded.

Furthermore, the Ministry of Finance revealed 200 billion yen ($1.6 billion) in hidden Yamaichi losses accumulated over the last decade, apparently some of it due to payoffs to gangsters. And this follows the surfacing of hidden trading losses in US Treasury bonds at Daiwa Bank and in copper at Sumitomo Corp. Given the Japanese concern with "face" and reluctance to admit mistakes, one wonders what additional nasty surprises will come out in the wash for other firms in financial difficulty.

I don't know of any honey bee equivalent to hiding losses, but current bad loans and financial deregulation in Japan are making it much tougher to cover up problems. Boom times cover a multitude of sins, but financial stress reveals reality.

CHART **15-8**

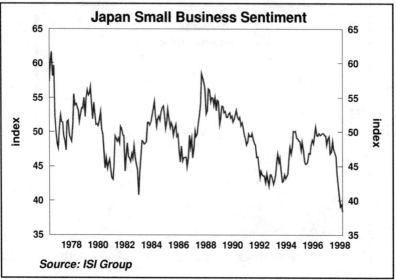

CHART **15-8**

Japan Small Business Sentiment

Source: ISI Group

A Big Shock

Note that the deregulation and competition now entering the Japanese financial area are also big shocks because, like most other industries, financial services have been carefully sheltered from domestic and foreign competition. Despite her reputation as an awesome exporter, Japan sends only 9% of all goods abroad through highly efficient firms that often dominate world markets. The rest are sold to domestic buyers by generally inefficient, cartel-structured producers, layers and layers of wholesalers, and inefficient mom and pop retailers, as noted earlier.

As banks quiver under the reality of coming competition, stricter capital requirements, more disclosure, and mountains of bad loans, borrowers are suffering as well. Small businesses, that have traditionally relied on close relationships with their banks to see them through thick and thin, are finding the lending window closed, and confidence there has plunged (Chart 15-8).

Scared bankers are curtailing loans to big businesses as well, as they devote their resources to cleaning up their balance sheets, just like US banks in the mid-1930s. Ironically, banks are only now facing the reality of real estate and other loans that went sour six or eight years ago after the bubble economy burst. But then only now is Japan ending the system in which banks

CHART 15-9

JAPANESE EXPORTS IN 1996	
US	27.2%
EU	15.3%
Germany	4.4%
UK	3.0%
France	1.3%
Italy	0.8%
Canada	1.2%
9 Asian NICs	42.4%
S. Korea	7.1%
Taiwan	6.3%
Hong Kong	6.2%
China	5.3%
Singapore	5.1%
Thailand	4.4%
Malaysia	3.7%
Indonesia	2.2%
Philippines	2.0%
Other	13.8%

Source: Ministry of Finance

lend to weak as well as strong borrowers with the assurance that the government will bail them out of any resulting problems.

And it's not only the banks that are in trouble. For years, interest rates in Japan have been well below those promised by life insurance companies to their policy holders. Over the last five years the industry's losses added up to $46 billion (see Chapter 22 for more).

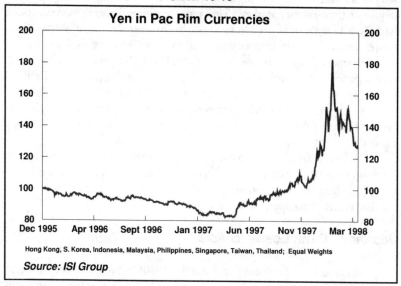

CHART 15-10

Yen in Pac Rim Currencies

Hong Kong, S. Korea, Indonesia, Malaysia, Philippines, Singapore, Taiwan, Thailand; Equal Weights

Source: ISI Group

Back to Recession?

Will Japan's fiscal policy tightening last year and the forced changes in her financial structure this year ensure renewed business slump? Will a 1998 recession parallel the 1937-38 swoon in the US? Probably, but the likelihood leaps even higher when the effects on Japan of other Asian problems are thrown in. Note that from 1992 through late 1997, before the Asian crisis really began to affect Japan seriously, real household income rose only 1% and real spending actually fell by 1% as scared consumers saved even more (Chart 2-9).

With 42% of Japanese merchandise exports destined for nine Asian lands (Chart 15-9), Asia matters a lot to Japan, especially South Korea, which takes 7.1% of her exports and accounts for 4.4% of Japan's imports. The rise of the yen against other Asian currencies (Chart 15-10) has put her at a competitive disadvantage, and her Asian trade is slumping seriously. For the first time in eight years, she had a trade deficit with Asia in January 1998.

The ongoing economic malaise in Japan, plus the Asian crisis, is wreaking havoc on Japan's electronics industry, one of her few bright spots of late. Lousy earnings of electronic companies will spawn capital spending cutbacks and even less domestic economic activity. The collapse in the South Korean won means that Japanese companies will lose out to their South Korean counterparts in third-country markets. This, plus the sliding South Korean economy, will slash Japan's steel exports to Korea by 80%, according to Nippon Steel Corp. The high cost of imported parts from Japan is killing Japanese motorcycle producers' assembly operations and sales in Thailand and Malaysia. A recent survey shows that only 17% of Japanese firms operating in Thailand have gains from the baht's fall while 80% have been hurt.

As exports to Asia slide, Japanese goods are redirected to the US. Recently, Japanese steel mills slashed prices on exports to this country to below those of domestic producers.

All this makes further drops in the yen attractive to Japan in order to catch up with the rest of Asia. Yet as the yen falls, the tigers will want even cheaper currencies to maintain their advantage vs. Japan, and so it goes in another round of competitive devaluations.

Japanese Bank Loans to Asia

The banks, still cleaning up from the 1980s bubble economy's break, now are faced with glass shards from their troubled loans to other Asian coun-

CHART 15-11

BANK LOANS TO DEVELOPING ASIAN COUNTRIES (MID-YEAR 1997)

NATIONALITY	$ BILLIONS	% OF TOTAL
German	47.2	12.1%
French	40.4	10.4%
British	29.7	7.6%
Dutch	12.8	3.3%
American	32.3	8.3%
Canadian	7.2	1.9%
Japanese	123.8	31.8%
Other	96.0	24.6%
Total	389.4	100.0%

Source: Bank for International Settlements

CHART **15-12**

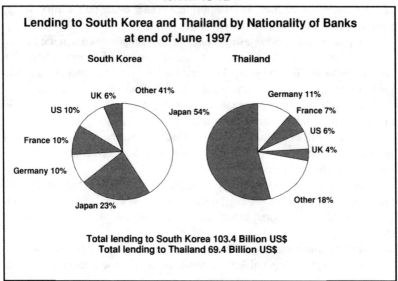

Lending to South Korea and Thailand by Nationality of Banks at end of June 1997

Total lending to South Korea 103.4 Billion US$
Total lending to Thailand 69.4 Billion US$

tries. In mid 1997, banks in Japan accounted for 32% of bank loans to the smaller Asian countries, while North American banks were saddled with only 10% (Chart 15-11). Japan's exposure in troubled South Korea and Thailand is especially heavy (Chart 15-12) with $24 billion in loans to Korea and $37 billion to Thailand (and $23 billion more to Indonesia). And Japan has a lot tied up in plant and equipment elsewhere in Asia that can't be easily extracted. The cumulative effects of this direct investment over the years are huge (Chart 13-3).

How Now Hashimoto?

The government of Prime Minister Hashimoto has been reluctant to stimulate enough to restore Japan to financial and economic health, much less make her strong enough to help revive the rest of Asia, as noted in Chapter 2. As an example of half-hearted attempts, the tax cut for individuals proposed in late 1997 equals only 35% of the tax increase of April 1997. That cut and more recently-announced individual tax reductions are "one-shot" affairs, while the increase is permanent—so people will probably simply save the extra money, figuring that their taxes will be back up later. Note that the top individual tax rate in Japan remains about 65% compared to 40% in the US. Furthermore, the more recent government proposals, as usual, contain much less stimulus than the numbers suggest and tax cuts that are only temporary. Some of the money will be used to shore-up real estate, while public surveys say people want lower property prices.

Japan is also backing away from some financial reforms in the face of financial weakness. Punitive actions against banks with inadequate capital will be postponed for one year. The new $225 billion bank bailout fund will preserve poorly managed institutions rather than guarantee the funds of depositors and let competition separate the efficient from the corpses. This will obviously delay needed bank consolidations.

Japan's Finance Minister recently said the government would consider rules to curtail short selling of stocks. I wonder if he's also considering measures to hold back the tide.

A lot more is needed to revive the Japanese economy, but if it doesn't take place, don't blame the government entirely. As noted earlier, this seems to be what the voters want, or at least stoically accept. Remember, 96% of their literary heroes die.

The Japanese may be willing to suffer prolonged deflationary depression, but even they seem unlikely to brook economic and financial collapse. Bailout programs designed to prevent widespread financial failures are being enacted. Despite financial problems, Japan has huge financial strength. Her reserves of gold and foreign exchange total over $200 billion, and private ownership of foreign assets is gigantic and appreciating as the yen falls. Personal savings amounted to a gigantic $8 trillion as of last September, with $1.8 trillion of it in the postal savings system. The thrifty Japanese put aside so much that, even after offsetting big government deficits as well as domestic investment, plenty is left over to invest abroad (Chart 12-15).

Also, what looks like an endless and futile public debate among Japanese politicians over what to do to rejuvenate the economy, may be a Westerners misconception of what's really going on. This may simply be another *ringi*, the slow decision making by consensus that is normal in Japan, as mentioned earlier. If so, once they make up their collective mind, they'll all support the plan, but what will it be? My hunch is continuing orientation toward export-led growth and continuing stimulus to the domestic economy of only modest proportions. On balance, then, the Japanese will still probably resemble honey bees, and that nation will remain more a part of the Asian problem than its solution. You'll learn in Chapter 16 about how the sum and substance of the entire crisis there is to export Asia's lack of growth and excess capacity to Western developed countries. They are exporting deflation.

CHAPTER 16

THE ASIAN FLU SPREADS

With or without devaluation in China, with or without meaningful government stimulus and economic revival in Japan, one thing is clear. The economic and financial health of the many developing countries in Asia, Eastern Europe, and Latin America that have been infested by the Asian flu has deteriorated significantly. As a result, they will cease borrowing abroad for big national projects and instead scrounge for money to service their immense foreign debts, with or without IMF help. They will also slash imports from hard currency areas, due to the much higher costs in their devalued currency terms. They will cut imports from weak currency countries as well, as their economies stumble.

At the same time, these lands will emphasize exports, exports, and more exports as the only way to keep their citizens employed and earning precious hard currencies. The export advantages of 30%, 50%, and even 70% devaluations against the dollar will still be large after some offsets from higher domestic inflation and imported material costs. And most important, the sudden economic changes in Asia will have immense effects on the rest of the world. East Asia accounts for 27% of global output (Chart 14-2) and 25% of exports, and cannot suffer these ongoing setbacks in isolation.

Like Mexico—Initially

What lies ahead may be very like the immediate aftermath of the 1994 Mexican devaluation (but not the later effects, as you'll learn later). That devaluation, too, went much further than officials thought possible, over 60% so far (Chart 16-1), and as in Asia, the first crack revealed many hidden problems. The Mexican economic collapse that followed also occurred despite the rapid and huge international bailout, $20 billion, largely financed by the US. Mexican imports collapsed overnight (Chart 16-2). Exports leaped but more gradually, not surprising since it takes time to crank up export production. Also, until the initial shock of the peso crisis subsided, many exporters, especially smaller ones, lacked the dollars needed to first import essential raw materials.

Similarly in Asia, imports have dropped like rocks, and some exporters can't get financing for raw material and component imports. They can't cut and sew the garments if they can't pay for and import the cloth. Asian countries are so short of credit that some exporters are resorting to the highly inefficient barter system to sell their goods abroad. But those are short-term problems. Developed country governments are working hard to insure that their goods keep flowing to Asia. The US and Australia are extending trade finance guarantees to their exporters in South Korea; Japan is doing the same with Indonesia, and other similar arrangements by Western countries are likely.

Already, South Korea's current account balance has swung to a $3.06 billion surplus in January 1998 from a $3.05 billion year-earlier deficit. And the swing was much greater in won, of course, which nosedived against the dollar in that time period. Exports are also leaping in Malaysia and Thailand as imports plummet.

CHART 16-1

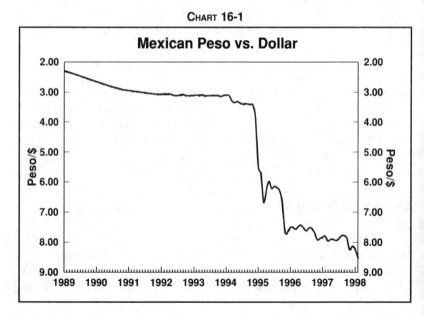

Global Glut

The net result is to add to already excessive global supplies of almost everything. For example, US computer capacity has leaped in recent years and is now rising at a 40% annual rate (Chart 16-3), and China's big production of electronic products, scheduled to come on line next year, will add much more to the worldwide total. This will be further augmented by other Asian lands which already are heavy exporters of electronic products (Chart 16-4) and want to export even more to offset weak domestic demand. Asian countries want to accelerate their shares of global exports, which have jumped in past decades (Chart 16-5). Unless other countries cut their production substantially, which is highly unlikely, excess capacity will leap.

Too Many Cars

In America, Japan, and Western Europe car sales are basically static as new cars are purchased mainly to replace junked vehicles (see Chapter 8). The world's automakers have been looking to the emerging markets of Asia and Latin America for their growth, and have made huge investments in production facilities in those areas. The US producers have invested heavily in Asia and Latin America, Japanese automakers in Asia, Western European

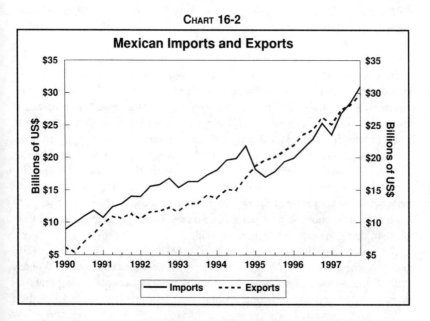

CHART 16-2

Mexican Imports and Exports

Imports · · · · Exports

CHART 16-3

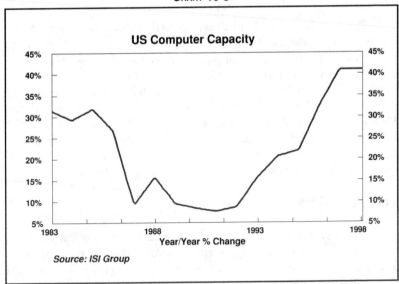

US Computer Capacity

Year/Year % Change

Source: ISI Group

automakers in Asia, and the North Korean automakers in Latin America and Eastern Europe. Asian production facilities are scheduled to add 6 million cars to capacity in the next five years. While worldwide supply is scheduled to increase to 80 million autos over the next five years, it's estimated that demand will only rise to 75% of that total, and that estimate was made before the Asian meltdown.

Before the crisis, South Korean auto production capacity was scheduled to reach 5.2 million in 2002. This would have been 1.9 million above domestic demand, so 1.9 million would have been destined for export. Now financial straits have forced Samsung Group and other South Korean auto makers to scale back capacity additions, but domestic demand has dropped even faster. It looks like capacity will exceed domestic sales by 2 million even earlier, in 1999. Japan produced 10.4 million vehicles last year, 3.3 million below capacity. India also has more capacity than is needed domestically. Toyota recently cut auto production in Thailand when local demand fell, but has since resumed operations with more locally made parts to avoid costly imports, and re-aimed output at exports. Other Japanese auto companies are doing the same elsewhere in Asia.

Excess capacity is, of course, a powerful deflationary force, and even more so when so much of it is in countries with devalued currencies. Where will all the goods and services that these developing countries desperately want to export end up? Obviously, not in their fellow sufferers. In 1996, the

CHART 16-4

ELECTRONIC PRODUCTS AS % OF TOTAL EXPORTS, 1995

	%
Singapore	66
Malaysia	52
Philippines	41
Taiwan	36
Thailand	24
South Korea	17
Hong Kong	16

Source:
International Monetary Fund

CHART 16-5

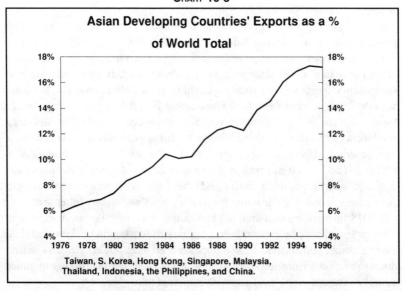

Asian Developing Countries' Exports as a % of World Total

Taiwan, S. Korea, Hong Kong, Singapore, Malaysia, Thailand, Indonesia, the Philippines, and China.

nine developing East Asian countries sold 40% of their exports among themselves. As that source of export demand drops, the pressure increases further to sell to the only remaining buyers—Western developed countries, especially the US.

Chart 16-6 shows, in the first column, how important exports are to each of the nine developing Asian countries in relation to their GDP, while the following columns list the amounts going to the various G-7 countries. For example, China's exports were 18.8% of her GDP in 1996, and her exports to the US were 3.3% of her total output.

Furthermore, as noted in Chapter 15, Japan remains part of the Asian problem, not the solution. Her domestic demand is lousy. Her instinct is to grow by exports, but her Asian markets are collapsing. Where do you think her export guns are trained?

Happy Dumping Ground

Without question, America is the happy dumping ground for the world's excess goods and services, the buyer of first and last resort. Just look at Chart 16-7. The US is running a merchandise excess of imports over exports of nearly $200 billion, while other countries, on balance, have a net surplus. China is at $44 billion and leaping, and Japan has the biggest, $104 billion. As the largest market in the world and one of the most open, the US is where the rest of the world comes to sell its surplus. Not surprisingly, Japan's trade surplus with the US is rising in lock-step with her declining surplus elsewhere.

But the US also exports, about 11% of all goods and services. Our goods exports to developing Asian countries account for 1.5% of total output, while Latin America takes an additional 1.3%. Even though the Asian crisis started only in mid 1997, the negative results are already apparent. Medical equipment exports to Asia were expected to grow 20% annually in the foreseeable future as countries there planned big hospital construction projects. Now, sales are lean and Asian buyers want price concessions that American producers can't afford. Athletic footwear maker Nike has seen its Asian orders nosedive. US casino operators fret over the demise of big rolling Asian visitors. The fiscal tightening in Brazil is beginning to hurt US exporters as well and is spreading to Argentina and other Latin American countries where American exports were growing twice as fast as those to any other area.

US farmers are now free to plant as much as they like, as discussed in Chapter 9, and have been counting on big exports to a booming class of middle income Asian consumers. Those hopes are gone as millers there switch to domestic tapioca from imported corn in some cases, and shrinking incomes curtail consumption of beef fed with imported corn.

CHART 16-6

ASIAN MERCHANDISE EXPORTS TO G-7
(AS A % OF EXPORTER'S GDP)

	TOTAL EXPORTS	US	GERMANY	FRANCE	ITALY	UK	CANADA	JAPAN
China	18.8%	3.3%	0.7%	0.2%	0.2%	0.4%	0.2%	3.8%
Hong Kong	116.0%	24.7%	4.9%	1.8%	1.1%	3.9%	1.6%	7.6%
Indonesia	21.7%	3.6%	0.9%	0.4%	0.4%	0.6%	0.2%	6.1%
Malaysia	81.2%	14.8%	2.4%	0.7%	0.6%	2.7%	0.6%	10.6%
Philippines	24.9%	8.4%	1.0%	0.3%	0.1%	1.1%	0.3%	4.4%
Singapore	135.2%	24.9%	4.1%	2.6%	0.5%	3.8%	0.4%	10.9%
S. Korea	26.8%	4.5%	1.0%	0.3%	0.2%	0.7%	0.3%	3.3%
Taiwan	37.8%	11.6%	2.0%	0.8%	0.5%	1.2%	0.8%	5.5%
Thailand	30.3%	5.4%	0.9%	0.5%	0.4%	1.0%	0.3%	5.1%

Source: International Monetary Fund

Asian troubles affect Western American states most since over half their exports are bound for Asia—compared to about 25% in the West North-Central and West South-Central states, and about 20% east of the Mississippi. On

CHART 16-7

MERCHANDISE TRADE BALANCES

	TRADE BAL. LATEST 12 MONTHS $BILLION		TRADE BAL. LATEST 12 MONTHS $BILLION
Australia	1.3	Greece	-18.7
Austria	-5.6	Israel	-7.5
Belgium	10.9	Portugal	-10.0
Britain	-20.6	S. Africa	2.9
Canada	16.0	Turkey	-21.1
Denmark	3.7	Czech Republic	-3.8
France	31.2	Hungary	-2.2
Germany	70.5	Poland	-11.3
Italy	29.8	Russia	21.2
Japan	103.8		
Netherlands	16.7	China	43.7
Spain	-18.3	Hong Kong	-19.5
Sweden	16.9	India	-5.8
Switzerland	0.3	Indonesia	11.9
		Malaysia	1.0
US	-199.4	Philippines	-10.3
		Singapore	-6.5
Argentina	-5.4	S. Korea	6.2
Brazil	-7.7	Taiwan	6.0
Chile	-2.0	Thailand	-5.3
Colombia	-2.9		
Mexico	-1.6		
Venezuela	11.5	*Source: The Economist*	

average, 2.4% of US gross state produce is exported to Asia, but for Washington state and Alaska, it is over 10%. Louisiana, Oregon, California, and Arizona are all in the 4.4% to 7.4% range.

Tourism-dominated Hawaii is already on the ropes. The weakening yen has kept many Hawaii-loving Japanese at home, and the length of stays of those who do come has fallen to 5.5 days from 6.5 in 1995. The effects have sped throughout the Hawaiian economy. In Oahu, existing home sales have dropped 55% since 1990, when the Japanese bubble economy burst, and prices are down 11%. And yet, the effects of the Asian collapse outside Japan are yet to be felt in the Aloha state.

Europe and Canada Are in the Same Boat

If you think that the Asian crisis is a much bigger problem for the US than other developed countries, think again. True, Asian lands send more of their exports to the US and Japan, but those are the globes' two biggest economies. Other developed countries get their share, as shown in Chart 16-8, which shows imports from Asia as a percentage of each G-7 country's GDP. Continental European countries tend to be more closed to Asian imports than the US, but they will end up with more incoming goods as prices drop.

CHART 16-8

1996 G-7 MERCHANDISE IMPORTS FROM ASIA (AS A % OF IMPORTER'S GDP)

	ASIAN 9	ASIAN 9 PLUS JAPAN
US	2.6%	4.2%
Canada	2.1%	3.4%
Germany	1.5%	2.5%
France	1.1%	1.7%
Italy	0.8%	1.1%
UK	2.6%	3.8%
Japan	2.7%	NA

Source: IMF Direction of Trade Statistics

And perhaps surprising to you, weakened exports to Asia will hurt European and Canadian economies about as much as America's. Even more so in the case of Continental European countries, when you consider that in recent years they have depended on exports for over 100% of their total growth (Chart 5-11).

Some may say that the US sends 29% of her exports to Asia while Germany sends only 9.7% (Chart 16-9). That's true, but look at the second column, exports as a percentage of GDP. That's the one that really measures the importance of exports to Asia for these economies. The US exports 2.4% of GDP to Asia, but Western countries have similar involvement with 2.2% for Germany, 2.1% for the UK, Canada with 2.7%, Italy at 1.9%, and France with 1.4%. Conservative estimates have the Asian crisis cutting German GDP output 0.3% this year compared to 0.5% in the US as a result of more imports and fewer exports. These estimates may prove far too low.

Europe is already feeling the Asian crisis. Because of Asian weakness, German foreign orders have been falling since September 1997. European air traffic to Asia is on the wane as are sales of luxury European cars and Scotch whisky. South Korean conglomerates are postponing new factories in France and Scotland. Whether Europe, especially Continental countries, can absorb the impact of the Asian crisis and still continue their expansions is debatable, and those who expect European growth to offset Asian weakness may be sadly disappointed. Chart 2-6 showed that German employment continues to fall and real retail sales are dropping, while UK leading indicators point to slower growth.

The Commodity Price Effect

Industrial commodities are traded on a global basis and are very price sensitive to demand. So, the weaknesses in Asian demand so far, and that which is anticipated, are pushing many commodity prices through the floor, as observed in Chapter 13. Paper and pulp prices are sliding. US producers are shifting output previously sent to Asia to Europe, pushing down prices there. In sugar, big world production is meeting shrinking Asian demand head-on, and prices have gone off the top of the roller coaster (Chart 16-10).

As chemical demand in Asia falls, global prices are under heavy pressure. Furthermore, Asia has huge chemical capacity, much of it developed by US, European, and Japanese companies. Asian companies, desperate for cash, are dumping inventories and killing prices. Dupont was selling 90% of the output of a South Korean plant on the local market, but now with weak South Korean demand, it is exporting 40%. Note, that one-third of US chemical exports go to Asia (Chart 16-11).

CHART 16-9

1996 MERCHANDISE EXPORTS TO ASIA BY MAJOR COUNTRIES

	EXPORTS AS % OF TOTAL EXPORTS	EXPORTS AS % OF NOMINAL GDP
US		
9 Asian Developing Countries	18.2%	1.5%
Japan	10.8%	0.9%
Total Asia	29.0%	2.4%
Global Total	100.0%	8.2%
Germany		
9 Asian Developing Countries	7.0%	1.6%
Japan	2.7%	0.6%
Total Asia	9.7%	2.2%
Global Total	100.0%	22.1%
France		
9 Asian Developing Countries	5.6%	1.0%
Japan	1.9%	0.3%
Total Asia	7.4%	1.4%
Global Total	100.0%	18.7%
Italy		
9 Asian Developing Countries	6.9%	1.4%
Japan	2.2%	0.5%
Total Asia	9.2%	1.9%
Global Total	100.0%	20.8%
UK		
9 Asian Developing Countries	6.9%	1.6%
Japan	2.6%	0.6%
Total Asia	9.4%	2.1%
Global Total	100.0%	22.8%
Canada		
9 Asian Developing Countries	3.9%	1.4%
Japan	3.7%	1.3%
Total Asia	7.7%	2.7%
Global Total	100.0%	34.6%

Source: IMF Direction of Trade Statistics

CHART **16-10**

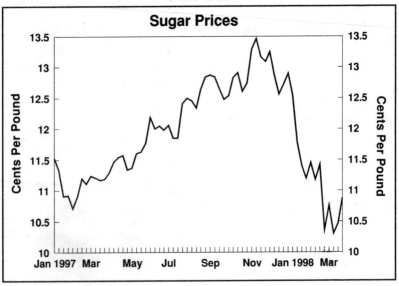

Even the global diamond market is affected by Asian troubles. In the second half of 1997, the DeBeers cartel suffered a 16% drop in sales due to weak demand in Japan and elsewhere in the region. And in Antwerp, the world's leading diamond center, sales fell last year for the first time in two decades due to weak Asian demand for luxury goods.

Canada has been clobbered due to its Pacific exposure and high dependence on commodity exports. Our neighbor to the north is the world's biggest exporter of construction-bound softwood lumber, with British Columbia accounting for 30% of global exports. Residential construction weakness, especially in Japan, knocked down prices about 30% last year and more of the same is likely. Mining accounts for 16% of Canadian exports, much more than most other developed countries, and the price declines of gold, lead, zinc, copper, etc., are devastating. It's no wonder that the Canadian dollar (Chart 16-12) has hit its lowest level since it replaced pounds, shillings, and pence in 1858. I knew they were in trouble when they abandoned the "shilling."

And, of course, Australia and New Zealand, due to their geographic locations, are hard hit by the Asian crisis. Asia takes two-thirds of Australian exports—60% of her coal and iron output is accounted for by exports which are tumbling along with steel production in Japan and South Korea. Live cattle exports are also falling. Adding insult to injury, not only are the vol-

CHART 16-11

US CHEMICAL EXPORTS TO ASIA-PACIFIC REGION IN 1996

COUNTRY	% SHARE OF US EXPORTS TO ASIA-PACIFIC	% SHARE OF TOTAL CHEMICAL EXPORTS
Australia	8.1%	2.7%
China	8.4%	2.7%
Hong Kong	6.9%	2.2%
India	2.3%	0.7%
Indonesia	2.7%	0.9%
Japan	28.6%	9.3%
Malaysia	2.6%	0.8%
Singapore	6.6%	2.2%
South Korea	12.7%	4.1%
Taiwan	11.4%	3.7%
Thailand	3.4%	1.1%
Other Asia-Pacific	6.2%	2.2%
Total Asia-Pacific	100%	32.6%

Source: Chemical Manufacturers Association

umes but also the prices of diamonds, nickel, coal, and iron ore exports declining.

Falling commodity prices aren't confined to industrial raw materials. Global grain prices are down 20% to 30% since the Asian crisis started, to the detriment of big developing country exporters like Argentina, but also hurtful to the likes of Canada, Australia, and the US.

The Banks, Too

Europe exports not only goods but also money to Asia (Chart 15-11). German banks more than tripled their exposure from the end of 1993 to the

CHART **16-12**

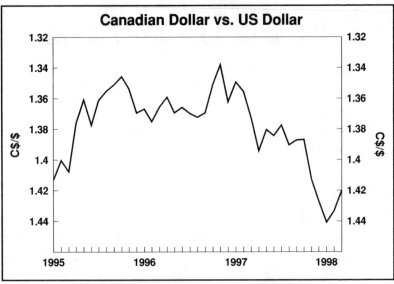

middle of 1997 and, along with the French, have more exposure there than US banks. Deutsche Bank has set aside $773 million to cover Asian losses, Societe Generale earmarked $162 million, Dresdner Bank $55 million, and Commerzbank $492 million. Standard & Poor's Ratings Group expect Asia's problems to cut the pretax earnings of 20 European banks by 75% this year. And, with loan defaults in Asia growing, the credit ratings of Asian-debt laden European banks are being slashed.

And don't forget the losses, present and potential, for developed country firms that have made direct investments in Asian production facilities. Those investments don't get the press attention of sour bank loans, but they can suffer even bigger losses as both the demand for their output and the prices at which it can be sold drop. Then there are the Western investors who own Asian stocks and bonds at much higher prices. There losses in local currencies are bad enough, but excruciating when the devaluations in those currencies are also considered (Chart 16-13).

You'll hear me say this again later, but I think it's worth repeating. Asia may account for only a minority of the globe's demand for raw materials, loans from Western banks, and sales by G-7 countries, but a big majority of expected worldwide growth in all of these areas. Earlier, few comprehended this completely. Only now is the reality becoming manifest through collapsing commodity prices, sour bank loans, and nosedives in the stock prices of companies suffering Asian setbacks, as it becomes clear that Asia has zipped from boom to bust.

Asian Recovery—When?

As noted in Chapters 14 and 15, to some degree recovery in Asia depends on the region's two heavyweights—China and Japan. But even if China doesn't devalue and Japan promotes a speedy recovery, revival in the rest of Asia will take time. Perhaps a lot of time.

Many disagree. They note that rapidly developing countries periodically overexpand, then suffer setbacks, but revive quickly. That happened in the US in the 19th century, in Japan in earlier postwar days, in Mexico and Brazil repeatedly, and in the original four Asian tigers—Taiwan, South Korea, Hong Kong, and Singapore. Why not in Asia this time? Certainly, the legendary Asian work ethic and high saving habits will survive the current crisis. And if the IMF continues to bail out those countries and, indirectly, international banks and other foreign lenders and investors, why won't they go right back to supplying Asia with ample credit and play one more round of *Heads I win, tails Western governments* (read, taxpayers) *make me whole*? That happened in Mexico in 1982, 1986, and 1994.

CHART 16-13

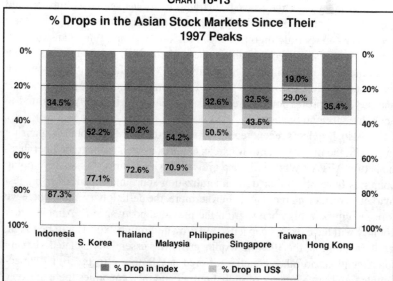

Further, those who look for a quick recovery in Asia point to the fast rebound in Mexico after the 1994 peso collapse, which allowed that country to float bonds promptly and use the proceeds to repay US bailout money. Why not a repeat in Asia?

Mexico Is No Model

Indeed, some are already venturing back into Asia, figuring the worst is over. Legendary global investor Sir John Templeton put money into South Korean stocks early in 1998. Some mutual funds are doing the same in South Korea and Hong Kong. A trickle of bond money is returning, figuring on a quick revival in Asian bonds that would rival Mexico's. Maybe they're right, but I'm not so sure.

To begin, don't confuse Mexico with Asia's developing countries. Mexico's ultimate and not so secret weapon is her 2,000 mile border with the US. Whenever she gets into financial difficulty, all she needs to do to get American aid, and promptly, is to point out that an economic collapse south of the border will result in another million illegals heading north of the border each year.

No such border exists in Asia between developing countries and Japan, the only close-by advanced nation, which is, of course, a group of islands. Besides, the US, despite recent concerns over illegal immigrants, is populated by outsiders and has always had a soft-spot for immigrants. As you read in Chapter 15, the Japanese and honey bees have some interesting similarities. And, like honey bees, they have been traditionally suspicious of outsiders and quick to repel them. Honey bees sting any intruder in their hive, even their beekeeper—nasty little ingrates, if you ask me. The first Europeans to reach Japan, usually shipwrecked sailors, were often killed on the beaches. Even today there is no such thing as an immigration visa in Japan, although foreign work permits do exist. About 99% of the population are of pure Japanese ancestry, and professional baseball teams there are each only permitted to have three foreign players.

Also, Mexico's recent recovery came in the midst of a robust expansion in the US, the major buyer of Mexican exports, as well as the trade liberalizations of NAFTA. When America grows, Mexico booms. Asian developing countries have no similar trade liberalization spur, and Japan, their biggest market, is reentering recession. Furthermore, the deflationary atmosphere we foresee will be a big change from the previous postwar era. Almost every country will have excess capacity, and growth through exports will be tough.

In addition, the 1994-95 tequila crisis was essentially isolated. Except for Argentina, no other country suffered any lasting effects. But Asia accounts for about a quarter of global output and the economics there are very interrelated, unlike Latin American countries until quite recently. And we've all seen how these interrelationships lead to domino-like behavior. South Korea may appear stabilized at present, but what if China devalues? Singapore has been dragged down by Malaysia and Indonesia, as noted in Chapter 13. Bear in mind that after the Latin American debt crisis of the 1980s, the whole region went into eclipse for a decade—and that was during a period of strong growth elsewhere in the world.

Also, unlike Mexico, it seems unlikely that the IMF bailout of Asia will let foreign investors off scot free. Congress is baulking over further money for the IMF, and Administration leaders agree that lenders must pay for their risk taking. As noted in Chapter 13, in Latin America foreign borrowing tends to be by governments, but in Asia it's by private enterprises that garner less international sympathy when financial rescues are needed.

Is Reform Welcome?

Finally, a major reason for rapid recovery in Mexico was rapid reform. Banks, telecommunications, and other key industries (but not petroleum) were privatized. Foreign competition was allowed in, and foreign ownership became possible. It's far from clear that Asian countries, including Japan (see Chapter 15), really have similar plans.

Most of these countries are semi-dictatorships, and if they really wanted financial reforms, they'd have instituted them long ago. But why should they? For years, their growth prospects were so mouth watering that foreigners showered them with money, while accepting opaque accounting, capricious or nonexisting financial regulation, severe limits on foreign ownership, nepotism, graft, corruption, and also government guidance on investments and financing.

No wonder that these leaders regard the reforms required by IMF bailouts as offensive. And, of course, like all humans, they tend to blame their problems on others, embracing free global markets when they work in their favor, but pining for other systems, even regional self-sufficiency, when times are rough.

Prime Minister Mahathir of Malaysia blasted international investors last summer by saying, "We are not going to allow these people to manipulate our economy as if they have a right to have a free ride with us. My view is that this level of manipulation must be made illegal." Interesting words from a man whose country's growth has been largely fueled by foreign investment. I guess money coming in is fine, but money going out is evil. Maybe he hasn't a clue about free markets. Or, maybe he enjoys letting off steam, but each outburst was lethal to Malaysian stocks and the ringgit. Furthermore, recent political, as opposed to market driven, mergers of troubled Malaysian companies suggest that "crony capitalism" remains alive and well.

Indonesia President Suharto said, "We have 30 years' experience in building a strong foundation. Then in six months it collapses, not because of an internal crisis but because there is manipulation of (our) currency." His comments cost the rupiah 25% of its value. And, despite promises to the IMF, Indonesia is dismantling cartels controlled by Suharto's family and friends in name only, and the promised removal of food subsidies has been delayed. A Senior Thai Official said, "The US has been a major proponent of liberalization and globalization for the past decade, and now the perception is that it is reaping greater benefit from it." The West, especially the US, has been branded as the bad guy.

South Korea, a financial basket-case that is now completely at the mercy of the IMF, is antagonistic. Students there have protested against the US and the "humiliating" IMF agreement. An array of matronly women, South Korea's anti-consumption league, has assailed imports and oversees travel. This is not surprising given their traditional hostility to outsiders, but don't we still have troops there protecting them from North Korea?

The new Hindu, nationalist-led government of India promises to continue free market reforms but also plans to limit foreign investment and be less accommodating on foreign trade agreements. It looks like the recent trend toward lower import tariffs will be stopped, if not reversed, and the nation will go back to ad hoc approval of foreign investments as opposed to clearly delineated guidelines.

In the final analysis, Asian countries can, to a considerable degree, blackmail the West. They have no Rio Grande to send millions of illegals across, but they can and do point out that without bailouts, their economies and financial systems will probably collapse completely and could very well take the West with them. This is a threat to be taken seriously. It's a mistake to assume that economic growth is at the top of those countries' leaders' agendas, as it is in America. Staying in power and alive probably ranks first, and amassing huge fortunes for their families and friends comes next.

But Some Reforms

Still, reforms are being made. Malaysia, under international pressure, has postponed some of her pet projects (see Chapter 13), including Linear City, which was to be the world's longest building, and a new international airport. Thailand is allowing foreigners to take bigger stakes in local banks and has lifted most currency restrictions on foreigners. Indonesia's Suharto, after rejecting IMF bailout conditions and still dragging his heals, did agree to halt 15 infrastructure projects, including some big investments that involve his children.

The door to foreign ownership in Asia is opening, slowly, as it's becoming clear that foreign capital is no longer available with no preconditions. Similarly, accounting standards are improving and financial statements are becoming more transparent in order to re-attract, they hope, foreign investors. Asian reforms are being made, but slowly and not by choice.

South Korea has agreed that foreign banks can buy South Korean banks, that the government will no longer direct bank loans into favored industries, South Korean firms will be permitted to borrow abroad, insolvent merchant and commercial banks will be closed or merged, tariff-lowering commitments will be honored, stock and bond markets will be opened to foreign investors, state-run companies will be privatized, trade subsidies will be eliminated, foreign ownership of South Korean firms allowed, and that accounting standards on banks and conglomerates will be introduced.

Gee, I had no idea a country could have so many restrictions and still have the growth that South Korea has enjoyed. I guess that if a developing country is loaded with dedicated, hard-working people and a stable currency, it can grow rapidly because foreign investors will throw money at it under regulatory conditions that would be totally unacceptable elsewhere. Let's see if South Korea honors these new agreements.

Newly elected President Kim has endorsed the IMF deal. He's also publically stated that the cozy relationships between the South Korean government and the *chaebols* (family conglomerates) were partly responsible for the severity of the nation's crisis and must be dismantled. Also, despite labor union opposition, he's backing measures to ease restrictions on layoffs, which are now almost impossible. As a result, monthly wages have risen four fold in the last decade and placed a heavy burden on South Korean firms. Still, Kim doesn't expect recovery from the financial crisis to start until the end of 1999. This may be an optimistic estimate for South Korea, much more so for other Asian lands that have yet to assess their problems realistically, much less take steps to solve them.

The world has been on the verge of deflation, and the Asian crisis probably pushed it over the edge. The Asian drama, including Japan and China as key players, is still on stage. Even if the play has reached its low point, it is unlikely to revive fast enough to prevent severe consequences elsewhere. And if a region that accounts for a quarter of the world's output and trade and a majority of its expected growth is in trouble, the world is in trouble. Now let us see how this will play out on the globe's biggest and most important stage, the US, in Chapter 17.

Chapter 17

US Consumers Will Switch From Borrowing and Spending To Saving

You've seen the large number of deflationary forces already at work in the world in earlier chapters. The Asian crisis (Chapters 13 to 16) is important, but much more so since it comes on top of the many other downward pressures on prices covered in Chapters 1 to 16. These 13 deflationary forces, listed in Chart I-7, are probably enough to push the world into chronic deflation, but if one more falls into place—a switch by US consumers from big borrowing and spending to big saving—deflation is assured.

Chart 17-1

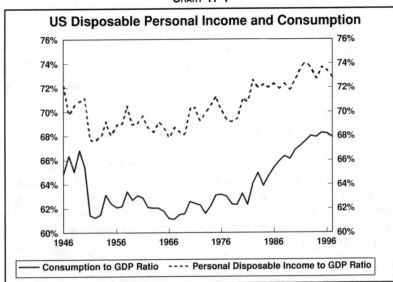

US Disposable Personal Income and Consumption

—— Consumption to GDP Ratio   - - - - Personal Disposable Income to GDP Ratio

The Spending Spree

Without question, US consumers have been on a spending spree for about three decades. Not only have their outlays increased as a share of GDP, but they have grown much faster than personal disposable, or after tax, income (Chart 17-1). Why?

Income Weakness

The purchasing power of the average American ended its rapid postwar growth in the early 1970s, despite the huge number of married women who entered the labor force in the years since then to try to keep alive the American Dream of ever-increasing purchasing power (Chart 17-2)[1]. Initially, growth was curtailed by commodity inflation, which transferred purchasing power abroad, and by very slow productivity growth. Then restructuring, starting in the 1980s, eliminated many high-paid but low-skilled jobs. Auto workers, who even 15 years ago made close to $80,000 annually including fringes, found themselves retrained as computer programmers but making half as much—if they were lucky and resourceful. Otherwise, they were flipping hamburgers at little more than the minimum wage.

Chart 17-3 shows the weakness in real wages for production and nonsupervisory workers since the early 1970s, and this weakness is found in each and every major industry (Charts 17-4 and 17-5). Furthermore, employment has been shifting from the higher paying sectors (Chart 17-6)—mining, construction, transportation, manufacturing, and wholesale trade—to the lower

---

[1]Chart 17-2 shows real median family income. "Real" means, of course, inflation adjusted. Median income is used to illustrate the income of people in the middle, since by definition, half the families have higher incomes and half lower. Pretax income is used because of data availability, but after-tax income would show the same or an even weaker pattern in the last two decades.

Due to increasing divorces, more single people, and other factors, the number of families has risen faster than the total US population since the early 1970s. This means that per capita real median income has risen more than family purchasing power. Still, we believe that family income, not per capita income, is the proper gauge of America's well-being, since a family, whether one person or 10, has certain minimal living costs. A divorced couple each needs a stove, a refrigerator, and a car. When a couple splits, each former spouse can't take half the bathroom to his or her new abode.

A family is defined by the Census Bureau as one or more related people living together. A household is defined similarly, as one or more people living together whether they are related or not. Income data for households and families show similar patterns.

paying sectors—services; retail; and finance, insurance, and real estate (Charts 17-7 and 17-8).

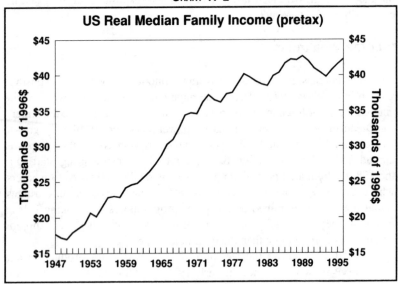

CHART 17-2

US Real Median Family Income (pretax)

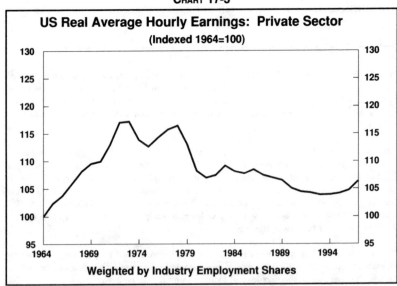

CHART 17-3

US Real Average Hourly Earnings: Private Sector
(Indexed 1964=100)

Weighted by Industry Employment Shares

In the last 15 years, these cuts in real earning are the result, as discussed in Chapter 5, of automating high-paid but low-skilled jobs out of existence and moving them to cheaper domestic or foreign sites; retiring early and/or

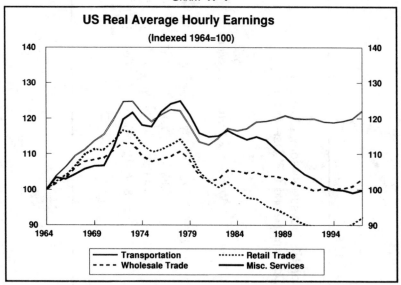

CHART 17-4

US Real Average Hourly Earnings
(Indexed 1964=100)

Legend: Transportation, Retail Trade, Wholesale Trade, Misc. Services

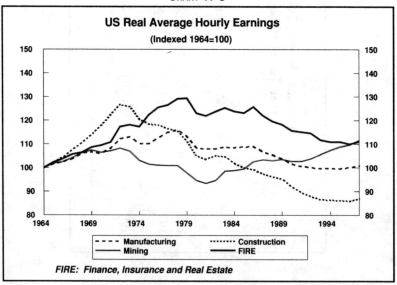

CHART 17-5

US Real Average Hourly Earnings
(Indexed 1964=100)

Legend: Manufacturing, Construction, Mining, FIRE

FIRE: Finance, Insurance and Real Estate

CHART 17-6

AVERAGE HOURLY EARNINGS OF US NONSUPERVISORY WORKERS
REAL TERMS 1982-1984 DOLLARS (USING CPI DEFLATOR)

	TOTAL PRIVATE	MINING	CONSTRUCT.	TRANS.	WHOLE.	FIRE	TOTAL SERVICES	RETAIL
1967	8.04	9.55	12.31	9.69	8.62	7.74	6.85	6.02
1977	8.62	11.44	13.35	11.53	8.88	7.49	7.67	6.35
1987	7.75	11.03	11.17	10.57	8.43	7.67	7.47	5.38
1997	7.64	10.04	9.95	9.27	8.36	8.28	7.65	5.19

FIRE—Finance, Insurance, and Real Estate

terminating expensive older people and replacing them with cheaper younger folks; supplanting union with non-union employees; using temporary and part-

CHART 17-7

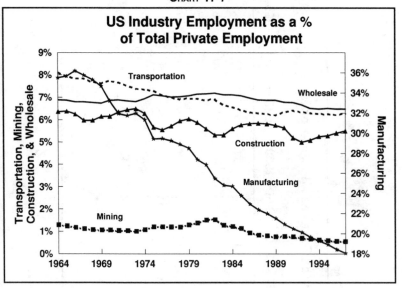

CHART 17-8

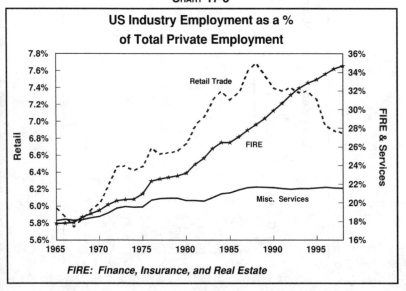

CHART 17-9

US FEMALE LABOR PARTICIPATION RATES AS A PERCENT OF MALE

AGE GROUP	1950	1955	1960	1965	1970	1975	1980	1985	1990	1995	1997
All Ages	39	42	45	49	54	59	67	73	75	78	86
16-19	65	67	70	71	78	83	87	96	90	88	96
20-24	52	53	52	58	69	76	80	86	86	87	89
25-34	35	36	37	40	47	58	69	76	81	87	83
35-44	40	42	44	47	53	58	69	77	80	85	86
45-64	36	42	48	51	55	57	62	67	71	75	87
65 & OVER	21	27	33	36	36	38	43	46	48	50	69

Source: Bureau of Labor Statistics

time people who are seldom paid expensive fringe benefits; and keeping money pay-hikes below price inflation rates.

Women to Work

American families have striven mightily to offset the loss in their real income. First, wives joined the labor force to help maintain purchasing power. As shown in Chart 17-9, up until 1970 most women in the 25-34 age group stayed home to raise families; their participating in the labor force was less than half the rate of men in the same age group. By 1985, however, their relative participation rate was up to 76%, and it has risen further since then. With or without children at home, they rushed out to earn money, and as necessity becomes a virtue, working outside the home became the socially accepted thing to do.

At the same time, women had fewer children and had them at older ages so that they could work longer and have more full-time jobs. Chart 17-10 shows the reduction in average family size, from 3.58 members in 1970 to 3.23 in 1985, as well as the rise in the percentage of births to women 30 and older, from 17.8% to 23.0%. Also note the rise in the percentage of working couples, from 49.3% to 60.2%, in those same years.

And jobs for these women became available because of the lack of productivity growth. Rather than more being produced per hour worked by men, who would then support their nonworking wives and children, more people, including many wives and teenagers, were hired to do the same amount of work.

The Next Option — Borrowing

All of these trends have continued into the 1990s, but failed to revive rapid growth in family purchasing power. No wonder that starting in the 1980s, middle class Americans resorted to borrowing to continue to enjoy the American Dream they felt they deserved, but could no longer afford (Chart 17-11)[2]. If a credit card issuer sends another piece of plastic, why not use it? The flip-side of more borrowing is reduced saving, and the personal saving rate has certainly declined (Chart 17-12).

In many ways, the 1980s were much worse for the middle class than the 1970s, which were already tough. In the 1980s, 36% of men saw their annual

---

[2] We're including all mortgage and home equity debt in this graph as well as credit card, auto, and other consumer borrowing to capture total debt by consumers in relation to their disposable incomes. The total also encompasses the changing character of borrowing. Today, for example, 15-year auto loans exist, although they're called home equity loans.

CHART **17-10**

US RESPONSES TO LAG IN REAL HOUSEHOLD INCOME GROWTH

	AVERAGE FAMILY SIZE	% OF BIRTHS TO WOMEN 30 AND OVER	% OF MARRIED COUPLES WHERE HUSBAND AND WIFE BOTH WORK
1950	3.54	27.4%	NA
1960	3.67	26.9%	NA
1970	3.58	17.8%	49.3%
1975	3.42	16.6%	52.0%
1980	3.29	19.8%	58.9%
1985	3.23	23.0%	60.2%
1990	3.17	30.2%	63.8%
1995	3.19	35.3%	65.1%
1996	3.20	36.2%	65.6%

Sources: Bureau of Census, Bureau of Labor Statistics, Department of Health and Human Services

CHART **17-11**

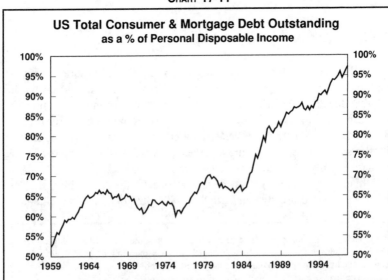

US Total Consumer & Mortgage Debt Outstanding
as a % of Personal Disposable Income

eal earnings fall, compared with 24% in the 1970s. Even college educations
idn't save people with restructuring in full swing in the 1980s, 20% of men
vith college degrees lost purchasing power, while 39% with some college

CHART 17-12

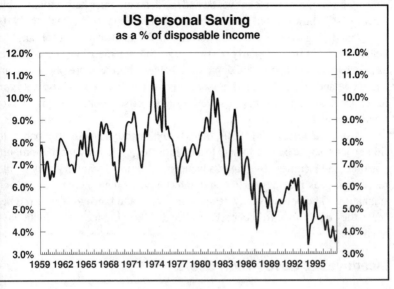

US Personal Saving
as a % of disposable income

CHART 17-13

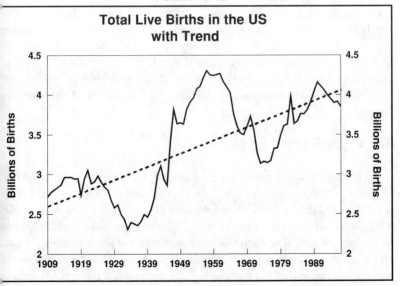

Total Live Births in the US
with Trend

experience saw their real incomes fall. In the 1970s, in contrast, 15% of college graduate men lost ground as did 27% of those with some college education.

The postwar babies have been especially frustrated by their lack of purchasing power gains in recent years, and the demographics help explain why Chart 17-13 shows actual live births versus the trend going back to 1910. Note that during the Great Depression and in World War II, the birthrate was below trend, but from the early postwar years through the 1960s it was above as postwar babies superceded depression babies. Furthermore, these two areas above and below the trend line are approximately equal. Those not born in the Depression and war years were roughly offset in numbers by above trend birthrates after World War II.

Consequently, in the 1970s, there weren't enough Depression babies to fill key jobs, so the baby boomers leaped into the gap and advanced rapidly in positions and incomes. But, rapid advancement simply meant that they would reach their peak incomes earlier, and in recent years their incomes have been stagnating. The boomers may be spending more and borrowing to do so because they don't want to accept the reality that their big income growth days are over.

Incentives to Save—High Debts

Despite the lack of it in recent years, there is ample incentive for Americans to save. High debts, in themselves, for one. Record levels of personal bankruptcies in recent years (Chart 17-14), to some extent, reflect the current legal ease of going bankrupt and the growing acceptance of bankrupts by the public and lenders. To some, especially younger people, bankruptcy is an acceptable debt management technique (Chart 17-15). Note that 30% of bankruptcies are filed by those 25 to 35. Nevertheless, these numbers also suggest that many are over their heads in debt and want to reduce or eliminate the burden.

The Piggy Bank Is Empty

Owner-occupied houses used to serve as a wonderful piggy bank that constantly refilled through capital appreciation and could be tapped for almost any need through refinancing or home equity loans, but no more. Chart 17-16 shows the owner equity in houses they occupy—the market value of the house and land after subtracting all mortgage and home equity debt outstanding, divided by the market value of the premises. Note the decline in the early 1960s, the end of the postwar housing-boom when mortgage financing by new homeowners drowned out the Depression survivors who had little or no mortgage debt and wanted even less.

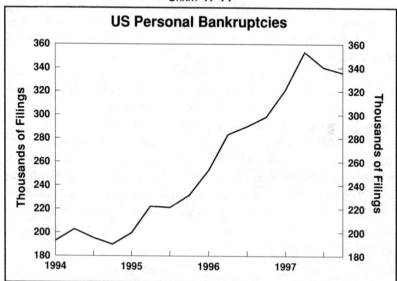

CHART 17-14

US Personal Bankruptcies

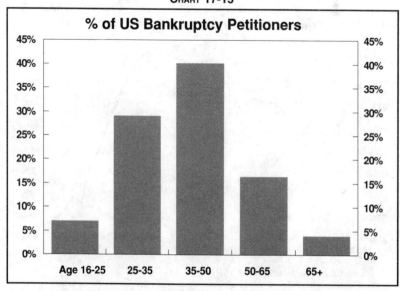

CHART 17-15

% of US Bankruptcy Petitioners

Then followed the inflation-related explosion in house prices in the late 1960s and 1970s, and homeowner equity leaped to 73%. With the 1980s disinflation, real house prices fell and, as part of their borrowing binge, homeowners drew out lots of their equity. Consequently, their net equity fell to 57%, but that's not all. About 40% of houses are owned free and clear, and an unknown but sizable number have old mortgages with low remaining principals. Subtracting both leaves many home owners with little, even negative, home equity.

Without question, house prices haven't kept up with inflation since the late 1970s. Sure, the average price of new homes sold has risen, even in inflation adjusted terms (Chart 17-17), but that's because houses have gotten bigger with more baths, appliances, plumbing, wiring, etc. The Census Bureau corrects for this, however, calculating the price of a quality-adjusted house which has the same number of baths, square feet, etc. through time. As shown, this price has actually fallen. The family that bought the average new house in 1979 could buy the same house today—but with all new appliances, wiring, and plumbing—for less in real terms. If houses no longer serve as automatically growing savings accounts, people have to save out of ongoing income or find another source.

CHART **17-16**

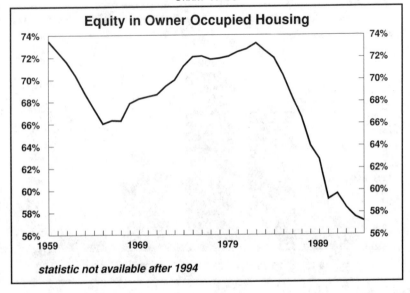

Equity in Owner Occupied Housing

statistic not available after 1994

The Big Savers Multiply

While middle-class purchasing power has been shrinking, compensation of all workers has been rising (Chart 17-18). Higher-end incomes have been the big winners, as shown in Chart 17-19. Consequently, the share of household income going to the top quintile (Chart 17-20) has been rising since 1980, the only quintile to do so. These are the people with the managerial and technical skills to compete in today's global economy, and they are paid increasing amounts for their services. They are also the big savers, and as income continues to move into their hands, the overall saving rate should rise.

Augmenting this income shift to higher income hands is a similar movement in net worth. The inflationary 1970s were clearly very beneficial to the prices of tangible assets such as coins, antiques, and real estate. And tangible assets are widely held—about two-thirds of American families own their own houses—so middle- and even lower-income homeowners benefitted, as well as the upper strata.

At the same time, the 1970s was a lousy decade for stocks, bonds, and other financial assets as interest rates rose and inflation transferred earnings to labor and government. Back then, 20% of households owned stocks, most of them with high incomes. With the dramatic decline in inflation rates in the 1980s, however, the action has reversed, and the winners are financial assets,

CHART 17-17

Real Price of New Homes Sold in the U.S.

— Average Price
- - - Census Bureau "Quality Adjusted" Average Price (Indexed 1977=100)

while tangibles languish. Financial assets, however, are still much more nar-
rowly held than houses. Over 40% of households now own stocks or mutual
funds, but holdings are concentrated among people with higher incomes. So

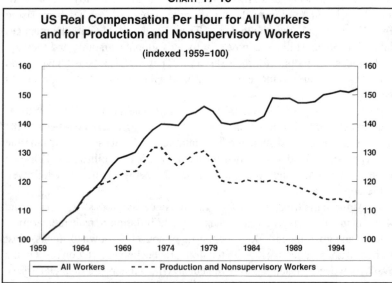

CHART 17-18

**US Real Compensation Per Hour for All Workers
and for Production and Nonsupervisory Workers**

(indexed 1959=100)

All Workers   - - - - Production and Nonsupervisory Workers

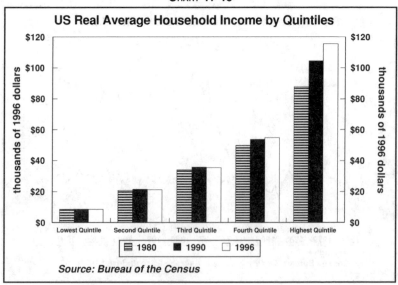

CHART 17-19

US Real Average Household Income by Quintiles

≡ 1980   ■ 1990   ☐ 1996

Source: Bureau of the Census

CHART 17-20

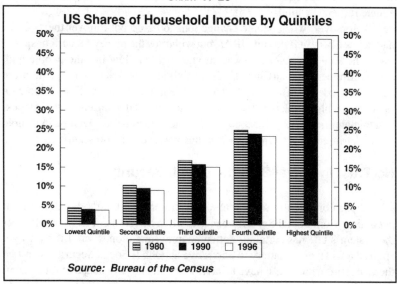

US Shares of Household Income by Quintiles

Source: Bureau of the Census

they have gained, relatively, from the shift in the value of assets toward financial and away from tangible assets.

Demographics

The postwar baby phenomenon is really a double whammy—a bulge of people followed by a decline (Chart 17-13). Obviously, this means that, in the years ahead, there will be fewer people in their 20s and 30s who spend a lot and save little as they form households and raise families. At the same time, there will be lots of postwar babies in their peak earning years who don't need to spend as much. Their children will be leaving home, so they won't have big tuition bills and, if their kids are anything like mine were, they won't have as many smashed-up cars to replace.

They will, then, be able to save more, and they need to. Postwar babies are already beginning to look retirement in the teeth and few have saved enough to maintain themselves in the styles they desire. They also may save more because, as I mentioned in Chapter 5, American business has turned toward 401(k) and other defined contribution retirement plans and away from defined benefit pensions. Under the former, retirement benefits are no longer guaranteed but depend in large part on the employees' investment skills. Employee-controlled pension plans now account for half of the total at the end of 1996, up from a quarter in the early 1980s. Added investment risk should encourage more saving while people are still working to insure adequate retirement funds.

Moreover, when people change jobs, 60% do not rollover their 401(k) and defined benefit funds into IRAs, but withdraw the money for current spending. The tendency to cash-out is strongest among low-income people with small retirement funds (Chart 17-21). With job changes now frequent, more saving is needed to offset this depletion of retirement money. Furthermore, in many cases, big chunks of 401(k) money are invested in the employer's stock, which magnifies risks. If the stock falls, the company may well be in trouble to the detriment of the employee's bonus and even his job security.

No Trust in Social Security or Job Security

Polls consistently show that almost no one working today thinks he'll get a dime from Social Security benefits when he retires. The publicity over the system's fate has certainly gotten people's attention, even if it hasn't yet spurred a widespread outcry to corrective action. If Social Security won't be there in retirement, you'll have to save yourself, and save ahead of retirement.

The ongoing threat of layoffs is another reason for employees to build up rainy day funds by saving more while people still have jobs. Some thought earlier that this phenomenon was over, but the recent upsurge in layoffs (Chart 5-7)—as well as what I hear from our corporate consulting clients—suggests

CHART **17-21**

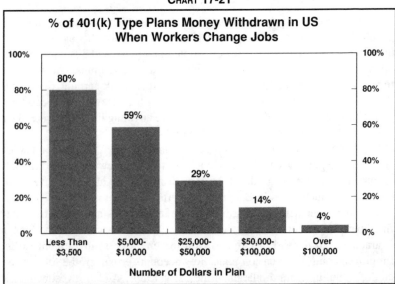

that it will be an ongoing reality, indefinitely. In fact, in the service sector, where three-quarters of us work, restructuring has just commenced. Note the layoffs, past and impending, at AT&T and at the banks as they consolidate, as examples.

Saving Becomes Worthwhile

Saving is also being encouraged by positive returns, even on ultra-safe three-month Treasury bills. Bill rates have fallen sharply in the last 15 years, but so has inflation and, on balance, tax rates, despite recent hikes. Chart 17-22 shows the real after-tax yield on Treasury bills for holders in the top income tax bracket over time. You'll note that from 1955 to 1983, the yield was negative. Only recently have those taxpayers gotten any positive returns.

Why Aren't Consumers Saving?

US consumers, then, have lots of incentives to save, but they haven't been. Why? Partly because they want to continue to enjoy the good life, regardless of whether they can afford it. And partly because their rapidly-appreciating stock holdings have, in recent years, been their savings accounts. This is the real-wealth effect. People don't have to sell their stocks to support current spending, but they are willing to save less and spend more of their

CHART 17-22

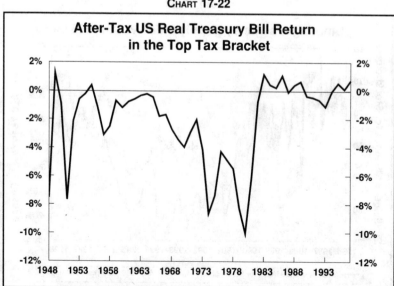

current incomes because their appreciated equity portfolios make them feel wealthier. In the government accounts, by the way, personal income includes wages and salaries; rent, interest, and dividends received; pensions, social security, welfare, and other transfer payments; but not appreciation in existing assets, including stocks and real estate.

This real-wealth concept makes sense when you note the close correlation between changes in stock prices and Sindlinger's money supply, or confidence, index for stockholders (Chart 17-23). Times of rising stock prices are times of prosperity, high employment and plentiful job opportunities, as in recent years. And these are times when people are especially willing to rely on their stock holdings to do their saving.

US stocks, of course, have been in a 15-year bull market (Chart 17-24), and people have been pouring money into stocks and equity mutual funds (Chart 17-25). One recent survey revealed that ownership of stocks and mutual funds by Americans doubled in the last seven years to 43% of adults. A separate Gallup poll shows a leap from 20% ownership in 1987 to 51% last summer. Between stock appreciation and increased investment in equities and mutual funds in recent years, household stock ownership has leaped in relation to incomes (Chart 17-26). Including employee-controlled pension plans, variable life insurance holdings, and other indirect ownership of stocks,

CHART 17-23

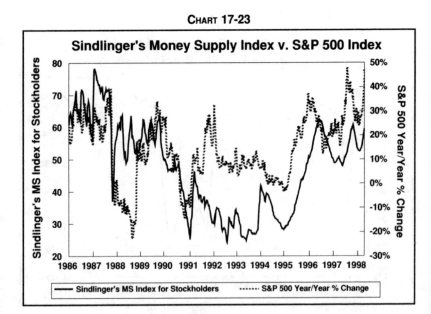

43% of household assets are now in equities, according to a recent Federal Reserve study, up from 39% in the 1960s when stocks were also red hot.

CHART **17-24**

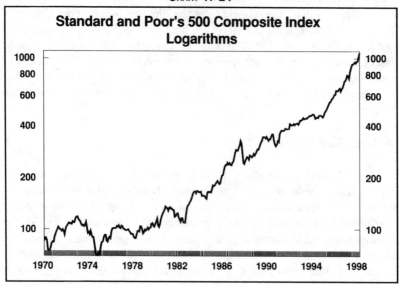

CHART **17-25**

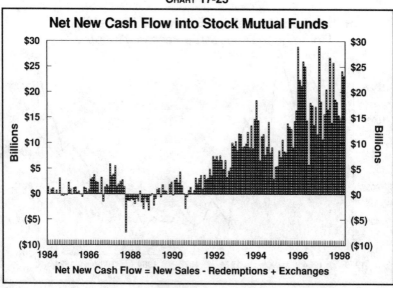

I've seen this real-wealth effect at work in recent years in our town, Short Hills, New Jersey. Brash, young Wall Street tycoons in their 30s, and ordinary citizens as well, are buying houses for the better part of $1 million, but they don't want the house, just the site. They promptly tear it down and then put another $1 million or more into a new edifice.

Our statistical analysis indicates that this real-wealth effect has only become important in the last ten years, but boy, has it gotten important and not just in Short Hills, NJ! Our numbers show that each 10% rise in stock prices has boosted consumer spending about one-half percent. With stocks returning over 30% on average in the last three years, this appreciation has increased consumer outlays about 1.6% a year. That's about a third of the total growth (Chart 17-27).

A Two-Way Street

The real-wealth effect works in the 1970s through owner-occupied houses and in the last decade through stocks, but there is no third major category of consumer assets. What can consumers do for an encore if stocks don't continue to jump or inflation and heady real estate don't return? This is an important consideration since this alternative to saving out of current income works both ways. The high portion of consumer spending growth in recent years that is attributable to stock appreciation makes this segment of

CHART 17-26

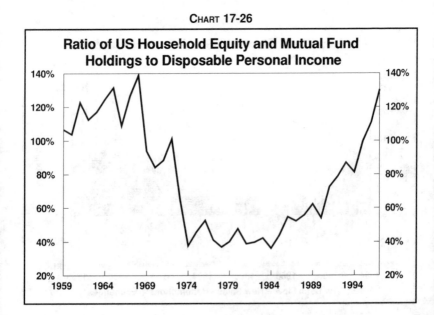

CHART 17-27

	STOCK GROWTH EFFECTS ON CONSUMPTION			
	S&P 500 TOTAL YEAR/YEAR RETURN	**% CHANGE IN CONSUMER SPENDING**	**PORTION DUE TO S&P 500 GAINS**	**RESIDUAL**
1995	37.6%	5.3%	1.9%	3.5%
1996	23.0%	5.2%	1.1%	4.1%
1997	33.4%	5.4%	1.7%	3.7%

the economy, two-thirds of GDP, highly vulnerable to any significant bear market. You'll see how the Asian crisis will probably make this vulnerability a reality in Chapter 18. And if it won't, sooner or later the Fed will.

CHAPTER 18

A BEAR MARKET IN US STOCKS WILL TRIGGER A CONSUMER SAVING SPREE AND ENSURE GLOBAL DEFLATION

Many still don't believe that the Asian crisis will have much effect on the US, or other Western developed countries, for that matter. The IMF recently lowered its forecast for 1998 real GDP growth in Japan from 2.1% to slightly negative, but expects only 0.2% slower growth in the US, Canada, and Western Europe, compared with earlier predictions. Fed Chairman Greenspan expects that the effect of the Asian crisis on the US will be "modest" but "not negligible." While estimates are being scaled back, Wall Street analysts still look for average earnings on companies they follow to rise by double digit amounts this year. The US stock market, that great distiller of all the wisdom of its participants, flattened when the Asian crisis became clear last August, but then took off again like a scalded dog in February (Chart 18-1). A recent poll shows that 57% of Americans believe that the effects of the Asian crisis on the US are only minor while 27% don't.

The Asian Impact Mounts

Still, evidence of the new-found zeal in Asia to step-up exports at deflated prices and curb imports is beginning to surface. The Fed's recent business survey found, in almost every one of its 12 regions, evidence of falling exports and more competition from cheaper Asian imports. Exporters to Asia of capital goods and auto parts were particularly hard hit. Ocean-shipping line traffic tells the same story. Asian bound US cargos were down 10% to 20% in late 1997, while shipments from Asia were up about 10%. Ship owners are concerned about empty back-hauls to Asia. Exports of construction-related equipment and lumber were very weak, but even apple shipments were down 20%. At the same time, imports of electronics and toys were up over 30%.

Although the Asian flu had barely infected the US last year, the trade deficit rose 2.4% from 1996. The gap with China leaped 26% to $50 billion while Japan's imbalance reached $56 billion, a jump of 17% (Chart 25-3).

Import prices are falling, especially for items from Japan and the Asian Tigers (Chart 18-2). This will force those who compete with imports to slash their prices. Since almost 30% of goods consumed in the US are imported (Charts 12-1 and 12-2), few domestic producers are immune from foreign competition. Note the particularly heavy onslaught from Asian Tigers (Chart 18-3). The purchasing managers' survey tells us that the fall in exports is just starting and the surge in imports will follow as the Asian export machine comes up to speed (Chart 18-4).

Multinationals Are Already Hit

Furthermore, many US companies have much bigger operations abroad than they have exports. Some 30% of S&P 500 companies' profits come from overseas, and 44% of large companies have some foreign exposure. In addition to weak sales in Asia, they are subjected to losses when the buck rises, since their foreign currency earnings translate into fewer dollars. Many, of course, do some currency hedging, but it's often unclear just how much is

CHART 18-1

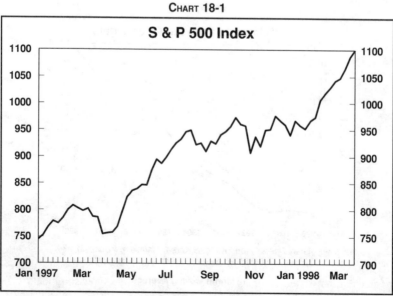

done. Do they match foreign assets and liabilities? In total? By country? Do they hedge this quarter's expected foreign earnings? Fine, but what about future quarters' earnings? Regardless, to hedge all or even a substantial por-

CHART **18-2**

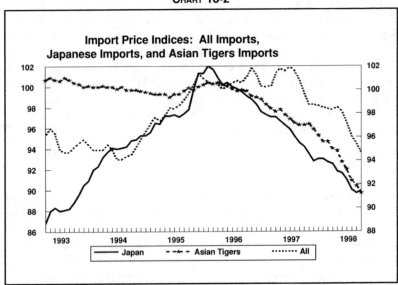

CHART **18-3**

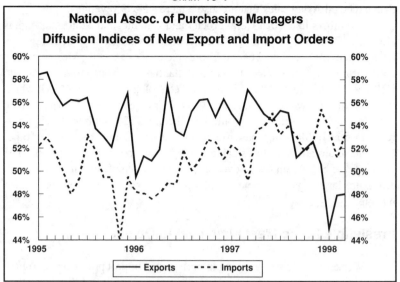

CHART **18-4**

National Assoc. of Purchasing Managers
Diffusion Indices of New Export and Import Orders

Exports   - - - - Imports

tion of their exposure is prohibitively expensive. The party on the other side of a hedge probably also expects a stronger greenback and demands a premium that equals the expected increase plus enough to cover risks—which are big in volatile times— and a profit.

Consequently, it's not surprising that a number of US multinational firms were already hurt in late 1997 by Asian flu exposure. 3M suffered from softer sales to Asia as well as Brazil. Asia is Boeing's principal market for 747s, and the firm expects the Asian crisis to lead airlines there to request delivery delays over the next three years. Philippine Airlines has already postponed orders indefinitely. United Airline's traffic to the Pacific fell 12% in February, and Northwest Airlines has suspended flights to Seoul and Japan and is holding back on planned new flights to Kuala Lumpur, Malaysia and Jakarta, Indonesia.

Impending economic weakness in Brazil worries security analysts covering GM. Intel and other semiconductor producers' stocks suffered as fading hopes for growth in Asian demand more than offset the falling cost of manufacturing there. As noted in Chapter 16, I see a critical point here. US firms may have only small current sales in Asia, but Wall Street analysts and investors have been counting heavily on those sales to mushroom. Otherwise their stocks wouldn't collapse when they announce soft sales in Asia. Oracle has only 12% of its sales in Asia but its stock dropped 29% last December when it announced softness there. Cummins Engine's stock fell 9% on March

23rd of this year after the firm announced a significant impact from weaker than expected Asian sales that are also a mere 12% of revenues.

For others like Coca-Cola, Procter and Gamble, and Motorola, Asia is already a big source of earnings, and that creates vulnerability. The region's turmoil late last year hurt Federal Express' earnings as well. More recently, Nike suffered the same fate. The strong dollar has proven negative for Kodak, Kellogg, McDonald's, Polaroid, Micron Technology, FMC, and IBM, which was also hurt by weak Asian sales. Coke's first quarter 1998 earnings rose 12% from a year earlier, but would have been up 22% without foreign currency losses. JP Morgan, Chase Manhattan, Citicorp, Bankers Trust, and other banks have already suffered sizable trading losses on Asian securities. The write-offs of bad Asian loans, over and above what the IMF will end up covering, are largely yet to come. Citicorp's big Asian retail business is also hurting.

Irresistible Force Meets Immovable Object

Weakening exports, growing imports, lower import prices, and currency translation losses are bad enough for corporate earnings. But they are worse because there is no offsetting give in US domestic costs, at least not in the short run. American labor markets remain drum tight. Jobs are plentiful

CHART 18-5

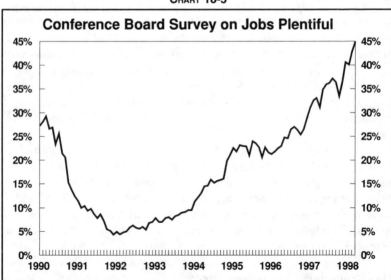

Conference Board Survey on Jobs Plentiful

(Chart 18-5), and with the unemployment rate low it's not surprising that hourly earnings are accelerating (Chart 18-6).

CHART 18-6

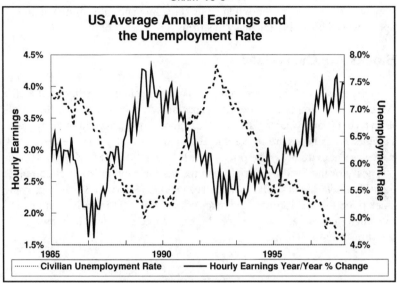

US Average Annual Earnings and the Unemployment Rate

- Civilian Unemployment Rate
- Hourly Earnings Year/Year % Change

CHART 18-7

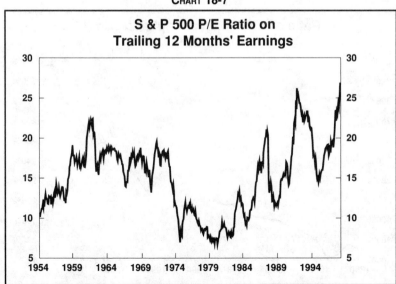

S & P 500 P/E Ratio on Trailing 12 Months' Earnings

So far, foreign and domestic competition have kept labor cost increases from being passed on in higher prices. In fact, for many firms, the combination of productivity growth, which is probably under reported, and falling interest costs, corporate taxes, and depreciation burdens are propelling profits in this non-inflationary atmosphere, as explored further in Chapter 26. But now with the effects of the Asian crisis spreading and intensifying, earnings appear very vulnerable for many US firms.

Stocks Are Overvalued

Even without the risk of a big corporate earnings slide, induced by the Asian crisis or simply the faltering of special factors that have propelled profits in recent years (Chapter 26), US stocks appear overpriced in so many ways. Price-earnings ratios are in nosebleed altitudes (Chart 18-7), price-to-book values are at extremes. The price-to-cash-flow ratio is 18% above its previous peak for the S&P industrials, and the market capitalization of corporate equities in relation to GDP has never been higher (Chart 18-8). Similarly, the stock price-to-sales ratio and the ratios of the S&P 500 to hourly earnings and to home prices are at or near record highs. At the same time, dividend yields are at historic lows (Chart 18-9).

CHART **18-8**

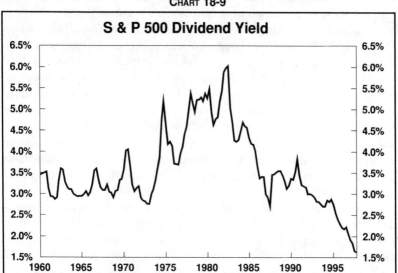

CHART 18-9

S & P 500 Dividend Yield

Success Breeds Excess

From the bull market start in August 1982 until the end of 1997, the S&P 500 index has had a compound annual total return (dividends plus appreciation) of 19.2%, about twice the historic norm. Sure, to a great extent, stocks have been celebrating the unwinding of inflation (see Chapter 27), and making up for the beating they suffered during the inflationary late 1960s and 1970s. Nevertheless, many investors feel that what has really been a catch-up will continue indefinitely.

Maybe the effects of the Asian crisis on corporate earnings will be minimal. Maybe, if Asia proves to be a non-event, the Fed will never, ever again tighten credit and precipitate a recession that is preceded by a bear market in stocks. Still, a number of self-reinforcing factors, common at major stock market tops, have convinced almost everyone that rising stock prices will continue forever. Those foolproof reasons cry out that the end is near.

Fear Is Gone

In the old saying, stocks are driven by greed, tempered with fear. In the scope of the 15-year bull market, (Chart 17-24), even the 1987 crash and the 1990 mini-crash were only temporary interruptions. They were so quickly retraced that they have trained, and I do mean trained, many to believe that sell-offs are wonderful opportunities to buy, not warnings to sell.

Indeed, on October 27, 1997, when the Down Jones Industrial Average plummeted 7.2%, individuals bought 178 shares for every 100 they sold, while the professional managers of pension and mutual funds did the reverse, buying 72 shares for every 100 they sold. On the following day, as stocks rebounded, individuals bought on balance, 4 to 1, while institutions continued to be net sellers. And small investors were right, at least in the immediate term, as the stock market spurted in early 1998. They learned from their "mistakes" in the 1987 case when individual holders of stocks sold some on balance and mutual fund holders dumped a lot. More recently, many have joined professional investors in returning to Asian markets to scoop up what they see as bargains.

Fear of anything but temporary losses has been replaced by the conviction that this trend will continue indefinitely. It's sort of a Newton's First Law of Stock Market behavior. His First Law of Motion says that a body in motion tends to stay in motion. That's been modified to read, Rising Stock Markets Continue to Rise Indefinitely. (You'll excuse the undergraduate physics major in me.) So you'd better be aboard the rolling train or you'll be left in the station.

Another sign of overconfidence may be the popularity of variable annuities, basically mutual funds wrapped in insurance blankets that provide tax advantages, but generally have higher fees. At the same time, sales have slumped for traditional cash value life insurance. Those policies are essentially backed by insurance company portfolios of bonds and mortgages, and guarantee a return, but one that is much lower than variable annuities have achieved in recent years. Buyers explain their choice by saying that they are not worried about death benefits but rather about outliving their retirement funds. I wonder, though, if this attitude isn't more indicative of unbridled confidence in stocks.

Most individual investors view themselves as long-term holders of equities. But history shows that many of those who think they have millennium-long time horizons quickly become panicked sellers in major and prolonged bear markets. They dump the last of their holdings at market bottoms, swearing that they'll never buy another stock again.

In my view, history is relevant because human nature changes very slowly, if at all, over time. Therefore, investors will react to similar circumstances in similar ways. As Sir John Templeton put it, the five most dangerous words in the English language are these: this time it is different.

In fact, scared investors make the stock market bottoms which occur when the last one who can be shaken out is shaken out. My good friend and colleague Dennis Gartman calls this the "puke point." Then the stock market is fresh out of sellers, faced with nothing but potential buyers, and therefore, ready for rebound. This is the exact reverse of a market top, which is formed when the last investor who can be sucked in has been sucked in. The market has run out of buyers and faces nothing but potential sellers. It's also true that a market pinnacle is reached when the last bear throws in the towel.

The problem is that those intending to be long-term investors panic on schedule, at bottoms, and then fail to reinvest until the recovery is well underway. Consequently, they realize far less appreciation than stock market indices suggest.

Bear Market Veterans Are Few

The last real for-sure bear market in US stocks was in the early 1970s, ancient history to all but a few active investors today. Furthermore, the majority of stock mutual-fund managers and investors have entered the game since the last meaningful sell-off in the early 1980s. The average age of mutual-fund managers today is 28. Studies show that the younger ones, many of even more tender years than that, have high SAT scores and take the most risks. They've also had above-average performance of late, but for them it's been only a bull market. Fearing something you've never experienced is difficult. I have repeatedly tried to explain just how devastating a bear market can be to my 31-year-old son, Drew, an analyst with a prestigious investment firm. Not much success.

Money Has No Place Else to Go

Like all previous rationales for an indefinite one-way market, the money-has-no-place-else-to-go concept has a basis in truth. Real estate is dead as a sure-fire investment, at least for most. Ditto for tax shelters, overrun by tax law changes and weak prices of their underlying assets in the 1980s. And who wants to accept 5% from Treasury bills when double-digit stock returns are there for the taking? Or bonds either, for that matter. Notice (Chart 18-10) the small flows into bond mutual funds in recent years compared with the huge flows into stock funds (Chart 17-25).

Many believe that demand for stocks will exceed supply indefinitely, especially as the postwar babies hit their saving strides, as noted in Chapters 17 and 27. Somehow, however, the supply of stocks seems always to catch up with demand, sooner or later. I remember well the devouring of stocks by pension funds and other institutional investors when they first started to buy them in size in the 1960s. They were accumulating equities at such a pace—

fueling a long stock rally in the process—that by the late 1960s, many Wall Street wizards were convinced that there would soon be a shortage of stocks. So, prices had only one way to go—up. Well, as they say, the rest is history. It took 277 months, over 23 years that is, for the S&P 500 index in real terms to get back to its December 1968 peak (Chart 5-1), and 127 months when dividends are included.

It's also interesting to note that Wall Street always is able to produce enough new paper to meet the demand. From the fall of 1991 to the fall of 1997, the number of publicly traded companies exploded by 87% from 6,103 to 11, 396. It's also true that new mutual funds have been launched at least as fast as growth in demand and now outnumber the individual stocks on the New York Stock Exchange. And, by the way, another possible sign of a peak: the New York Stock Exchange is thinking about building a big new trading floor to relieve overcrowding and to trade more foreign stocks. Finally, corporate insiders, officers and directors who are in the best positions to evaluate their companies' prospects, sold 3.34 shares of stock in the last quarter of 1997 for every one they purchased, a high ratio for the 1990s. Note that they similarly were unloading stock right before the 1997 crash.

CHART **18-10**

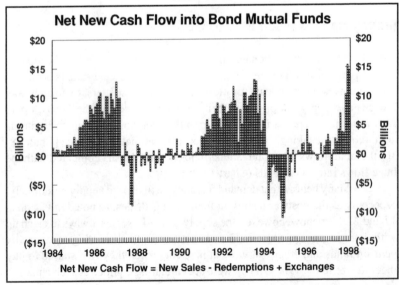

A 10% Annual Return on US Stocks Is a Sure Thing

To be sure, stocks have returned about 10%, on average, over long periods of time, but not every year as they have recently, and then some. Since its bottom in 1990, the stock market had no 10% setbacks in this decade until October 1997. This pattern has convinced many that there is little risk of a bear market's lasting the better part of a year or more. That may be one reason why most see themselves as long-term investors, come hell or high water.

Conviction of continuing steady growth in stock prices is rampant. Financial planners are advising individual investors to put more money into stocks, and some have curtailed purchases of houses and yachts to do so. Others are so convinced they can't lose that they are financing stock purchases with credit cards and home equity loans, and then using 50% margin debt to boot.

Investment consultants, armed with reams of statistics which go back only as far as the current bull market, are matter-of-factly advising public and private pension funds to do the same. More and more companies are making stock options a key part of executive compensation, under the assumption that good managements will always be rewarded with higher prices for their stocks. Led by "chainsaw" Al Dunlap, a number of corporations now pay directors only in stock options. Travelers Group, which plans to merge with Citicorp, requires directors and key officers to hold their company shares until they leave the firm. Sports stars who endorse products are foregoing cash in favor of stock options. Head hunters and consultants (but not this one) are in the same queue. Some politicians believe that the best way to fund Social Security benefits in the future is to forego stodgy old Treasuries in favor of common stocks.

A number of countries in Latin America, Europe, and Asia have already instituted such plans. Norway generates huge trade surpluses from petroleum exports. Earlier she directed unneeded funds to debt markets, but in the future, they'll be going to foreign equities. Canada is now starting to invest some of her national government pension plan funds in stocks. If equities falter, Ottawa is on the hook to make up the difference.

Wall Street Journal reporter Jonathan Clements reached the top of the tree in a June 27, 1995, column. He agreed with the time-honored idea of setting aside six month's worth of living expenses as a contingency, but keep it in cash or Treasury bills? No way! He recommended a well-diversified stock mutual fund. What if stocks hit a big bear market? Not to worry. He wrote,

...if that happens, I have no intention of dumping my fund shares at fire-sale prices. Instead, I figure that—if I really put my mind to it—I could get my hands on a fair amount of money fairly quickly by tapping into the equity in my home, getting a cash advance on my credit card or borrowing some of the money I have in my employer's profit-sharing plan. I would then pay back the money out of my paycheck, and maybe also by selling some stock-fund shares when the market rebounds.

The Sky Is the Limit for New Money Coming into US Stocks

With the huge inflow of mutual funds in recent years, even the biggest bulls realize that individual investors may be running out of ammunition. They salivate, however, over all those foreign investors who are fleeing Asia and who may jump into US stocks, especially as the dollar continues to rally and gives their US investments an additional reward. The bulls may be right, but if a bear market starts, foreign investors will probably depart, as usual.

Everybody's a Stock Expert

The story has it that just before the 1929 crash, Joe Kennedy knew the end was near when he got a stock tip from his shoeshine boy. Recently we were doing major renovation on our residence, and the carpenter, electrician, and plumber all asked my advice on investments—but gave me their own hot stocks as well. A rising market makes geniuses out of idiots, just as a falling market makes everyone a dunce. A recent poll found that 60% of individual investors think they have investment savvy. New investment clubs are springing up like weeds in the spring. The Beardstown Ladies have been dispensing stock tips along with their cookbook recipes—until it was revealed that the 10-year 23.4% average annual return on their investment club portfolio that helped them sell 800,000 copies of their book was really a disappointing 9.1%.

Indexed funds have mushroomed, increasing from 147 to 172 in 1997 alone, and their assets rose from $255 billion at the end of 1992 to $600 billion at the end of last year. Why pay an active portfolio manager when you can make 30% a year in a low-fee indexed fund? And this rush isn't just confined to individual investors. Now 28% of US corporate pension-fund stock portfolios are indexed, up from 21% in 1988. Furthermore, if you want to buy stocks yourself, why pay a broker for advice? Note the rapid growth in discount brokerage and on-line trading. Also, over 50 colleges now have real money run by students in investment classes, none of whom has ever seen a bear market. States like West Virginia and Michigan have instituted 401(k)-type equity plans for state employees.

Lessons of History

I've learned, repeatedly, that when a majority believe that a market will continue to move in one direction indefinitely, a reversal is at hand. Dennis Gartman has another wonderful statement: "When you're yelling, you should be selling; when you're crying, you should be buying." Of course, convictions that any declines are magnificent buying opportunities are so ingrained that it will take big losses over a long period to disabuse investors of their bullishness. Furthermore, nature is perverse and will give investors what they least expect. Consequently, the next bear market will probably be a Chinese water torture affair, with sell-offs met with buying that spawns weak rallies, followed by more sell-offs, etc.—a long and frustrating saw-toothed pattern along a declining trend. As usual, even the true believers will ultimately dump their stocks, and thereby create the final bear market bottom.

Whether you agree that US stocks are on thin ice, please note that in the past, investment atmospheres as euphoric as today's have ended with major declines. Also note what another great friend, Bruce McCowan, says. "Bad things happen to over-priced stock markets." When one problem surfaces, others erupt out of the briny deep.

A Big Shock

How do you think consumers would take a major loss in the appreciation in their stocks that have had big cumulative gains over many years—a loss that would destroy much of the wealth they've been counting on for retirement and other purposes that are normally funded by saving current income? My friend, Steve Leuthold of the Leuthold Group, calculated an excellent example of how devastating the loss would be.

Let's assume, he writes, that in late 1991, a couple became convinced that the stock market was their one and only route to a comfortable retirement. Starting in January 1992, they diligently invested $2,500 each quarter in a 401(k) plan, all in equity mutual funds, and the total returns to date have matched S&P 500 performance (better than the vast majority of equity funds). On February 1, 1998, including their 1997 fourth quarter contribution, the $62,500 invested for retirement had a portfolio value of about $122,603, a

CHART 18-11

THE SAVER'S REWARD

MARKET DECLINE	COST	VALUE	GAIN (LOSS)	PERCENT GAIN (LOSS)
Now	$62,500	$122,603	$60,103	96%
Down 10% Next 12 Months	$72,500	$118,272	$45,772	63%
Down 20% Next 12 Months	$72,500	$108,841	$36,341	50%
Down 25% Next 12 Months	$72,500	$104,160	$31,660	44%
Down 30% Next 12 Months	$72,500	$99,409	$26,909	37%
Down 35% Next 12 Months	$72,500	$94,658	$22,158	31%
Down 40% Next 12 Months	$72,500	$89,977	$17,477	24%
Down 50% Next 12 Months	$72,500	$80,546	$8,046	11%
Down 60% Next 12 Months	$72,500	$71,114	($1,386)	-2%

Source: The Leuthold Group

nice gain of $60,103, about 96% over cost. They doubled their money and can retire with ease if this trend continues (Chart 18-11).

But if the S&P 500 slides 25% over the next year and the couple continues to make disciplined quarterly investments, the $72,500 then contributed would have a portfolio value of $104,160, shaving the gain to $31,660 (about 44% over cost). This is a meager and demoralizing reward for almost seven years of diligent retirement saving. Even CDs or money market funds would have done as well!

And what's more, a 40% decline (a stock market retreat to closer to its median valuation levels) would shrink portfolio value to $89,977, only $17,477 more than the amount they had contributed over the last almost seven years, a gain over cost of 24%. CDs or money market funds would have done better. If stocks drop 50%, the gain is trivial. Money under the mattress would have been almost as good, even better on a risk adjusted basis. Thanks, Steve, for the wonderful example of a bear market's devastation!

Most believe, of course, that investors in 401(k) and other retirement funds will never desert stocks, even in the worst of bear markets. They'll simply ride it out in Jonathan Clements fashion. Steve Leuthold's example makes me think otherwise. And if investors become disillusioned by a debilitating decline in US stocks, they will enhance the fall by liquidating mutual funds. They didn't hesitate to dump international stock funds last year in reaction to the Asian markets meltdowns.

Most US stock funds are invested almost 100% in equities. They have to be, whether their managers like it or not. To hold cash is to hold an asset which has vastly underperformed stocks for years and to risk the displeasure of fund holders, already none too happy since few funds have beat the market averages consistently. So, many open-end funds have set up bank borrowing lines to provide emergency cash for redemptions. Nevertheless, if shareholders start to redeem their funds in size, managers eventually will be forced to sell stocks to raise the funds needed to meet those redemptions. This will push stocks lower, induce more fund redemptions, etc., in a downward spiral. In the trade, it's called forced liquidation of the mutual funds.

Furthermore, the long bull market has generated lots of unrealized capital gains for stock mutual funds. Forced portfolio sales would result in big capital gains tax bills, even for those long-term investors who remain in the funds until the next tax record dates. This could encourage them to bail out before those dates, forcing additional liquidations of the portfolios.

The Saving Spree...

Given the US stock market's lofty level, it looks like the negative effects of the Asian crisis on corporate earnings will touch-off a severe enough bear market to destroy considerable consumer wealth—and confidence in stock appreciation as a substitute for saving ongoing income. Alternatively, a Fed-induced recession and preceding stock market slide will have the same effect, as discussed later.

A big bear market would be the shock we've been waiting for to switch consumers from borrowing and spending to saving. And it will take a shock. Few are likely to wake up one day and say to their spouses, "Dear, we've been spending too much; time to cut back." With stocks leaping, their current game plan for building education funds for their kids or retirement nest eggs is working too well.

But if a big chunk of that stock appreciation is wiped out, all the inducements for savings discussed in Chapter 17 will be unleashed with full fury—the desire to spend to maintain the good life notwithstanding. And a switch to saving will make a big difference in the US economy. In the last 15 years, the consumer saving rate has fallen almost a half percentage point per year on average (Chart 17-12). Conversely, the spending rate has risen the same amount.

Suppose a saving spree breaks out and the saving rate rises by a half percentage point per year for ten years from its recent low of 3.5%. In a decade, that will bring saving back to 8.5% of after tax income, about in-line with earlier post-war experience, but still below the extreme you might expect with a big new trend. The shift from a minus ½% per year to a plus ½% is obviously a one percentage point net increase in the saving rate—and a one percentage point net fall per year in the spending rate.

...Would Have Big Consequences

That's a huge shift, considering that real consumer spending has only been growing at a 2½% rate in the last decade, but it has plenty of precedence. Note that the destruction of Japanese real wealth in stocks and real estate may have a lot to do with the recent leap in their saving rate (Chart 2-9). US consumer spending is two-thirds of GDP, and a long-term change in consumer spending habits will have similar effects on the other one-third of spending. Housing will be directly dampened by consumer caution. Capital spending will grow more slowly, especially that which is oriented toward capacity expansion, as weaker consumer spending growth spawns excess capacity. Even government spending will rise more slowly if the zeal for balanced budgets survives as slower economic and deflation growth hold back tax collections,

CHART **18-12**

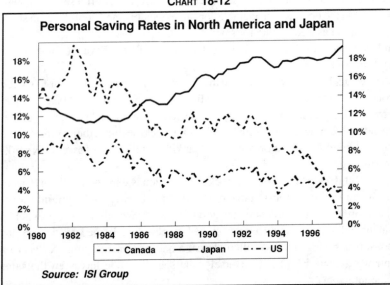

Personal Saving Rates in North America and Japan

- - - - Canada   —— Japan   - · - · - US

Source: ISI Group

CHART **18-13**

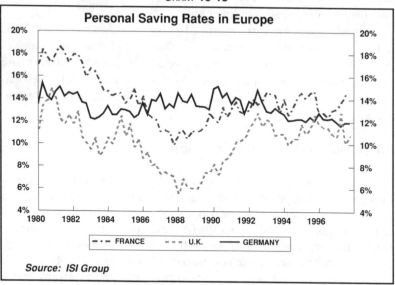

Source: *ISI Group*

as noted in Chapter 2. To be sure, economic sluggishness will curtail exports to the benefit of GDP. Nevertheless, the rising dollar we foresee and business weakness abroad, to say nothing of possible protectionism (Chapter 25), work the other way by encouraging cheaper imports to the detriment of domestic production.

A 1% or so slower annual growth in real GDP will reduce it from the 2½% of the last decade to 1½%. Let me be optimistic and move the forecast range up a bit to 1½% to 2%. Coming on top of other 13 deflationary forces already at work (See Charts I-7 and Chapters 1-16), this weakness will insure deflation in the US—and throughout the world. American consumer spending plus residential construction accounts for 70% of US GDP, which, in turn, is over 25% of the globe's total. So, 70% of 25%, or close to 20%, of all the goods and services produced in the world are bought by US consumers.

And, as discussed in Chapter 16, the US is the world's buyer of last resort. American consumer restraint will put downward pressure on US trade and current account deficits at a time that no replacement buyer for the world's excess is in sight. Except for Japan, developed country saving rates have fallen to such low levels (Charts 18-12 and 18-13), that it's unlikely that consumers in other major lands will slash their saving further to offset an uptrend in the US—especially as deflation encourages foreigners as well as Americans to save in anticipation of lower prices.

In addition to America's quarter of global output, another 10% or 20%, at least, is accounted for by commodities that are traded in dollars, such as crude oil, many metals, and agricultural products. With the buck likely to rise in the years ahead (see Chapters 12 and 13), this huge share of dollar-denominated production and consumption will spawn considerable further deflationary pressures.

When Do You Know It's Deflation?

A very wise economist once said that if you have to forecast an event, forecast it in detail, or forecast its timing, but not both. I'll take his advice. American consumer retrenchment will seal the case for deflation, so let's concentrate on this initiator of chronically falling prices, not to try to pinpoint the timing of deflation ,but to figure out when we'll know it is firmly established.

As noted earlier, a major bear market in US stocks will probably scare consumers into a saving spree, and that switch to saving in an economy geared to rapid growth will likely initiate a recession. Now, I know that US recessions, at least in the post-war period, have always been touched off by Fed tightening, and none is likely in this scenario. However, we are in a global economy, and the credit authorities that are doing the tightening this time are foreign lenders to Asian lands. Also, as often in the past, there is an initiating financial crisis, but it, too, is in Asia. Different location, same effect.

Prices would decline in a recession but that wouldn't insure deflation, since prices always decelerate in business dips. If inflation is running at 10%, it drops to, say, 7% or 8% rates in a recession; if at 4%, it falls to 1% or 2% in a downturn. Inflation is now about zero, so price declines of 2% or 3% in the next recession are likely, but don't guarantee deflation. If in the recovery that follows, however, US consumers remain cautions and prices continue to fall 1% or 2% per year, then chronic deflation has arrived. As usual, though, security markets will anticipate the facts.

Back to Waiting for the Fed

There is, of course, a slim, remote, infinitesimal, highly unlikely, insignificant, trivial chance that I'm dead wrong on deflation's trigger mechanism. Contrary to my belief, the Asian crisis may have limited detrimental effects on US corporate profits, and may be laughed-off by the US stock market. Maybe I'm wrong and recent rapid earnings growth is sustainable even without a spillover from Asia. Then consumer confidence and spending would remain intact, but continuing tight labor markets would again threaten a future surge in inflation, at least in the Fed's eyes. So we'd be back to waiting for the credit authorities to raise interest rates and, as is normal, precipitate a recession. Chairman Greenspan has made it clear that only the threat of meaningful and lasting spillover from the Asian crisis has kept the Fed at bay in recent quarters.

As usual, that recession would be preceded by a bear market in US stocks. Given stocks' lofty levels, the sell-off would probably destroy enough of individuals' wealth to chase consumers out of spending and into a saving spree. Then, as with the case of an Asian-initiated bear market, the end result would be deflation. Damned if you do, damned if you don't. I see deflation in the cards one way or another.

Washington's Reaction

Many say deflation is impossible because Washington and other major governments and central banks simply won't allow it. Really? Chapter 2 notes that developed country governments are hell bent to reduce spending and deficits, with a lot of voter steel in their ribs to do so. It would take considerable deflation to change their minds. Ditto for the Fed and other central banks. As discussed in Chapter 3, they're all still fighting the last war, inflation, and not the next, deflation. And in any event, the Fed probably won't ease until deflation is firmly established.

The credit authorities change their policy on the basis of reality, not forecasts—theirs or anyone else's. Years ago, when people still had faith in big econometric models of the economy (those mentioned in Chapter 6), the Fed was criticized because they didn't have one. Why would they? They wouldn't have used it for policy decisions anyway. Of course, knowing the long lead times between monetary ease and its effects on the economy, the Fed always tries to act promptly—once the case for ease is clear, but not until then.

Monetary Ease Won't Help

Furthermore, unlike the experience in inflationary times, monetary ease won't do much to stimulate an economy beset with declining prices and global excess capacity. In the postwar era to date, interest rate declines were initiated by the Fed, after they'd killed the economy with credit stringency. Those rate declines preceded economic revivals that were anticipated by bull stock markets.

Once the excess inventories built up in the early stages of the recession were liquidated, the economy was ready for revival. Pent up demand for consumer goods and housing was unleashed, encouraged by lower borrowing rates. Similarly, business soon needed more capacity to meet growing demand, and lower interest rates made capital investments more attractive. During inflationary periods like the postwar era, fundamental demand exceeds supply, by definition, so anything that cuts effective costs, including lower financing rates, considerably augments strong underlying demand.

In contrast, supply exceeds demand chronically in deflation. Most things are in abundance and buyers are waiting for lower prices. If you've already got too much, lower costs of financing won't make you rush out to buy more of it. Since interest rates are unlikely to go below zero, real interest costs remain high when prices are falling (see Chapter 26). I'm describing, of course, the classic liquidity trap of 1930s fame—one that Japan is struggling with today. Note that even a ridiculously low ½% discount rate (Chart 12-10) has done almost nothing to increase money supply growth in Japan (Chart 3-6).

We also see this principle at work in the statistical models of US capital spending we've developed over the years. They always show operating rates to be the prime driver of plant and equipment outlays, with profits and interest rates of little importance. And for good reason. When operating rates are high, business people are optimistic. They need more capacity to meet demand. They're sure they'll get the selling prices needed to justify it. If they don't expand, the competition will grab their market shares. But, in contrast, when capacity is excessive, who needs more? The profit outlook is grim and selling prices are uncertain. Not surprisingly, then, low and falling interest rates in themselves don't stimulate much capital spending.

None of this says that interest rates don't influence economic activity. Tight credit will slow any economy, especially a booming inflationary climate in which credit demand is already straining supply. But easing credit doesn't do much to stimulate economic activity unless there is strong underlying purchasing power. It's the old string analogy. By pulling on it, tightening credit, the Fed gets a response, but easing credit is like pushing on the string—little effect.

To be sure, if a US financial collapse were to unfold, Washington would be galvanized into aggressive monetary and fiscal stimulus. But as you'll find in Chapter 22, in my deflationary crystal ball, I see a good chance of avoiding major financial difficulties in America and other Western developed countries. Meanwhile, the next chapter will show you how deflation reinforces itself.

CHAPTER 19

DEFLATION IS SELF-FEEDING

In Chapters 1 through 18, I've made the case for deflation. Yet, you, like most people today, may still think that deflation just isn't possible in the modern world—despite my argument, at the end of the last chapter, that fiscal and monetary responses will be limited and late unless there are also big financial problems. Developed economies have too many built-in stabilizers, both public and private, to experience chronic and widespread price declines, you may believe. Private spending is predominately on services, which have an inflationary bias. Government spending in today's developed countries runs a third to a half or more of economic activity, so its very size will prevent widespread falling prices.

Living Examples of Deflation

But before your opinion gets cast in concrete, look at two real-life examples of deflation today—Japan and Switzerland. You already saw in Chapter 15 that Japan remains mired in a deflationary depression—with falling prices of real estate (Chart 15-4) and other tangibles, financial assets like stocks (Chart 15-3), and many goods and services—despite an unbelievably low central bank discount rate of ½% (Chart 12-10). Wholesale prices have fallen 6% in the last seven years. Even at ridiculously low interest rates, no one wants to buy much of anything that is falling in price. Blame it on a government and bureaucracy that hate deficits so much that meaningful fiscal stimulation remains a no-no. Blame it on a populace that sits still for economic malaise. Blame it on a strong yen which has depressed imports and therefore domestic prices (Chart 12-12). Regardless, Japan has suffered eight years of deflation and more is in prospect as she slips back into recession.

Switzerland has also suffered from deflation in recent years (Chart 19-1), in large part because of the strength of the Swiss franc, especially against the currency of her major trading partner, Germany (Chart 19-2). Much of

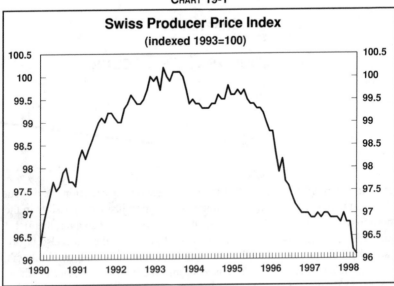

CHART **19-1**

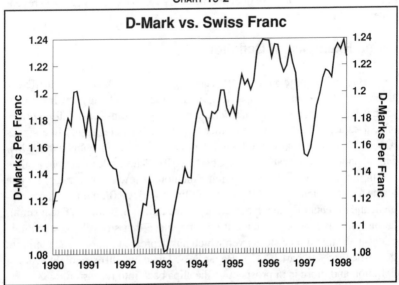

CHART **19-2**

that strength was due to money seeking a safe haven from the uncertainty over the new Euro currency that is due next year and the associated disappearance of the trusted D-mark. Big deal, you may be thinking, Switzerland is just one big bank, and a strong currency attracts even more deposits, both cold and hot money. But Switzerland also relies heavily on manufactured exports and tourism, both of which are priced out of their markets by the robust Swiss franc.

No wonder that like Japan, she has seen nothing but economic weakness in the 1990s (Chart 19-3). Unlike the rest of Europe, Switzerland never recovered from the early 1990s recession and the economy has gone nowhere since. Swiss joblessness (Chart 19-4) used to be so low that they didn't count the unemployed, they named them. Now that rate is at previously unknown heights. It's no wonder that Swiss officials have suggested that they want a weaker currency to curb the deflationary cycle. The decline in the Swiss franc against the dollar since 1995 has been to little avail. Also, like Japan, super-low interest rates (Chart 19-5) have been of little help. It's hard to believe that the previously hard money-oriented Swiss want a weaker currency. What's the world coming to? But they desperately need something to stop deflation and rekindle their economy.

CHART 19-3

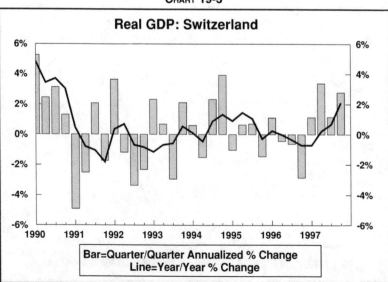

Real GDP: Switzerland

Bar=Quarter/Quarter Annualized % Change
Line=Year/Year % Change

Deflation Is Self-Feeding

Switzerland and Japan are clear cut examples of not only modern day deflation, but also its self-feeding nature. Consumer spending in both countries is static. As buyers wait for still lower prices, the resulting excess capacity and unwanted inventories lead to further price cutting. Suspicions are confirmed, so buyers wait for still lower prices in a self-perpetuating spiral. To put it another way, just as a saving spree by US consumers will reduce demand and encourage deflation, deflation in turn will foster saving as people wait for lower prices before buying. And, the likely high real returns on fixed income instruments during deflation (see Chapters 17 and 26) will further reward saving and discourage spending.

The self-feeding cycle applies to services as well as goods. An airplane full of empty seats is just as much an inducement to cutting prices as is a dealer's lot full of unsold cars. Chart 19-6 shows that in the last year, despite the strong US economy, service price inflation continued to atrophy.

In Services As Well As Goods

Auto insurance premiums offer an example of deflation's potential self-feeding nature. State Farm, which insures about one-quarter of US cars, in-

CHART 19-4

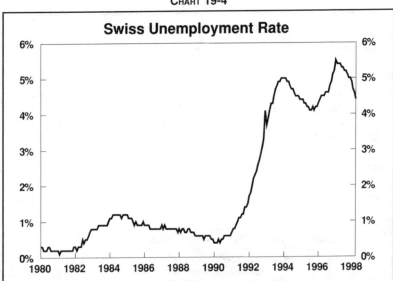

creased its premiums about 2% last year, a big change from 8% annual hikes in the earlier 1990s. Of course, part of the deceleration was due to fewer and less costly accidents. The aging postwar babies drive more carefully, and

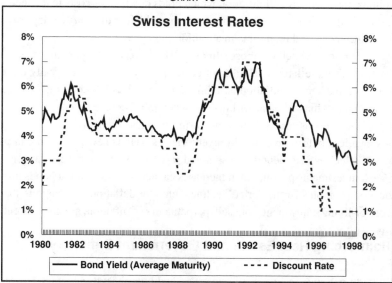

CHART 19-5

Swiss Interest Rates

Bond Yield (Average Maturity) — — — Discount Rate

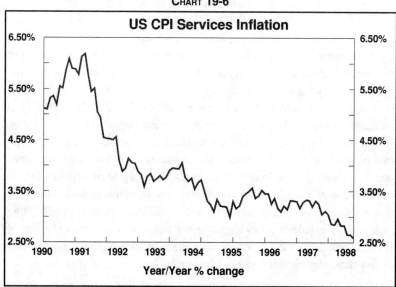

CHART 19-6

US CPI Services Inflation

Year/Year % change

there aren't as many young hot rodders as earlier. Air bags, seat belts, and more rigorous enforcement of drunk driving laws also help. But so, too, do declining medical costs for accident victims and moderating costs of vehicle repair. Regardless of the reasons for smaller increases in auto insurance premiums, they depress CPI inflation which holds down labor costs in the medical and auto repair industries, among others, which in turn further depresses insurance costs and premiums in a reinforcing cycle.

Services, which compose almost 60% of consumer spending, tend to have much more labor content than goods production. So, it's really quite amazing that service inflation is falling at a time when US labor markets are drum tight. Think of what will happen when jobs become less plentiful.

Deflation is also self-feeding in the business arena as firms wait for lower prices before investing in inventories as well as new plant and equipment, which is also depressed, as noted in Chapter 18, by excess capacity. Weak investment spending then increases capacity among capital goods producers, promotes further price declines, etc. In deflation it's obvious that cost-of-living adjustments, big self-perpetuators of inflation, are nonexistent.

Reinforcing Real Estate and Government Deflation

In deflation, as prices of real estate and other heavily-leveraged assets fall, defaults will be more common and lenders will be much more cautious. So, construction will be depressed, leading to more excess capacity in that industry and falling prices in real estate markets that will be already subdued by deflation. Of course, dull markets in tangibles discourage investment and speculation there and turn attention to saving and productivity-enhancing investments. That, too, cuts costs and prices. Speculation in tangibles is further discouraged by the high real cost of borrowing.

Deflation is self-feeding in government as well. With flat or only small increases in money wages and salaries, personal tax collections grow more slowly and fewer people are pushed into higher tax brackets. Taxable corporate profits also rise more modestly as basic earnings advances in nominal terms are slower. Also in deflation, inventory losses occur as prices fall and depreciation overstates the cost of replacement equipment. Both reduce taxable earnings. Assuming that voter zeal for balanced budgets persists, sluggish growth in federal revenues will force even more government spending restraint and further cut Washington's share of the economic pie, which is also deflationary, as discussed in Chapter 2.

No Longer Any Place to Hide

Also gone in deflation is the coverup that inflation provides for many problems and abuses. We see that clearly today in Japan, as discussed in Chapter 15. It's easy to say that Japan's economy is quite difference from those in the West, but deflation has a way of introducing unwanted discipline to any system and opening untold cans of worms. Recall that when the S&L bailout started in the late 1980s, it was estimated to cost $50 billion tops. The final bill was about $250 billion. By exposing problems and forcing their solutions, deflation is once again self-reinforcing. As the king said in Hamlet, "When sorrows come, they come not single spies, but in battalions!"

The Reverse of Inflationary Expectations

To appreciate fully the self-feeding aspects of deflation, it may be helpful to recall the exact opposite, self-feeding inflation. During the high inflation of the 1970s, people became convinced that it would last indefinitely, and indeed that prices would accelerate. So they borrowed heavily to beat rising interest rates and used the money to invest in leaping tangibles. This strained credit supplies and pushed up interest rates, while rampant demand for real estate, coins, antiques, and art works propelled prices. Suspicions were confirmed, spawning more of the same.

Similarly, consumers and businesses bought more goods than they needed to in anticipation of rising prices. That put pressure on supplies, pushed up prices, and encouraged even bigger hedge buying. Productive work and investments gave way to speculation, so there was little productivity growth to offset rising costs. This, too, added fat to the fires of inflation. Businesses didn't care much what it paid for labor and materials because cost increases could be passed through with ease, and with markups to boot. This practice fed on itself since costs accelerated as they moved through the production system and encouraged even bigger markups. Meanwhile, the resulting leaping inflation induced widespread cost of living adjustments and even high labor costs.

During those years I told clients how I'd succumbed to inflationary expectations even though I was predicting their demise. After the October 1973 energy price leap, I knew that drastically higher fertilizer prices would follow since natural gas is used in making its nitrogen component. But my local garden center owner hadn't caught on. So, as he was closing at Thanksgiving for the winter, I bought his remaining supply, and he even gave me a discount to avoid holding the inventory over the winter.

There it was, stacked up in my garage from the floor almost to the ceiling. I used part of it on my lawn the next summer, but still had room for another stack, so I returned the following fall. His prices had risen, but not much, so I repeated the exercise. I'm sure I would have kept repeating it until prices broke and I would have been stuck with a ten-year supply of fertilizer, but fortunately, I ran out of garage space first.

Half Way There

These inflationary expectations ruled in the 1970s and are the precise opposite of the deflationary expectations I see developing. Indeed, the business attitude toward cost pass-through has already made at least half of the transition. Very few American businesses today expect their customers to cover their cost increases. It's gotten to the point that most suppliers don't even bother asking for price relief. And this doesn't just refer to manufacturers facing withering foreign competition. Medical services, lawyers, and regrettably, economic consultants, are in the same boat.

When a business can't get its customers to pay more, it in turn tells its suppliers that their cost increases are their problems to be offset by their own cost cuts and productivity increases. In fact, the only price discussions many firms have today with their suppliers concern how much the vendors' prices will be *cut*. This, of course, is the introduction of deflationary pass-through, which will expand considerably in deflation as widespread price declines are pushed backward through the supplier chain.

Deflationary Expectations

As you've seen by now, deflation, like inflation, is self-feeding in many ways. A key, but by no means the only self-perpetuation mechanism, is the anticipation of lower prices. But how much deflation does it take for consumers and businesses to wait for lower prices before buying? This is the same question we used to ask, in reverse, about inflation, and in either case, there is no simple answer. It depends on at least four factors.

1. The breadth of deflation. Prices per unit of computing power have been declining for years and so have TV, appliance, and video and audio product prices (Chart I-4). But decreasing prices haven't been broad enough yet to convince people that they will spread across a wide spectrum of goods and services.

2. The chronic nature of deflation. Producer prices of goods have fallen over the past year (Chart I-2) as have the prices of many consumer goods. Yet, against the background of the high inflation 1970s, this recent experience is obviously not long standing enough to convince people that it will persist.

3. Decelerating prices, at least in short run. Most Americans have vivid memories of the near runaway inflation of the 1970s, and many, including the Fed, assume that a return to serious inflation remains a greater threat than deflation, as discussed in the Introduction. This probably means that it will take a continuation of the recent price pattern to persuade them that deflation is to be anticipated, a pattern of smaller and smaller rates of inflation turning into bigger and bigger rates of deflation.

In other words, inflation rates have fallen from double digits to essentially zero in the past 15 years. If deflation sets in, but at a steady rate of say 1% per year, it would probably take a number of years before people believed in its permanence. More immediately convincing would be 1% deflation followed by a 2% decline in general prices the next year and 3% the following year.

4. The amount of deflation. Of course, the deeper the deflation, the more convincing it becomes. Deep deflation would be a big persuader as it promotes big drops in interest rates and tangible asset and commodity prices, and unbelievable consumer bargains, but also job losses in firms that don't cut their costs and prices. Those living on fixed incomes would feel like kings as their purchasing power grows while highly leveraged individuals and corporations fail.

In addition, deflation, like inflation, must be significant enough to spur action. Even if you are convinced that a decline in shoe prices is in the offing, it may not be enough to make you wait to buy. Waiting could entail another trip to the shoe store, and besides, if you buy a pair now, you get the use of them in the meanwhile.

To be sure, the cost and discretionary nature of a good or service influences your sensitivity to deflation. An expected 5% decline in car prices may make you wait. If you're spending $30,000, that's a cool $1,500 in your pocket, and you can probably nurse your old bus along for another year any way. Recall how rebate programs have pushed vehicle sales up and down like ping pong balls. But an expected 10% drop in toothpaste prices may not make you get out the pliers so you can, by vigorous squeezing, make the old tube last until the lower price is in effect.

The Trigger Point for Deflationary Expectations

Taking these four factors into account, what would it take to trigger deflation expectations? Probably not as big a decline in prices as the 3% inflation rate level that seemed to touch off inflationary expectations in the

1970s. Even before that decade, folks had gained familiarity with rising prices throughout the postwar era, and were sensitive to the inflationary beast. Been there, done that. Deflation, however, is a different animal, not seen since the 1930s, and few of us today had first-hand experience with it. Widespread and chronic falling prices would be such a shock to most, that it probably would take less deflation today than it took inflation earlier to get people's attention.

My judgment is that declines in the prices of most goods and a fair number of services, averaging 1% to 2% and lasting for several years, would do the job. Then, anticipation of lower prices by buyers and all of the other self-feeding aspects of deflation would kick in.

I think we'll see this degree of deflation because, among other reasons, it's usual at this stage of the 50- to 60-year Kondratieff Wave, as you'll learn in the next chapter.

CHAPTER 20

DEFLATION IS NORMAL AT THIS STAGE OF THE KONDRATIEFF WAVE

Deflation isn't as new, strange, rare, or exotic as many believe. Indeed, as noted in the Introduction, it's the norm in the US in peacetime. It's also usual for this stage of the Kondratieff Wave, named for the Russian economist, Nikolai Kondratieff.

As a result of his work in the 1920s, he correctly predicted big problems for the capitalist countries in the 1930s, but he made a strategic blunder for a Soviet by suggesting that the capitalist world would survive. The reaction of the Kremlin was predictable, and Kondratieff spent the rest of his career in Siberia—making little rocks out of big rocks, by some reports.

The Kondratieff Wave shows that capitalist countries have consistently been subject to 50-to 60-year cycles of extended growth and decline, commodity price peaks and troughs, and rising and falling interest rates. After studying more than 100 years of data on commodity prices in industrialized countries, Kondratieff found that after a long period of expansion, approximately 25 years, a long decline ensued, lasting about 30 years. To date, this Long Wave seems intact, with a few modifications. Chart 20-1 shows a stylized Kondratieff Wave and the dates of its four phases in the US as well as wholesale and stock prices.

The Upswing

The upswing, or first phase, of the Long Wave starts with a popular war, which is typically short and inexpensive and serves to spur economic activity. It is fought against a weak foe at the time when public confidence is at an ebb, when the nation wants to be sure it can be victorious. The first US trough war was the Mexican War, which started in 1846. The second was the

CHART 20-1

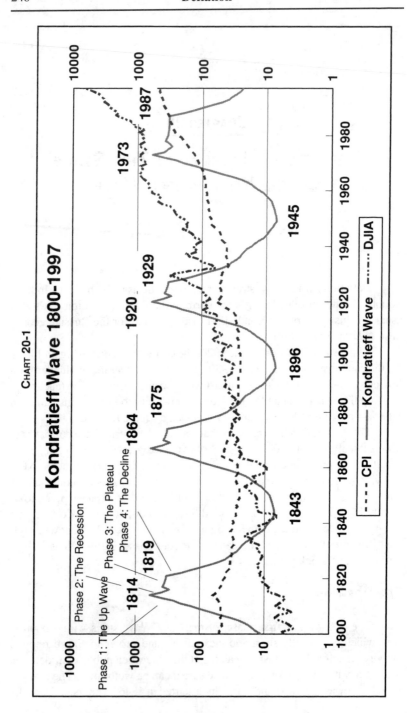

Spanish-American War in 1898, and the third, World War II. This up-phase is dominated by strong growth and fairly mild recessions, and ends about two and half decades later with an unpopular war—the War of 1812, the Civil War, World War I, and most recently, the Vietnam War. They all started at the height of public confidence and in the pursuit of some great cause, but ended with nothing but disillusionment.

The Civil War, World War I, and the Vietnam War all began with a "crusader" spirit. The Civil War, of course, was fought to end slavery. In the beginning of US involvement in World War I, American soldiers marched off to war because, as Woodrow Wilson said, "the world must be made safe for democracy." The rationale for the Vietnam War was to prevent falling dominoes in Southeast Asia and to stop the spread of communism. The enthusiasm for all three wars evaporated quickly, and they became highly unpopular. Consider the draft riots of the Civil War and Lincoln's near reelection defeat in 1864 and the enormous trauma of the Vietnam War.

The Downswing

Those unpopular wars are followed by a surge in commodity prices and then collapse, and then continuing price weakness for the balance of the downswing. This happened after the War of 1812, the Civil War, and World War I. The leap in the early 1970s, after the end of the Vietnam War, and then the commodity price nosedive were right on schedule. But widespread price declines have been delayed until now by two factors. First, the Cold War that began soon after World War II and only ended in the late 1980s. Second, expanding government spending on social programs, the legacy of the 1930s and the New Deal, which has only more recently begun to be reversed. The voter tide against big government began to turn in the late 1970s, as you saw in Chapter 2, but the restraints on public medical and welfare spending and the end of farm subsidies in the last several years are the first concrete evidences of federal government downsizing. As long as defense and nondefense spending were robust, the economy had a strong inflationary bias.

The price explosion at the end of unpopular wars results in a self-feeding inventory building spree that ultimately breaks into the sharpest recession of the wave, phase 2, as excess inventories are discarded and prices collapse. This was true after World War I when the 1919 explosion was promptly followed by the 1920-21 recession, the fastest decline on record when prices nosedived (Chart 20-2). Similarly, the 1973-75 recession, the sharpest and deepest of the postwar era, followed the gigantic inventory buildup of the early 1970s.

Then comes phase 3, the plateau decade, when prices fall back and "normalcy" seems to return. Kondratieff called it "secondary prosperity."

CHART 20-2

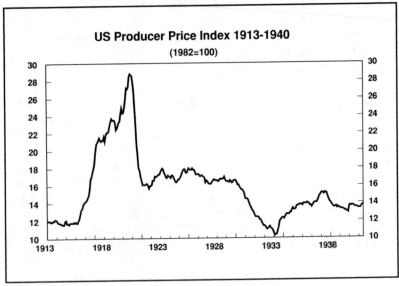

US Producer Price Index 1913-1940

(1982=100)

This was, of course, the "Roaring '20s" and the mid-1970s to mid-1980s decade of greed and glitz. It's also often an era of intense speculation—stocks in the 1920s. With inflation persisting in the 1970s, the objects of endearment were tangible assets.

The final, depression, phase of the Kondratieff Wave starts with financial difficulties that usher in a period of slower economic growth and often some out-and-out hard times, like the "Hungry 1840s," the difficult years in the 1870s, and, of course, the 1930s. Deflation is a definite hallmark of this phase.

In the present Kondratieff Wave depression phase, which probably started in the late 1980s, the financial corrections of previous excesses have been spread out much more than in previous counterparts. As I discuss in Chapter 22, the domestic economy saw in the 1980s and early 1990s a rolling correction of earlier agricultural, oil patch, and real estate over exuberance. Now only over-leveraged consumers are yet vulnerable. Note that farmland usually suffers earlier than other real estate in the downswing, and the plight of American farmers in the midst of the "Roaring '20s" and in the early 1980s is typical.

Protectionism in the Down Phases

Protectionism and isolationism appear consistently during the Kondratieff depression phase. As pointed out by James B. Shuman and David Rosenau in *The Kondratieff Wave*, "in the years after the peaks, when declining prices activated the downward spiral, when both business and labor felt the pinch, public attitudes swung towards restrictive imports." For instance, after the first Kondratieff cycle peak, tariffs were increased in 1816 and again in 1828—sometimes called the "tariff of abomination." In the second down cycle, tariffs were raised once again. The McKinley Tariff Act of 1890, the Wilson tariff of 1894, and the Kingley tariff of 1897 were blatantly protectionist (see Chart 23-1).

The next cycle also had its protectionist legislation, of course, the Smoot-Hawley Tariff Act of 1930, involving more than 20,000 items. Whether protectionist legislation actually led to the Depression or not, the "beggar-thy-neighbor" policies that most governments pursued in the 1930s certainly made matters worse. As world economies slumped, many nations tried to export their problems to other countries, much as Asia is doing today.

Currencies were devalued in the Depression to make exports more competitive, and the wealthy nations, particularly the United States, stopped extending credit to the less-developed countries. This caused financially weak lands to default on their loans, which exacerbated the US banking crisis and worsened the deflation and depression. The reaction to the crisis by the wealthy nations was to balance their budgets, reduce welfare payments (particularly in Great Britain), and increase interest rates, thereby accelerating the downturn.

To be sure, memories of the tariff walls of the 1930s have spurred the postwar movement toward free trade and made it possible for technology and capital to move around the globe in search of the most cost-effective sites of production (Chapters 10 and 23). Nevertheless, the ongoing polarization of income in the US and the growing trade deficits, especially with Japan and China, may well resurrect the popularity of Pat Buchanan, Dick Gephardt, Ross Perot, and other protectionists when jobs become less plentiful (Chapter 25).

Political Scandals and Gold

Political scandals occur in the plateau phase of the Kondratieff Wave, maybe because the previous high prosperity encourages a lax attitude toward graft and corruption. Grant's second term was scandal ridden, Harding's Administration suffered numerous corruption problems including the Teapot Dome scandal, and Nixon resigned under fire as a result of Watergate.

During the beginning of the upswing, the production of gold increases, probably swept along with rising prices and surging economic activity. But gold production declines during the down phase as prices in general fall, and there is no inflation against which it can serve as a hedge. Note that recently even central banks have been dumping gold as a sterile commodity that continues to fall in price and provides little return (see Chapter 27).

What Creates the Wave?

During phase 3 and 4, the old technologies that drove the previous upswing have been fully exploited and overbuilt. The technologies that will drive the next upswing are already known, but not yet commercially exploited to their full degree. Kondratieff himself offered no causal explanation for the Long Wave, and his work was purely statistical. Yet this technology cycle offers an explanation of the Kondratieff Wave. The upswing is driven by the surge of investment in new technologies—canals and river boats in the early 1800s, railroads and the American Industrial Revolution in the late 1800s, and autos in the early twentieth century.

Then, investment in these areas gets so excessive that it falters, and economic growth wanes. The investment in the next technology has already begun, but isn't yet big enough to sustain rapid overall business growth. The result is the down phases of the long wave which are, in effect, the gaps between the full exploitation of one technology and the onset of massive investment in the next. For example, railroads were developing in the early 19th century and pushing down transportation costs, but they did not become major economic driving forces until the second half of the century, when the transcontinental routes were built and opened up the American West. But by late in the century, too many coast-to-coast and other tracks had been laid, and the sector consolidated. Similarly, autos were being made before the turn of the century but didn't dominate growth until decades later, and, then, finally saturated demand by the 1930s.

Postwar Catchup in Spending

The most recent upswing, beginning after World War II, was driven by post-war booms in construction, consumer durables, capital spending, Cold-War defense spending, and the flight to the suburbs. During the 1930s and 1940s, construction had been held down by the Depression and then the war, during which unspendable consumer purchasing power was channeled into war bonds. This fueled the huge postwar catch-up spending, especially in construction.

CHART **20-3**

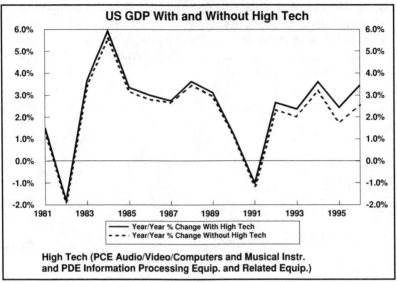

High Tech (PCE Audio/Video/Computers and Musical Instr.
and PDE Information Processing Equip. and Related Equip.)

One reason for the building surge was the proliferation of automobiles, another area of catch-up spending. With more cars came more roads and the interstate highway program, and the need for motels, diners, and service stations. Cars also enabled city dwellers, fed up with the annoyances of city life, to move to the countryside, which soon became suburbs. That meant big spending on houses, furniture, appliances, and other durables. Needless to say, these Kondratieff Wave driving forces are long exhausted.

Similarly, the Cold War ended in the late 1980s, and with it, the huge postwar military buildup. As noted in Chapter 1, the Cold War spawned entire industries, like aerospace, that have limited civilian counterparts. So, with the military stand-down, these industries atrophied, unable to move easily to production of civilian goods and services. Finally, the third big postwar stimulus, government social spending, appears to be waning, as mentioned earlier.

Granted, today's new technologies, such as telecommunications, computers, semiconductors, and biotech are mushrooming, but they aren't yet strong enough to drive the US economy by themselves. Spending on high tech by consumers and business is still less than 10% of GDP, and has had little effect on overall economic growth until quite recently (Chart 20-3). Nevertheless, this doesn't mean that the US economy is about to collapse. Chapter 22 notes that a financial crisis, like the one that initiated the Kondratieff Wave depression of the 1930s, is unlikely in Western countries any time soon.

In any event, the Kondratieff Wave shows us two points of current relevance. First, in the ongoing final down phase, deflation is the norm. Second, the new technologies that will drive the next up phase are already well known and growing in importance. The first point is, of course, the thesis of this book. The second was touched on in Chapter 6 and will be fleshed out in the next and succeeding chapters.

CHAPTER 21

DEFLATION CAN BE GOOD
AS WELL AS BAD

Whenever Americans hear the word "deflation," most immediately think of the Great Depression in the 1930s. Images of soup lines, shanty towns, and apple sellers are so vivid that any other idea of deflation pales by comparison. Indeed, the Great Depression did occur during the deflationary part of a Kondratieff Wave, with the typical attendant forces of excess capacity, fully exploited technologies, and new technologies only in the budding stage. Yet, the huge price declines in the early 1930s were the result of the financial collapse starting in 1929, not the cause. The stock market crash revealed quickly the over-leveraged nature of the financial system. Bankruptcies spread rapidly and were followed by massive layoffs and pay cuts for those still working. Deflation is, of course, the result of supply exceeding demand. In the 1930s, the fundamental cause was the shortfall of demand as incomes vanished.

The 1930s Collapse in Demand

To be sure, the 1930s started with some excess capacity. It was already overabundant in agriculture when the 1920s dawned, as noted in Chapter 20. American farmers had expanded acres in cultivation and production hugely during World War I to feed Europe. After the war, however, European agriculture recovered and the Americans were stuck with so much excess agricultural capacity—and farm debt—that farming entered big deflation and financial crisis long before the drought of the dust bowl years of the 1930s augmented their woes.

Also, in the 1920s, as discussed below, industries like electricity generation mushroomed as the nation got wired and developed considerable excess capacity in the process. The same was true in autos. Rapid and over expansion occurred at Ford, GM, and dozens of other manufacturers, whose

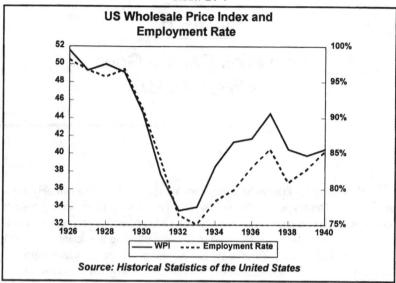

CHART 21-1

US Wholesale Price Index and Employment Rate

Legend: —— WPI · · · · Employment Rate

Source: Historical Statistics of the United States

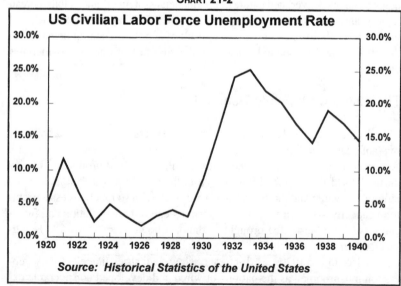

CHART 21-2

US Civilian Labor Force Unemployment Rate

Source: Historical Statistics of the United States

names are now only found in history books and in the wonderful collection of antique cars in the Henry Ford museum in Dearborn, Michigan.

Nevertheless, it was the collapse in incomes and demand that primarily drove the bad deflation of the 1930s, not over supply. Let me tell you why. Following the Crash, wholesale prices and employment (Chart 21-1) nosedived in tandem as unemployment leaped. The American Federation of Labor estimated that in October 1930 there were approximately 4.6 million unemployed workers. In October 1931, the number rose to 7.8 million, to 11.6 million in October 1932, and early in 1933 to more than 13.0 million, almost 25% of the civilian labor force (Chart 21-2).

The wages of those still working fell faster than prices, even more so when periods of unemployment are included (Chart 21-3). Also, the declines had to be spread over a lot of unemployed people as well, especially at a time when government relief programs were tiny. My friend told me about his father, who managed to keep his job as a delivery truck driver during the Depression. His wages were good, but because he was the only person in the extended family who was employed, he supported not only his wife and children but also his brother and his family and his parents. Obviously, many people could only afford the bare necessities of life.

To get a perspective on just how severe this shortfall in demand really was, compare changes in real consumption and real gross national product

CHART 21-3

US Real Average Annual Earnings of Employees

— After Deduction for Unemployment   - - - - When Employed

Source: Historical Statistics of the United States

then with changes between 1839 and 1843, a similar depression phase of the first Kondratieff Wave, the "Hungry '40s" (Chart 21-4). Even at that worst phase of that deflation, real consumption and real GNP increased. Notice that the declines in the money stock, prices, and number of banks were similar in the two periods. As discussed in Chapter 3, it's hard to pin the depth of the 1930s Depression solely on the decline in the money supply and the Fed.

It's also hard to pin it on American business or even the Hoover Administration. Since the federal government ran a budget surplus in 1929, there was leeway to offset the weakening economy with fiscal stimulus. In November 1929, President Hoover called for tax cuts and expanded public works programs. He also gathered the captains of industry and made them promise to help sustain purchasing power by maintaining wage levels and increasing capital spending. After that meeting, Henry Ford raised the wages of his auto workers from his celebrated $5 per day to $7 per day. Nevertheless, neither Ford nor other manufacturers could withstand the onslaught of the Depression. The average hourly wage of those production workers lucky enough to keep their jobs in manufacturing fell 21% from 1929 to 1932, and since hours were cut as well, average weekly earnings fell 32%. Many weren't so lucky. By 1932, 38% of those production jobs in manufacturing that existed in 1929 had been eliminated.

CHART 21-4

COMPARISON OF **1839-1843** WITH **1929-1933** IN US

	1839-43	1929-33
Change in money stock	-34%	-27%
Change in prices	-42%	-32%
Change in number of banks	-23%	-42%
Change in real gross investment	-23%	-91%
Change in real consumption	+21%	-19%
Change in real gross national product	+15%	-30%

Source: Mancur Olson, The Rise and Decline of Nations, Yale University, 1982

Post-Civil War Deflation without Collapse

Deflation, however, doesn't have to be the bad kind caused by deficient demand. In the down phases of the second Kondratieff wave (1864-1896), it was good deflation caused by excess supply. At the end of the Civil War, the country moved into the American Industrial Revolution, following the first to industrialize, the United Kingdom, by about 50 years. Agricultural value added was almost twice that of manufacturing at the beginning of that conflict (Chart 21-5), but the explosion of factory output equalized the shares of the two by the mid 1880s. At the end of the century, factories out-produced farms by almost two to one. Between 1860 and 1914 employment in manufacturing and construction tripled, and the physical output of manufacturing rose six times.

What were all these factories producing? In 1860, common products included planed and sawed lumber; cast, forged, and wrought iron; steam engines; textiles, including cotton goods, woolen goods such as yarn, and clothing; foodstuffs such as flour and meal; and leather goods, including boots and shoes. By 1914, many of these industries had mushroomed, and others

CHART 21-5

**VALUE ADDED IN COMMODITY US OUTPUT
BY SECTORS 1859-99
(PERCENT)**

	AGRICULTURE	MANUFACTURING	MINING	CONSTRUCTION
1859	56	32	1	11
1869	53	33	2	12
1874	46	39	2	12
1879	49	37	3	11
1884	41	44	3	12
1889	37	48	4	11
1894	32	53	4	11
1899	33	53	5	9

*Source: Robert E. Gallman, Trends in the American Economy in the Nineteenth
         Century*

had been added, including meat packing, automobiles, printing and publishing, smelted and refined copper, and liquors.

Technology on the Rise

Industrial growth was spurred, of course, by the needs of the Civil War, but after the war, the boom continued, fueled by rapidly changing industrial technology and rapidly expanding railroads, which provided an ever-increasing market potential. The number of patents granted in the nation grew from 25, 200 in the 1850s decade to 234,956 between 1890 and 1900. Examples of some of the most influential changes were as follows:

- roller grinding revolutionized flour milling
- new types of spinning and weaving equipment increased output of cloth
- invention of equipment to manufacture seamless hosiery
- adaptation of sewing machine to leather reduced dramatically the price of shoes and boots
- carpets made on power looms replaced handmade rugs
- new ways of making stoves, ice boxes, and plumbing fixtures reduced their prices
- invention of the linotype coupled with the discovery of processes to make cheap paper mushroomed the supply of books, magazines, and newspapers at lower costs

For years, observers have bemoaned the fact that Americans have not been at the forefront of basic science. The only one of serious note was Joseph Henry who discovered electrical induction in 1830. Even Henry, who served as the first head of the Smithsonian Institution for 32 years, was hardly considered a world beater at the time. He failed to publish his findings until he learned a year later that Britain's Michael Faraday had discovered the same phenomenon. None of the scientists whose theoretical work made the atomic bomb possible were American born.

Yet for all the pioneering scientific work of such British luminaries as Faraday, Henry Cavendish, Sir Humphrey Davy, Lord Rutherford, Sir Joseph Banks, James Prescott Joule, Lord Rayleigh, and James Clerk Maxwell, and the commanding lead that Britain had as the first industrialized nation, Americans were the ones with the uncanny ability to turn scientific discoveries into technologies and apply them to industry in the post Civil War period—and ever since. Consider Thomas Edison in this regard. He had an unbelievable lead time of 10 to 15 years over his global rivals in practical inventions.

Drinking Glasses for All

Typical of what was happening to manufacturing in the United States between 1860 and 1890 is the pressed-glass industry. During that time, glass manufacturers of all kinds began to experiment with gas furnaces and continuous glass melting tanks. Coal was firmly established as the best glass-making fuel, but natural gas proved to be perfect for glass-melting: it burns at intense heat, leaves no residue, has no bad effects on the glass, and made continuous melting tanks possible in 1879.

In addition to these general improvements, pressed-glass manufacturing benefitted from new discoveries in glass chemistry. The use of lime instead of flint in the glass mixture reduced metal costs and gave rise to mechanical innovations that enhanced its properties. The straight wooden press lever, spiral springs, the adjustable mold guide, and the water-cooled plunger—all of which, I'm sure, are familiar to you—were among the new devices that became commonplace during this period.

Here Comes the Choo-Choo

At the same time, railroads pushed across the continent, uniting first North and South, then East and West. In 1860, the US had 30,626 miles of track, mostly in the East, Midwest, and South. But Americans knew there was a vast land of resources stretching toward the Pacific Ocean, and in a valiant competitive effort, railroad companies rushed to reach the West—with, to be sure, considerable government subsidies in the form of free land along the rights of way. The dramatic increase in miles of track occurred in three building spurts: 1866-1873, 30,000 miles were built; 1879-1883, 40,000 miles more; and 1886-1892, 50,000 additional miles were constructed. By 1900, the US had 198,964 miles of track (Chart 21-6).

Trains crisscrossing the nation carried people west and brought agricultural products and minerals east, thus opening up vast acreage for farmers, ranchers, and miners. Before the war, cattle and hogs were primarily raised in the Ohio Valley, making Cincinnati the leading center of pork packing, with the meat products moving to market via the Ohio and Mississippi rivers. With the railroads and the invention of the refrigerated freight car, livestock production shifted westward, and Chicago became a leading shipping point for livestock and meat products. All of those cowboys in the old West weren't

CHART 21-6

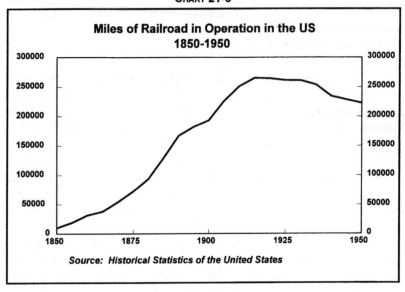

Miles of Railroad in Operation in the US
1850-1950

Source: Historical Statistics of the United States

raising cattle for chuck wagon dinners, but for Eastern markets that were only accessible by rail.

Agriculture in Bloom

Accessibility of Eastern markets also caused a great expansion of wheat growing, which, combined with cattle raising, fed the exploding labor force concentrated in industrialized cities. Food surpluses created a marketable export which became more important than cotton. After 1873, the American balance of trade turned favorable, because of wheat and wheat flour, meat products and live cattle exports. Although agricultural products were becoming a smaller percentage of US output, agricultural productivity increased 40% from 1869 to 1899 as farm technology blossomed.

In the mid-1800s, John Deere of Illinois developed and sold a plow whose moldboard, share, and landslide were made of cast steel strong enough to break the tough sod of the prairies. In the late 1860s, John Oliver, also of Illinois, developed a plow of chilled iron (a soft-center steel), which was more durable and cheaper. Obed Hussey of Ohio and Cyrus H. McCormick of Virginia both came up with the same idea which would truly revolutionize the wheat-growing industry: the mechanical horse-drawn reaper. Hussey is credited with being first (1833), but McCormick was close behind (1834), and was a better marketer. When he began manufacturing in Chicago in 1847, he knew how to advertise and offer credit as well as instructions in maintenance and repairs. The number of reapers in use in the US grew from 70,000 in 1858 to 250,000 in 1865. Improvement followed fast. Improved reapers raked the cut grain and gathered it for a man on the reaper to bind. Harvester and thresher were combined (hence the term "combine") in the 1890s.

An example of the productivity leap attributed to farm equipment is the drop in man-hours needed to prepare and harvest one acre of grain. In 1829-30 the time required in Illinois was 61 hours, 5 minutes. By 1893, a Red River Valley spring-wheat farm took only 8 hours, 46 minutes to do the same thing. Largely because of mechanization, output per farm worker in wheat, corn , and oats increased between three and four times between 1840 and 1910, or at compound annual rates of 1.5% to 2.0%.

More Productivity Equals Lower Prices

Overall, US productivity after the Civil War grew at a sustained rate unequaled at any other period of history. Real GNP per capita grew at an average annual rate of 2.1% from 1869 to 1898, and the population rose at about the same rate, encouraged by waves of immigrants. Consequently, real GNP grew 4.3% per year, about twice today's growth rate (Chart 21-7).

Notice, in comparison, the much slower growth in the UK and France during the latter part of the 19th and early 20th centuries (Chart 21-8). Without meaningful immigration, population growth was much slower than in the US, and the industrial revolution bloom was off the rose, especially in the pioneer industrializer, the UK. Canada, naturally, resembled the US. After Bismark assembled the various German states into one nation and industrialization commenced, growth was strong but the immigrant population growth of the US was missing. The same was true of Japan, after Commodore Perry's show

CHART 21-7

US ECONOMIC GROWTH 1869-1898
(AVERAGE ANNUAL GROWTH RATES)

POPULATION (%)	GNP (%)	GNP (PER CAPITA) (%)	CONSUMP- TION (%)	CONSUMPTION PER FULL CONSUMER (%)
2.17	4.32	2.11	4.75	2.33

Source: *US Congress Hearings before the Joint Economic Committee*

CHART 21-8

GROWTH BY COUNTRY 1869-1913

COUNTRY	PERIOD	GNP (%)	GNP (%) PER CAPITA	POPULATION (%)
United States	1869-1878 to 1904-1913	56.0	27.5	22.3
United Kingdom	1860-1869 to 1905-1914	25.0	12.5	11.1
France	1841-1850 to 1901-1910	18.6	16.3	1.9
Germany	1860-1869 to 1905-1914	35.6	21.6	11.5
Canada	1870-1879 to 1905-1914	47.1	24.7	17.8
Japan	1878-1887 to 1903-1912	49.2	33.7	11.6

Source: S.S. Kuznets, Economic Development and Social Change, Oct 1956

of American naval and industrial firepower in 1854 convinced the leaders there that feudalism had to go in favor of industrialization.

The availability of so much output produced at such lower costs depressed prices considerably—even though the reduced prices vastly expanded sales, and ordinary Americans could afford to eat better and buy manufactured goods for the first time ever. Innovations in glass manufacture, detailed earlier, compressed the retail prices of pressed-glassware by as much as 89% between 1864 and 1888, as shown in the top row of Chart 21-9. Prices of food staples plunged dramatically. The overall Wholesale Price Index dropped 49.7% between 1870 and 1896 (Chart 21-10) or at a 2.6% annual rate. The wholesale price of a bushel of wheat fell from $1.58 in 1871 to 56 cents in 1894. Nails dropped from $4.52 for 50 pounds in 1871 to $2.00 in 1889.

CHART 21-9

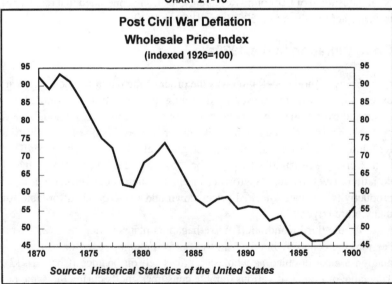

RETAIL PRICES PER DOZEN OF PRESSED GLASSWARE
1864-1888

	1864	1874	1888	% FALL IN PRICE 1864-1888
Goblets	$3.50	$0.78	$0.40	89
Tumblers	$1.30	$0.55	$0.37	72
Wine Glasses	$1.73	$0.50	$0.30	83

Source: National Glass Budget, May 6, 1899

CHART 21-10

Post Civil War Deflation
Wholesale Price Index
(indexed 1926=100)

Source: Historical Statistics of the United States

Prices that farmers received for their products also fell. Between 1879 and 1889, wheat fell 37% and corn 25%. Farmers thought they were really getting short-changed by these declines, but non-farm prices fell as rapidly as farm prices in many cases, and in some cases more rapidly. Fortunately for farmers, rates for railroad transportation were declining during the period despite concern over freight rate gouging. Between 1866 and 1897, the charge for carrying wheat from Chicago to New York fell from 65 cents per 100 pounds to 20 cents, or a 70% decline. Between 1870 and 1899, the charge for dressed beef transport declined from 90 to 40 cents, or 55%. Farm machine prices also dropped by 60% between 1870 and 1900.

Lower Prices Lead to Lower Nominal But Higher Real Wages

Nominal or money wages after 1870 began to fall along with prices for many occupations, such as carpenters, painters, and blacksmiths (Chart 21-11). Overall, nonfarm employees saw their money pay decline from $489 per year in 1870 to $420 in 1894, a fall of 14% (Chart 21-12). But prices were falling faster than wages, so real pay grew 29%, or at 1.1% annual rate during those years. If we extend the period to 1900 and pick up the Spanish American War effects, money wages were still down slightly, 1.2% over 30 years, while real incomes grew 1.4% annually. In an analysis conducted under the National Bureau of Economic Research, C.D. Long concluded that real wages in manufacturing went up 50% from 1860 to 1890.

Good Deflation in the 1920s

So even though deflation was the order of the day after the Civil War, excess supply was the cause, not declining demand. In fact, as noted, demand and overall growth were nothing short of flamboyant. Although we'll probably never again see anything like the growth explosion of the Industrial Revolution and the opening of the West, good deflation has not been confined to that era. As mentioned earlier, the "Roaring '20s" were also a time of deflation driven by supply growing faster than demand, even though rapid productivity advance knocked prices down and made goods affordable for many more buyers.

As the third Kondratieff Wave began its plateau after the 1920-21 recession, the economy boomed. In the following eight years, industrial production almost doubled as wholesale prices fell on balance (Chart 21-13). The value of output of various durable consumer goods during the same period jumped anywhere from 29 % to 200% (Chart 21-14). New technologies, especially electricity, were responsible for much of the boom. Electrification of factory power equipment grew from 33% in 1914 to 74% in 1929.

Not to be left behind, the American housewife got her efficiency improved through electricity as it powered such appliances as electric irons, washing machines, vacuum cleaners, and refrigerators. The manufacture of electric machinery and appliances became one of the decade's leading industries. Not surprising, the production of electric power more than doubled during this period.

CHART 21-11

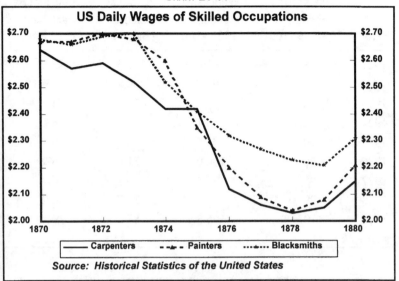

US Daily Wages of Skilled Occupations

—— Carpenters - -▲- - Painters ······· Blacksmiths

Source: Historical Statistics of the United States

CHART 21-12

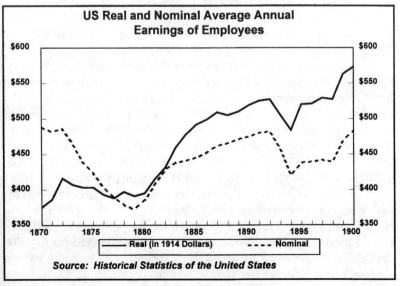

US Real and Nominal Average Annual Earnings of Employees

—— Real (in 1914 Dollars) - - - - Nominal

Source: Historical Statistics of the United States

CHART 21-13

US ECONOMIC GROWTH, 1921-1929

YEAR	INDUSTRIAL PRODUCTION 1933-39=100	WHOLESALE PRICES 1926=100	NATIONAL INCOME (BILLIONS)	REAL INCOME PER CAPITA (1929 PRICES)
1921	58	97.6	$59.4	$522
1922	73	96.7	60.7	553
1923	88	100.6	71.6	634
1924	82	98.1	72.1	633
1925	90	103.5	76.0	644
1926	96	100.0	81.6	678
1927	95	95.4	80.1	674
1928	99	96.7	81.7	676
1929	110	95.3	87.2	716

Construction also took off during the 1920s. Normal construction had slowed during World War I, so builders were ready to go once money was available, and modern improvements made even recently-constructed buildings old fashioned. Building construction in 120 cities (one-third of which was in New York City) climbed from $373 million in 1918 to $3.4 billion in 1925.

Of course, the granddaddy of all boom industries during the 1920s was the automobile. Henry Ford's application of interchangeable parts and his introduction of the moving assembly line increased the production of cars by the whole industry from 65,000 in 1908 to 1,000,000 in 1915. Between 1913 and 1914, the labor time required to put together a Model T chassis dropped from 2 hours and 38 minutes (down from an original 12 hours and 28 minutes) to 1 hour and 33 minutes. Consequently, the price of the Model T runabout dropped from $500 on August 1, 1913 to $260 on December 2, 1924.

As noted earlier, Henry Ford paid his workers an unprecedented $5 per day. He reasoned that if they couldn't afford to buy the cars they were assembling, he wouldn't sell many. I've known this for years, but never figured how $5 per day would buy anyone a car. Now I know. At $5 per day, 300 days a year (they worked Saturdays then), the assembler made $1,500 and paid few taxes. A Model T at $260 was definitely affordable.

CHART 21-14

US CONSUMER GOODS OUTPUT 1921-1929 (IN MILLIONS OF DOLLARS)			
	1921	**1929**	**% CHANGE**
Electrical refrigerators, washing machines, and stoves	$63	$177	179%
Radios	$12	$37	200%
Automobiles	$1,116	$2,567	130%
Automobile Accessories	$170	$408	140%
Household Furniture	$467	$600	29%
Heating and Cooking Apparatus	$187	$347	86%
House furnishings	$375	$643	72%
China and Household Utensils	$167	$274	64%

Source: Historical Statistics of the United States

Other prices fell as well in the 1920s, even after the 1920-21 collapse, including items like home furnishings and apparel. Food prices rose a bit after the 1920-21 plunge, in which they fell much more than individual prices, but the weakness in the latter after that collapse made the "Roaring '20s" a time of overall deflation, the good deflation of excess supply (Chart 21-15).

Good and Bad Deflation—The Textbook View

You must have concluded by now that I'm not much of a textbook economist. But to justify my economic credentials (or, in all likelihood, tarnish if not destroy them in the eyes of my academic brethren), I've put together two supply-demand graphs to show how our deflation ideas work out in chart form.

First look at the 1930s-style bad deflation (Chart 21-16). S1 and D1 represent overall supply and demand curves in the late 1920s. I've concentrated on the US economy with these curves because at that time, America was much more self-contained than now. Besides, the tariff walls of the early 1930s sealed her off even further from the rest of the world. This domestic orientation may not seem applicable today, but in the unlikely event that a US financial crisis develops and precipitates a collapse in American demand, you can bet your bottom dollar that the tariff walls will go up, and fast.

CHART **21-15**

US Wholesale Price Indices of All Commodities, Industrial Commodities, and Farm Commodities
(indexed 1967 = 100)

All Commodities — — Industrial ···•··· Farm

Source: Historical Statistics of the United States

CHART **21-16**

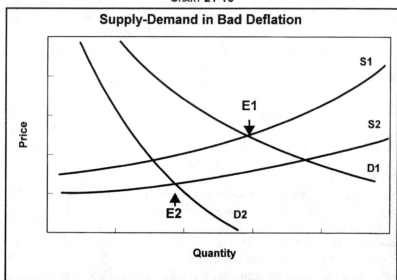

Supply-Demand in Bad Deflation

When things go to hell in the bad deflation case, the demand curve shifts down a far piece as incomes plummet. It also steepens because the loss of income tends to be proportionally greater for those on the bottom of the spectrum. Still, the steepening is limited because those on the top get hurt too. Remember the previous millionaires who peddled apples in Wall Street in the early 1930s? The net effect is D2.

Meanwhile, the supply curve moves down as labor and material costs fall with deflation (S2), but not as much as the demand curve since some costs are fixed overhead. It also flattens somewhat as high cost producers exit via bankruptcies. The net effect is the move in the equilibrium point from E1 to E2—lower prices and a lot less quantity sold.

The good deflation that I foresee is quite different, as shown in Chart 21-17. Again, S1 and D1 are the initial supply and demand curves, but now our scope is global, as fits the current world. The demand curve shifts down somewhat with deflation as US consumers pull in their horns (D2). It also steepens as competitive devaluations and weak economies in Asia and else- where leave those marginal buyers with less cash to purchase the world's goods and services.

Continuing restraint on government spending further moves the demand curve down and steepens it, making quantity more sensitive to price. Govern- ment spending isn't exactly price sensitive—recall the $200 hammers and

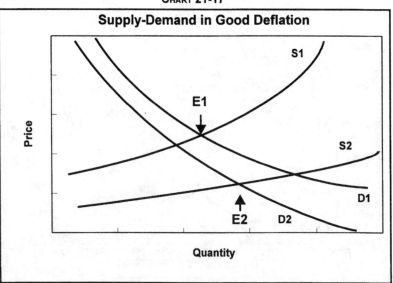

CHART 21-17

Supply-Demand in Good Deflation

$600 toilet seats the Pentagon bought during the Cold War—and even more recently. So, the less government spending, the bigger the portion of aggregate demand that is generated by the private sector and the more responsive it is to price.

In contrast to bad deflation, the real action in good deflation is on the supply side. Big exports from developing countries and competitive devaluations push the supply curve down and flatten it, as does expanding capacity in developed countries and global sourcing. Adding to this downward shift are international and domestic deregulation in developed countries, leaping mass distribution, growing use of the Internet, rapid technological advances and restructuring, as well as the shift of important economies like China to market status. As you see, the equilibrium point moves down to lower prices, as in bad deflation, but what a difference in quantity. It rises in good deflation. Lower prices stimulate volume growth, but supply still exceeds demand. So much for the textbook treatment of deflation, bad and good. Class dismissed!

If the deflation I see ahead is to be the good deflation of the post Civil War era and the 1920s, not the bad deflation of the 1930s, overall demand needs to hold up. That, in turn, requires the nation's financial structure to remain intact. To see why this is likely, turn to Chapter 22, but before doing so, consider a modern day vivid example of the difference between good and bad deflation. Japan and Switzerland have both seen deflation in the 1990s

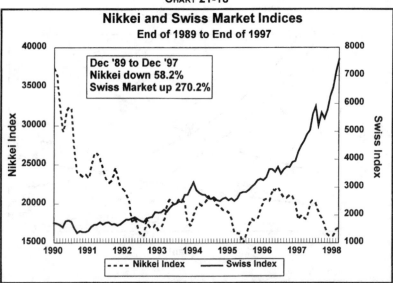

CHART 21-18

Nikkei and Swiss Market Indices
End of 1989 to End of 1997

Dec '89 to Dec '97
Nikkei down 58.2%
Swiss Market up 270.2%

(Chapter 19). Japan suffered the bad kind, touched off at the beginning of the decade by severe financial problems. Japanese stocks fell 58% in the 1990-97 years. In Switzerland, where the financial structure remained sound, it's been good deflation with stocks rising 270% in the same years (Chart 21-18).

CHAPTER 22

FINANCIAL COLLAPSES ARE UNLIKELY IN THE US AND OTHER WESTERN COUNTRIES

Deflation has not always been linked to financial collapse, as you saw in Chapter 21. Will it be this time? Probably not. Nevertheless, most people believe that any deflation in future years will be the bad deflation of the 1930s that followed the demand-killing financial collapse, not the good deflation of the 1920s and the post Civil War era that resulted from mushrooming supply.

The 1930s Phobia

Listen to George Melloan, the *Wall Street Journal* columnist, who I believe is one of the most astute observers of the political, financial, and economic scene. In the November 25, 1997, edition he said, "Deflation, a general decline in prices,...feeds on itself, wiping out returns on investments, forcing producers out of business, and piling up bad debts. People lose their jobs or their businesses." I wonder what Melloan thinks about the tremendous prosperity of the post Civil War years that allowed men to build fortunes which, by the standard of their day, makes everybody but Bill Gates look poor. Men like Cornelius Vanderbilt, Leland Stanford, and Collis P. Huntington in railroads; Andrew Carnegie in steel, and E. I. DuPont in chemicals. And how does he view Henry Ford's empire in autos and everything related to it in the 1920s? All those guys may have taken healthy slices of their industrial pies, but they couldn't have accumulated the vast fortunes they did if the pies hadn't grown quickly to enormous size through technology- driven explosions in supply.

Melloan continues, "Deflation usually begins with sharp drops in asset values, which result in a loss of liquidity, or, to oversimplify, money. The 1930s deflation followed the 1929 stock market crash, exacerbated by the failure of the US monetary authorities to replace the lost dollar liquidity." As you saw in Chapter 3, I'm not as quick as Melloan to make the Fed the villain of the 1930s, but his point about deflation's starting with financial crisis does have some validity.

In a sense, a Kondratieff Wave sense, it all started in the US in the 1980s, as noted in Chapter 20. One by one the various sectors that had over-expanded and over-leveraged themselves in the 1970s heyday of inflation went through the deflationary wringer. Just like the collapse in agriculture in the 1920s, stratospheric farmland prices were the first to go in the early 1980s. Then followed the collapse in oil prices in the mid 1980s that took oil patch real estate and economies with it. By the late 1980s, it was overbuilt real estate nationwide that hit the fan with tax laws changed in 1986, and in the process, the bank lenders, which were already weakened by bad Latin American loans, were humbled. The S&Ls were virtually eliminated.

It was a tough period and financial difficulties then dominated the American scene. In fact, even though the US economy entered a recession with real GDP falling in late 1989, we felt at the time that the basic problems lay not with excessive inventories and other GNP components, nor with corporate income statements, but with balance sheets. We went so far as to send this message to our clients and friends via T-shirts as Christmas presents, the front of which is shown in Chart 22-1.

CHART 22-1

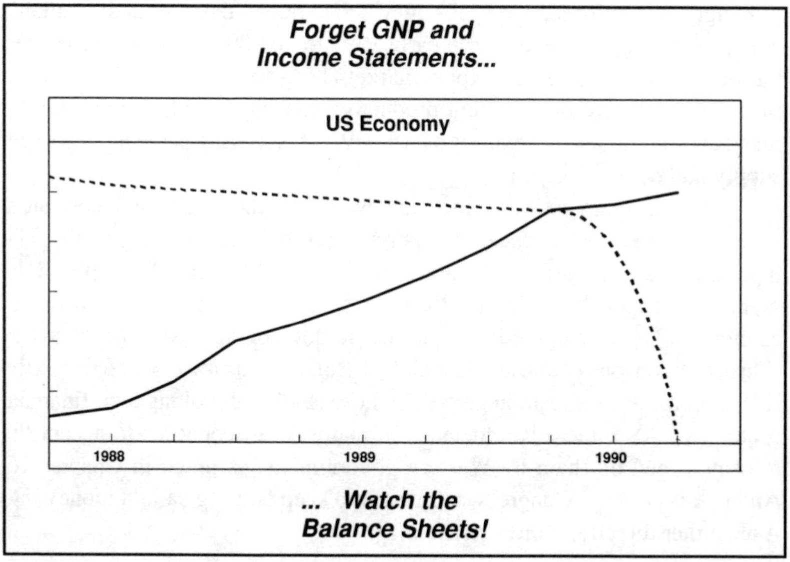

*Forget GNP and
Income Statements...*

US Economy

| 1988 | 1989 | 1990 |

*... Watch the
Balance Sheets!*

None of these crises sank the US financial ship, maybe because they occurred in rotation so all the problems didn't erupt at once and compound each other. Also the federal government provided easy credit to avoid widespread foreclosures on farm mortgages. It filled the strategic oil reserve to limit the damage of oil price collapse. The S&Ls were, of course, bailed out at huge taxpayer expense. And the Fed kept short-term interest rates low in the early 1990s so banks could rebuild their capital by borrowing cheap and lending at much higher long-term rates.

It's the 1930s in Asia

Now, the financial crisis is in Asia, first in Japan and now in many other lands, and since the economy is global, that crisis has global ramifications. In many ways, what's happening in Asia resembles events in Western countries in the 1930s. Then and now, over expansion has given way to financial collapse, which in turn has dried-up credit and left unpayable debts, bankruptcies, and widespread unemployment in its wake. Then and now, countries have attempted to unload their troubles on others through competitive devaluations. Then and now, the net result is the augmentation of already considerable global gluts of almost everything. Back then in the West it came as a great shock to the multitude that expected the "Roaring '20s" to last forever. Now, it's disabusing those who had similar faith in the Asian miracle.

Look at Indonesia to see the similarity of the US in the 1930s and Asia today. Basic domestic demand in early 1998 is ample. There is no shortage of hungry mouths to feed or backs on which to put clothes. With the rupiah's collapse from 2,500 per dollar in early 1997 to 16,000 at its low a year later, the opportunities to sell in export markets became fabulous. At the same time, there is more than enough productive capacity to fulfill domestic demand and facilitate huge exports as well. What is lacking is the money to get supply and demand together.

In fact, it may be worse in Asia now than in the American Depression, given their high dependence on exports to promote economic growth. The high tariffs and competitive devaluations of the 1930s certainly deepened the global depression, but at least at the time the US was largely a self-sufficient economy. To be sure, the IMF is trying hard to contain Asia's problems by shoring up various countries financially. But, as you saw in Chapter 13, the IMF conditions may restrain growth in those lands and prolong their financial problems. Also, there is reluctance in many Asian countries to accept the reforms urged on them by Western governments, as noted in Chapter 16. And in this country, Congress is reluctant to keep pouring bailout money into Asia, either directly or through the IMF.

Can It Spread Here?

Finally, even if the Asian financial crises are contained, they can still spread to the US and other Western countries if Western financial institutions are vulnerable. I don't see this as a likely outcome, however. To begin, US exposure to Asia's bad debts is limited. Chart 15-11 shows that American banks were only owed $32.3 billion by Asian countries outside of Japan at mid 1997, or 1.1% of total loans. This is far less than their relative exposure to Latin America, 6.3% of total loans, when it imploded in the mid 1980s and trapped many US banks that were in the middle of the petro-dollar recycling game. And back at the ranch, most over-leveraged US sectors already had their comeuppances in the 1980s and early 1990s, as noted earlier.

Elsewhere, the US has returned to much better financial condition as well. The federal budget is moving into surplus. Real estate debts are not big problems. Overall, the net debt increase by nonfinancial sectors of the economy—consumers, businesses, and government—is back to the 10% ratio of GDP it has averaged in this century (Chart 22-2). Note that the climb that started in the late 1960s and peaked in the 1980s almost reached the heights of the two World Wars when government borrowing was astronomical. The 1920s debt expansion pales in comparison—in part because unlike the 1970s and 1980s, the federal government was then running a surplus, so private debt alone was in excess.

CHART 22-2

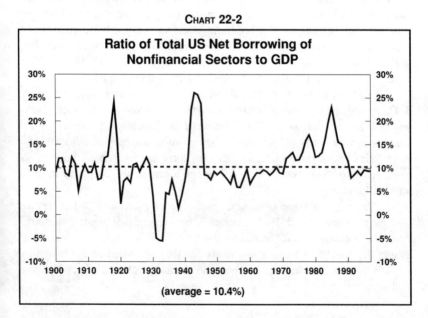

The only two sectors of the US economy which remain vulnerable are consumers and stocks. But as noted in Chapter 18, we expect American consumers to retrench and reduce their excessive borrowing. That's part of our deflation scenario. Sure, credit card delinquencies and personal bankruptcies could leap even from current lofty levels, but massive foreclosures that would ignite a downward spiral in consumers' finances seem unlikely, and politically unacceptable. Indeed, there is evidence, in credit card delinquencies and other data, that consumers are already starting to take a more cautious attitude toward debt.

Chapter 18 also notes my conviction that US stocks are significantly overpriced and headed for a substantial fall. Still, a genuine bear market of the extent not seen since the early 1970s with a nosedive of 40% to 50% in stock prices wouldn't in itself be the end of the financial world—unless it touches off a forced unwinding of all the derivatives that have permeated the financial structures in recent years.

The Caveat — Derivatives

Derivatives are a huge, multifaceted, interrelated market that few comprehend completely. I surely don't. I know something about the simpler forms, such as futures contracts on stocks, bonds, currencies, and commodities like soybeans, copper, and crude oil. I also know a bit about straightforward puts and calls. We use these in the portfolios we manage to implement our investment themes. They're dangerous enough because of their leverage. Just ask Nick Leeson, formerly of Barings and now behind bars, who literally destroyed his 233-year-old firm in 1995 when he was age 25 by accumulating a huge long position in futures on the Japanese Nikkei stock index. Then came the Kobe earthquake and the collapse in Japanese equities.

I haven't a clue, however, about all the exotic interest rate swaps and OTC options on currencies or almost anything else you can think of. These are all based on, derived from, real financial instruments like corporate loans and foreign currency obligations. They promise not only to convert long-term loans into short-term obligations, to eliminate foreign currency exposure, and to perform other feats of financial legerdemain, but to do so in almost riskless ways.

The names of some of these derivatives, however, suggest that they are less than riskless: "death-backed bonds," "heaven and hell bonds," "limbos," "harmful warrants," and "worthless warrants." Nevertheless, their creators assure the holders of these investments that they are based on mathematical models that precisely define the risks and ensure that those risks can be controlled.

The big derivative blowup of the mid 1990s that hurt GE, Procter & Gamble, Gibson Greetings, Mead Corp., German-controlled MG Trading, and Orange County, California among others, is, of course, history—except to the lawyers who are still cleaning up the mess at their full billing rates. Still, the derivatives markets continue to grow, like Harriet Beecher Stowe's Topsy. Note (see Chapter 13), that the financial crisis in developing countries is revealing much broader use of derivatives in countries like Brazil and Indonesia and the havoc they can wreak than was known earlier. And as with most new financial wrinkles, their devotees believe that derivatives are the best things since sliced bread since they eliminate risk while ensuring great returns.

There's no such thing as a free lunch, however. Risk can be transferred, but not eliminated. The only question is, is it being transferred to weaker or stronger hands? My hunch is, and recent evidence suggests, that it's moving to weaker hands. This means that the whole system may be in for another severe test if US stocks take a header.

The New Portfolio Insurance

In the 1980s, portfolio insurance was all the rage. The idea was that to avoid big losses in their stock portfolios, financial institutions, guided by mathematical models, would execute a series of sales if equity prices fell. But rather than reduce risk, portfolio insurance actually increased it. With everyone following the same strategy at the same time, the rush for the exit resulted in chain-reaction selling in the 1987 crash. Furthermore, the inherent market-wide risks of portfolio insurance were increased by trust in the system. Portfolio managers who were concerned about the speculative leap in stocks in early 1987 nevertheless remained loaded to the gills with equities, figuring that portfolio insurance would offset any major stock market decline.

Today stock options have provided a sequel to portfolio insurance for professional and individual investors. And again, investors are so convinced that the puts they own against their long stock positions will preclude big losses that many have thrown caution to the wind. The Chicago Board Options Exchange recently ran large ads promoting its new puts on the Dow Jones Industrial Average as shields against market volatility. In other words, don't sell your large capitalization stocks—simply buy puts on the Dow Jones to insulate them from a possible bear market, is the message.

Of course, someone must write those puts—*i.e.,* sell them to investors—and whatever the buyer gains in a falling stock market, the seller loses. The sellers, many of them Wall Street houses, do get paid well for the insurance they provide, as long as stocks don't fall. If they do fall, the sellers will enact their "dynamic hedging" programs, essentially selling stocks short to offset the puts they've written. This works fine in isolated cases, but if tons of stocks are sold under these programs, the result could be a self-reinforcing downward spiral, much like the portfolio insurance fiasco of 1987.

The odds of an options-driven stock market swoon are probably small, but certainly enhanced by the possibility, discussed in Chapter 18, that many green investors may eventually run for cover when the devastating effects of their first bear market sink in. Those who are leveraged may throw in the towel when they receive their first margin calls, and that selling would push stocks still lower. Even those without leverage may, as in the past, eventually panic and liquidate their mutual funds, forcing the funds to discard stocks in order to meet redemptions. As also noted in Chapter 18, few funds have meaningful cash customs. Those that did underperformed in the raging bull market of recent years and were abandoned by fund holders. The rest took the clue.

On balance, however, I don't expect major US financial problems to accompany and reinforce the deflation we foresee. Even if big difficulties develop with excessive consumer debt, overblown stocks, or lethal derivatives, the odds are against a 1930s-style financial collapse. Chart 21-4 shows the depth of the first Kondratieff Wave depression, 1839-43, witnessed economic growth despite widespread financial distress. Similarly, the worst years of the second Kondratieff Wave depressions, 1873-79, were mild compared to the early 1930s. A simple average of these three traumatic periods is much less severe than the early 1930s collapse. It seems more appropriate as today's absolutely worst case scenario than does a rerun of the Great Depression.

What about Other Developed Countries?

How about the financial health of other Western countries? Canada and Europe are somewhat less exposed to Asia than the US in terms of imports (Chart 16-8) and have about the same export exposure (Chart 16-9). On the financial side, European banks are more involved (Chart 15-11). Still, I don't think that any of these lands have big enough financial or economic imbalances at home to succumb financially to the Asian flu. Canada will continue to suffer from weak commodity prices, but she has her financial house in fairly good order. The UK economy is perking along, so far without rampant speculation, while the European continent is finally recovering from the early 1990s recession and has yet to develop meaningful excesses. The Asian meltdown might disrupt, even postpone, the introduction of the Euro currency, but I don't see it doing much permanent damage.

And Japan?

Japan will, of course, get the biggest fallout from Asia of any developed countries. She has the largest trade exposure (Chart 15-9). Her banks are the most involved (Chart 15-11) with 32% of developing Asian country loans, at mid 1997— compared with 12% for German banks, 10% for French, 8% for British, and 8% for US banks. On top of this, as noted in Chapter 15, Japan has considerable structural and financial problems at home. We believe, however, that her high domestic saving, and immense holdings of foreign exchange and assets abroad can take care of her fallout from the Asian crisis, and prevent Japan's domestic difficulties from cascading into a financial whirlpool.

Still, many fear that Japan's domestic and Asian financial woes will spread here as she dumps US securities and carts the money home to shore-up faltering financial institutions. Indeed, she dumped $44 billion in foreign bonds in the November 1997-January 1998 period. Is this a harbinger? I think not. To begin, Japan's investments in US bonds, especially Treasuries, continue to be much more rewarding than what's available at home, more so when the rising dollar against the yen is considered (Chart 22-3). Furthermore, Japanese insurance companies are obligated to pay policyholders 4% returns. They can't invest in domestic bonds at the current and almost unbelievably low 1½% yield—and make up the difference on volume!

CHART 22-3

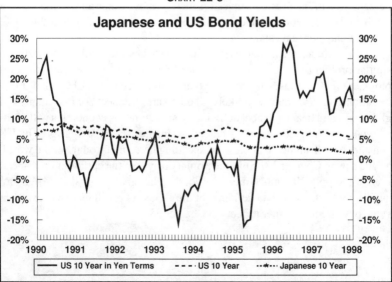

Furthermore, Japan is running a $94 billion current account surplus. This may decline somewhat as her Asian exports dwindle and if she introduces enough fiscal stimulus to spur domestic spending and imports. Still, this current surplus isn't going to disappear anytime soon, especially with her traditional, and still current, policy of promoting economic growth by encouraging exports and retarding imports, as explained in Chapter 15.

The Current Account Deficit Must Come Home

A $94 billion current account surplus in 1997 means that Japan ends up with $94 billion in foreign exchange that year. What can she do with it? The only choices I see are to convert it to paper currency, cut up the bills, and flush them down the toilet—or invest the surplus abroad. Of course, Japanese holders of dollars, the principal component of that surplus, don't have to buy Treasuries. They can buy US stocks or, as in yesteryear, American farm land, hotels, Rockefeller Center, or build Honda plants in Ohio.

They don't even have to invest in dollar assets. Let's say they prefer German bonds. But then the Germans end up with the dollars, and what will they do with them? As long as the US has a current account deficit, one way or the other, foreigners must invest an equal amount in US assets. Like chickens, the bucks come home to roost. Furthermore, the buck's rising value since 1995, despite the growing current account deficit, says that foreigners want to invest even more than that deficit amount in the US and are bidding up the dollar to do so. And, that zeal may rise now that Big Bang financial deregulation in Japan allows investors there to move funds abroad much more freely and enjoy returns that are vastly superior to those available in Japanese stocks, bonds, or real estate.

I conclude, then, that Asia's financial woes are unlikely to result in similar problems in developed countries. Consequently, the leap in unemployment and collapses in incomes that characterized the 1930s and drove deflation then are equally unlikely. To be sure, I expect some weakness in global demand to aid and abet deflation. Asian domestic economies will probably take years to recover, as discussed in Chapter 16. A saving spree by US consumers will subdue incomes and spending here and throughout the world, as you saw in Chapter 18. Still, the primary driver of the deflation I see ahead is excess supply. It's much more the good deflation of the post Civil War era and the 1920s than the bad deflation of the 1930s, as you'll learn as I examine some of deflation's other aspects in Chapter 23.

CHAPTER 23

THE INDUSTRIAL REVOLUTION HAS BEEN EXPORTED

After the Civil War, the transcontinental railroads opened huge, new supplies of agricultural products and minerals in the American West, while the Industrial Revolution mushroomed the supply of manufactured goods. (See Chapter 21). In the 1920s, exploding industries like automobiles and electricity generation had the same supply-enhancing effects.

Where Technology and Capital Roam

Now, suppose for a minute that the western border of the US is extended across the Pacific Ocean, across East Asia, across India, and stops at the Ural mountains in Russia. Also suppose that the eastern border is extended across Latin America (most of which lies east of the US, of course), across the Atlantic and Western Europe, across Eastern Europe, and stops at those same Ural mountains. We'd own the world. Of course, this movement of borders to encompass the world hasn't happened politically, but it has happened economically. And just to prove that I'm not a provincial American, I'll happily make the same border-shifting argument for Western Europe and Japan.

Since the General Agreement on Tariffs and Trade (GATT) was signed in 1947 at Bretton Woods, New Hampshire, there have been eight rounds of negotiations involving 123 participating nations, the most recent of which is the Uruguay Round, which began in 1986. This round's major accomplishments include tariffs reductions of 36% on average; tariffs completely eliminated in several sectors; non-tariff barriers converted into tariffs, which are more visible, predictable, and easier to monitor; introduction of a maximum level of tariffs and a minimum quantity of imports; and establishment of the

World Trade Organization (WTO), which oversees arbitration between countries in order to discourage trade wars. Developed country import tariffs are slated to fall to under 4% and developing country duties, averaging 34% in 1984-87, to drop to 14%.

Although some countries have set tariffs that are higher than the non-tariff barriers they replaced, and others have reduced their lowest tariffs the most in percentage terms and left their higher tariffs as is, the majority of countries have reduced protection levels for many major products. The US, as shown in Chart 23-1, has maintained a consistently low tariff rate since the 1980s. Altogether, this new GATT agreement has made it harder to impose trade barriers on imports, thereby opening markets. Obviously, this reduces the cost of goods to importers, increases competition, and culminates in even lower prices. The US Treasury Department estimates that this treaty will increase international trade by nearly $750 billion over the next decade. WTO members have agreed to begin the next round of negotiations in 1999, which may result in a further lowering of tariffs and the opening of more markets to exported goods, assuming global protectionism doesn't intervene (see Chapter 25).

The North American Free Trade Agreement (NAFTA), signed in December 1993, added Mexico to the free trade arena already inhabited by the US and Canada. Although some feel that this treaty will benefit Mexico at the US's expense, its main result is increased competition, which lowers prices

CHART 23-1

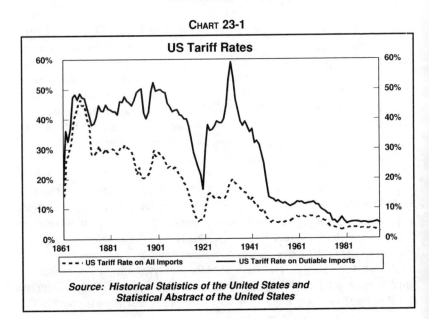

US Tariff Rates

Source: *Historical Statistics of the United States and Statistical Abstract of the United States*

for consumers. It also lowers costs for producers, wholesalers, and retailers, who are free to produce and buy goods and services wherever they choose within the three countries. This mobility will be helped by North American rail mergers that will probably produce companies with tracks in all three countries. In South America, the Southern Cone Common Market, or Mercosur (Argentina, Brazil, Paraguay, and Uruguay), recently agreed on the framework of a free trade accord with the Andean Community (Colombia, Equador, Peru, Bolivia, and Venezuela).

Furthermore, in 1970, 34 countries were free of exchange controls on imports; in 1997 the number was 137. Technology and deregulation have reduced the real unit cost of sea freight by 70% between the early 1980s and 1996; and there have been further declines since then, as shown by the Baltic Freight Index which measures ocean shipping rates (Chart 23-2). Since 1991, there have been 570 liberalizing changes in direct investment regulations and a tripling in investment treaties, which numbered 1,330 among 162 countries in 1996.

Put these economic barrier-slashing developments together with rapid advances in telecommunications and travel and what have you got? An open invitation for capital and technology to roam the world in search of the most cost-effective sites for production—and production of services as well as goods, as you saw in Chapter 10.

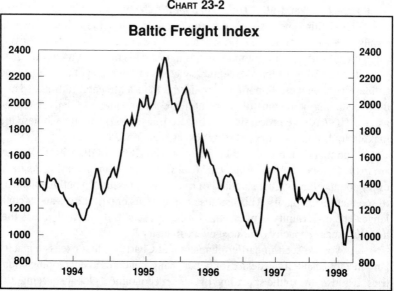

CHART 23-2

And roam the world technology and capital have. Foreign direct investment has grown at a 12% annual rate between 1991 and 1996, compared to 7% for global exports, to reach $3.2 trillion. And 37% of it went to developing countries in 1996. Production soon followed investment. In 1995, $7 trillion in global sales was made by 280,000 foreign affiliates of multinational companies, 20% more than worldwide exports. Those multinationals accounted for 7.5% of global output in 1995, up from 4.5% in 1970.

Exporting the Industrial Revolution

In effect, the Industrial Revolution has been exported to the non-developed countries by the advanced lands, and their low-cost output of goods and services imported in return. With fewer physical or governmental barriers to entry, developed economies have moved quickly to absorb new territories with even more cheap resources than the lush treasure trove of the American West in the 19th century—especially when you consider the cost of human capital.

This is even more true as the world's output contains less and less raw materials and more and more value added per pound. A century ago, the typical economic output was manufactured like steel or grown like wheat. Steel requires coke, limestone, and iron ore as well as transport to ship out the finished product. Pittsburgh became the American steel center due to its strategic location in relation to all of those factors. Wheat takes good land and climate to grow and water or rail transport to move, and the American Midwest fit the bill beautifully. Today, in contrast, the typical products are things like DRAM chips and software programming. Needless to say, their raw materials do not determine the production site. One 747 air freighter can move a lot of chips, and all a programmer needs to move his output is a satellite disk.

In the middle of the 19th century, victims of the Irish potato famine and Chinese coolies were imported to build the transcontinental railroads. Now they're staying home but still working for US companies at relatively cheap wages. The Irish are processing credit card transactions, and the Chinese are making tools and consumer electronics, as mentioned in Chapter 5.

And there's more to come. To quote the CEO of GE, John F. Welch, Jr., in the October 1, 1997, *Financial Times*: "There is an increasing desire in every country for a higher standard of living, and pressure on political leaders to see that this happens. This creates an enormous opportunity—and a challenge. The opportunity is in the size of the markets. But the challenge is that there is excess capacity in almost every industry."

As you've seen in earlier chapters and Chart I-7, that excess capacity isn't just the result of the desire for better living standards in developing countries. It's also due to the spreading of market economies, global sourcing, the booming buck, growing efficiencies in distribution, technology-induced productivity growth, ongoing deregulation, and the pressure on Asian countries to dump their exports just to keep employment from collapsing. Also significant in augmenting excess capacity are the constraints on demand caused by global defense spending cuts, tight monetary and fiscal policies in developed countries, restructuring-related layoffs, and soon, I think, big US consumer saving.

They Love the Old Technologies

The globalization of production reinforces other deflationary forces. You saw in Chapter 20 that in the last stages of the Kondratieff Wave, economic growth slows and deflation sets in because investment falters in the over-built old technology industries. Investment is leaping in new technologies which will dominate the next economic upswing, but they are not yet big enough to offset the slipping old technologies and carry the economic ball.

In the current Kondratieff Wave, however, investment in the over-built technologies isn't falling, but rising as developing lands industrialize. I'm referring to old technology products like steel, ships, cars, textiles, basic chemicals, glassware, basic capital equipment, and industrial commodities. Even Japan, perhaps due to cultural orientation, is in large part still playing the old technology game, as noted in Chapter 12. The massive production resulting from this investment glut in old technologies just has to be deflationary. New technologies, of course, are also contributing to deflation, as you learned in Chapter 6.

US Excess Capacity

Furthermore, excess capacity creation isn't just confined to developing economies. Look at the recent leap in US manufacturing capacity (Chart 23-3). This will continue to push down utilization rates, and is one of the reasons that producer prices are falling while labor markets are drum tight and compensation is jumping. Industries with big addition hikes include computers (Chart 16-3), office equipment, industrial and electrical machinery, oil and gas drilling, lumber and forest products, synthetic fibers, aircraft, steel, and chemicals.

US steel maker Nucor and Canadian steel producer Ipsco each recently announced plans for new steel plate mills that would add 20% capacity in North America. Both agree that little domestic demand growth is in sight, so the planned addition will lead to excess capacity. Nevertheless, they figure the new efficient capacity will replace competitors' old inefficient mills and

CHART **23-3**

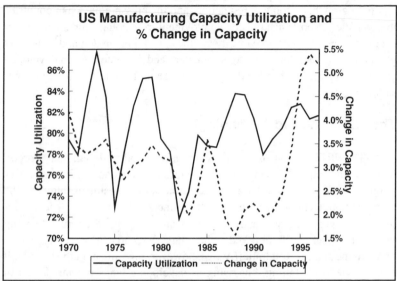

back out imports, which equaled 37% of domestic production in 1996. But where will those backed-out imports go? Not back to Korea and other lands from whence they came, but to some other developed countries at distress prices, in all likelihood.

Similarly, Phelps Dodge is sticking to its plans for a 36% increase in capacity by 2002, despite the collapse in copper prices and prospective weak demand from Asia. Meanwhile, excess capacity drove residential insulation prices down 10% last year and Owens-Corning hopes the fall this year is only 5%.

Another key factor that makes good deflation possible is rapid productivity growth. I'll address that likelihood in the next chapter.

Chapter 24

Productivity Growth Will Be Robust and Consistent With Good Deflation

By 1981 it began to look like inflation was starting to unwind, but the book we'd agreed to write in 1977 for McGraw-Hill on the subject wasn't even completely outlined—as I'd been busy getting A. Gary Shilling & Co. launched (in 1978). I'd been criticized for years for forecasting inflation's demise, and was about to be left in my own dust, I feared. By the time the book was published, it might be old hat. So I asked my friend, Bill Rukeyser, then Editor of *Fortune* magazine, if I could write an article, really a summary of the yet-to-be-written book. Bill readily agreed, and it appeared in the May 3, 1982, edition as "Disinflation—It's Not All Fun." In that article, I made a careful distinction between disinflation—declining rates of inflation but not below zero—and deflation. I argued that disinflation was in the cards but not deflation.

Why I Thought Prices Wouldn't Fall

Here was my argument.

The case for lower inflation, then, is strong, but will the trend go all the way to deflation—prices declining on a widespread and prolonged basis? Probably not. Deflation used to be the rule in peacetime, but that was before the 1930s when wages could fall as well as rise—even though real wages usually rose in either case, since wages rarely fell as much as prices.

Nationwide sentiments against falling wages as well as the growth of labor unions since the Depression have made general declines in wages nearly impossible. So, too, have minimum-wage laws, Social Security, welfare, and unemployment benefits. For the nation as a whole, labor costs account for over three-quarters of total costs. Consequently, if wages don't fall, the only way that overall prices can fall appreciably, unless productivity growth is rapid, is for profits to be wiped out—and that suggests a 1930s-style economic collapse that appears unlikely.

Now I'm forecasting actual deflation. And, for deflation to be worth writing a book about, it's got to be at least in the 1% to 2% range, enough to spawn deflationary expectations, with buyers waiting for lower prices and generating a self-feeding cycle (see Chapter 19). I believe that deflation range is in the cards.

Ah ha, you're probably thinking, Shilling's inconsistent. He's saying that we'll have meaningful deflation but without US financial crisis. Yet he implied, at least in 1982, that deflation would be curtains for corporate earnings because money wages can't fall and productivity growth won't be strong enough to offset falling prices. True, I wrote that, but now money wages are, in effect, falling, and productivity growth should be robust.

Money Wage Cuts without Cutting Money Wages

Money wages are being cut without cuts in money wages. Sure, in a few cases, money wages of individual workers in specific jobs have been reduced, but, the big action is elsewhere, as I discussed in Chapter 5. The compensation of specific individuals has fallen as their union shop jobs are outsourced and they end up working in lower-paying nonunion organizations; as they shift from full-time jobs to part-time and temporary jobs, often without benefits; and as jobs move to lower-cost areas of the country and people move as well. Also, the greater reliance on bonuses and other forms of incentive pay has reduced total compensation for some.

From the employer's viewpoint, labor costs are also being cut by moving jobs offshore and replacing older, more expensive employees with younger, cheaper ones. And from the economy's perspective, money compensation is falling as jobs shift from high paying industries, such as manufacturing and transportation, to lower wage industries, like retail trade and services (see Chapter 17).

In my 1982 *Fortune* article, I obviously was not thinking of all the methods that American business has utilized since then to reduce money wage costs without cutting the pay of ongoing employees. These techniques will probably continue to be employed since the social pressure against explicit wage cuts is well entrenched.

Less Pain for the Same Results

Irrespective, I happen to think that in many cases explicit wage cuts would be much less disruptive to employees as well as employers. Suppose the boss rounds up his staff and announces, "We're getting killed by foreign and domestic competition, but if we all take 10% pay cuts and work harder and smarter, I think we can compete and we'll all keep our jobs." That would avoid all of the trauma, loss of self-esteem, and disruption to family lives brought on by the alternative—layoffs.

Layoffs are destructive. Attempts to get relocated in similar jobs at the same pay in the same industry are usually fruitless because the whole industry is cutting staff. And lay-offs would not have been necessary in the first place if people weren't overpaid in relation to competitive conditions. Some are lucky at finding jobs in different industries at the same or higher pay. Some try their hands at entrepreneurial ventures, A few succeed—their terminations gave them the push to do what they should have done years before. Others dissipate their life savings trying to run their own businesses, and in order to say they're employed—a near psychological necessity in today's world, especially for men. But many, even with retraining, end up in lower paying jobs in the same or different industries, even in today's robust labor markets. Some do the same thing they did before on a part-time or temporary basis, even with their old employers.

The Virtues of Rising Productivity

Productivity has always been the key to increasing the economic pie that feeds consumers, corporate profits, and government spending. Rising output per unit of input allows all participants to get bigger slices without reducing anyone's share. Sure, more can be produced if a greater percentage of the population work and if people work more hours, but that approach soon runs out of steam. People become exhausted from overwork. Family life and leisure are disrupted and the pool of unemployed, but employable, people disappears.

Giving people more capital equipment to work with will also increase output, but this too has its limits. Building capital equipment takes resources that otherwise could be devoted to raising living standards, and unless new equipment embodies more productivity, diminishing returns set in. Giving a construction worker a second shovel won't help him dig faster. Both of these techniques have been utilized in developing Asian lands, but the current crisis there shows that economic growth through simply adding more men and machines only goes so far.

Productivity is embedded in the inputs of labor, capital, technology, management, organization, infrastructure, regulation, and so on. Studies suggest that historically, about half of productivity growth comes from better trained, educated, and managed labor, and about half from more efficient equipment.

Never Fun

Increasing productivity is never easy. As my good friend Ed Samek puts it, people love innovation but they hate change. Introducing new equipment and technology always involves risks, compared with the tried and true. Reorganizing people is disruptive. Terminating unneeded employees is difficult, at best. Consequently, even though most people have enjoyed the benefits of rising productivity over time, many have fought it tooth and nail. Recall that early in the Industrial Revolution, the Luddites in England smashed the machinery they saw replacing them. Similarly, modern-day trade unions complain about assembly line "speed ups."

To be sure, people have had trouble adapting to the changes that productivity increases require, and some have never successfully adapted. When trucks replaced horses and wagons, some teamsters became unemployed because they never learned to drive trucks. But those who did enjoyed higher living standards because the trucks they drove hauled more goods faster and cheaper, and the drivers got a share of the productivity increase.

No Recent Glory

Productivity growth in recent decades has been well below norm (Chart 24-1). Notice that in every decade from the 1900s to the 1960s—even, surprisingly, in the 1930s—output per man-hour rose 2% to 2½% per year on average. Starting in the 1970s, however, growth faltered. No one's quite sure why, but there are clues.

The 1970s were disrupted by oil shocks and uncertainty which inhibited capital investment. Ample labor in the form of the postwar babies and married women was a substitute. But those newcomers to the labor force were inexperienced recruits, and the work ethic was poor, as mentioned in Chapter 5. The growing share of government, due to its inherent inefficiency, deterred productivity as defense spending remained high and governments took over much of health care and other areas that otherwise would have gone to the bottom-line oriented private sector. High inflation in the 1970s discouraged productive work and investment in favor of tangible asset speculation.

CHART 24-1

**PRODUCTIVITY IN THE US NONFARM BUSINESS SECTOR
(AVERAGE ANNUAL GROWTH BY DECADE)**

	NBER*	BLS**
1901-1910	2.34%	NA
1911-1920	2.64%	NA
1921-1930	2.07%	NA
1931-1940	2.39%	NA
1941-1950	2.46%	NA
1951-1960	2.28%	2.17%
1961-1970	2.49%	2.85%
1971-1980	NA	1.71%
1981-1990	NA	1.13%
1991-1997	NA	1.18%

*National Bureau of Economic Research
**Bureau of Labor Statistics, Department of Labor

The 1980s saw many of these productivity drags from the 1970s persist, even though disinflation was under way. Old habits die hard. Also, the restructuring that commenced in the mid 1980s, even though ultimately very conducive to productivity growth, was initially very disruptive. Think of the big corporate writeoffs of restructuring costs and the difficulty people had in adapting to new flatter corporate structures. Also, some of the productivity growth generated by American restructuring in the last decade has occurred not at home but in foreign developing countries, as production moved to more cost-effective locations abroad. Some would also argue that as the US economy becomes more and more service oriented, it is doomed to slower productivity growth since services are more labor intensive.

But There's Hope

Nevertheless, as I noted in Chapter 5, services are just as susceptible to restructuring and productivity advances as goods-producing industries. Also, the trend toward a service economy isn't new (Chart 24-2). And, service pro-

CHART 24-2

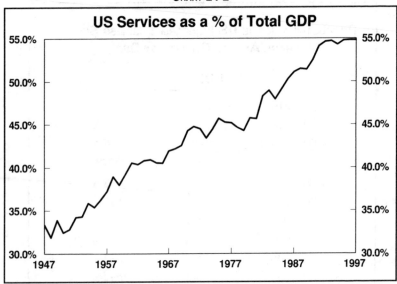

ductivity growth has been running well below trend (Chart 5-8), suggesting that a big catchup is possible.

Think about what the Walmarts, Home Depots, and other mass distributors are doing to cut costs by increasing productivity, as discussed in Chapter 8. Consider what software is doing to eliminate secretaries, receptionists, telephone operators, and even typesetters as desktop publishing is readily available and cheap. Galloping medical costs, seemingly with no hope of control in earlier years, are now being tamed as those that pay the bulk of the bills, government and businesses, demand efficiency. Note how airlines have changed route structures and procedures to improve productivity, including (ugh!) the recorded announcements of when your plane is *supposed* to take off—if you punch enough telephone buttons.

In services as well as goods, the expected surge in imports from Asia and elsewhere at lower prices will redouble American productivity-enhancing efforts. So, too, will weak export markets, and the buck's continuing rally against the yen and Continental currencies. Less government involvement in the economy will work in the same direction (Chapters 1 and 2). The postwar babies are now fully absorbed in the work force and entering their most productive years, while younger inexperienced newcomers are few in number. And low government deficits or even surpluses and rising consumer saving will insure more than ample funds for productivity-enhancing capital investment.

Finally, it stands to reason that all the restructuring, capital investment, labor training, and other productivity-enhancing activities of recent years should have had more of an impact than the reported numbers show. There is

CHART 24-3

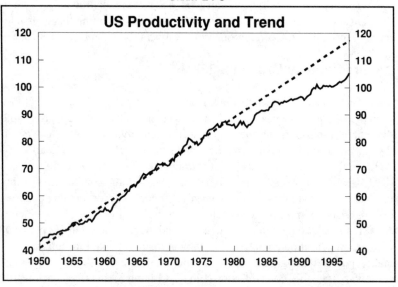

CHART 24-4

US PRODUCTIVITY GROWTH IN 1990s		
	NONFARM BUSINESS	MANUFACTURING
1990	0.5%	1.8%
1991	0.7%	2.3%
1992	3.2%	3.6%
1993	0.1%	2.2%
1994	0.5%	2.7%
1995	0.2%	3.1%
1996	1.9%	3.9%
1997	1.7%	4.4%

a technical explanation for why productivity measures are below postwar trend (Chart 24-3). It concerns reported inflation rates. As is well known, inflation, especially measured by the CPI, is overstated by over one percentage point per year. Price increases are subtracted from dollar sales to determine physical output in calculating output per man-hour or productivity. If inflation rates are overstated, output will be understated, and so too will productivity. Government statisticians are in the process of gradually correcting this overstatement of inflation, so future productivity numbers should appear stronger.

2% Productivity Growth Is Likely

On balance, I believe that in line with the past, 2% to 2½% productivity growth is likely in the years ahead and maybe more on a catch-up basis. Note that nonfarm business productivity rose 1.9% in 1996 and 1.7% last year in distinct contrast to some miserable numbers in the earlier 1990s (Chart 24-4) and manufacturing was considerably stronger.

Meaningful deflation is fully compatible with the combination of this productivity growth range, money wages that don't fall for ongoing employees, and rising corporate profits. Chart 24-5 shows why.

If annual productivity growth is 2% and overall prices fall 1% per year, money compensation could rise 1% without disturbing equilibrium and normal corporate earning gains (Line 2, Column 3). A 2% deflation rate would work with flat labor compensation (Line 2, Column 3). In effect, each sector

CHART 24-5

DEFLATION MATH
EQUILIBRIUM GROWTH RATES FOR COMPENSATION,
PRICES AND PRODUCTIVITY
(% ANNUAL CHANGES)

ANNUAL PRICE CHANGE	PRODUCTIVITY GROWTH			
	0	**+1%**	**+2%**	**+3%**
0	0	+1%	+2%	+3%
-1%	-1%	0	+1%	+2%
-2%	-2%	-1%	0	+1%

Numbers in boxes are equilibrium growth rates in labor compensation

Chart 24-6

US PRICES, EARNINGS, AND PRODUCTIVITY GROWTH AVERAGE ANNUAL RATES OF CHANGE 1870-1900

Consumer Prices	-1.3%
Nominal Earnings	0.0%
Real Earnings	1.4%
Productivity (1874-1900)	2.0%

Source: Historical Statistics of the United States

of the economy would maintain its share of the overall pie which would grow with productivity, or 2% per year for participants. Real pay would rise 2% annually even with zero nominal wage gains because prices were falling 2% per year. Real corporate profits would rise 4% to 4.5% per year (see Chapter 26). If productivity grows 3% per year, 1% money compensation gains would fit with 2% deflation (Line 3, Column 4). In effect then, 1% to 2% deflation rates are consistent with money compensation not falling, maybe even rising a bit, as long as productivity growth is in the 2% or greater range, which seems highly likely. This was very much the pattern in the post Civil War era, as shown in Chart 24-6. Note that money pay was flat, but real earnings rose 1.4% annually.

Regardless, you and I will know for sure that the nation is fully dedicated to productivity and efficiency when parking lots, which speak volumes about the orientation and structure of businesses and institutions, look much different from the way many do today. My October 9, 1995, *Forbes* column notes that hospitals tell you that they're oriented toward their patients' welfare and efficient care, but I question whom they're really working for. Next time you visit one, look at those most desirable parking places right next to the entrance. They're marked, "Doctors Only."

You may be aware that Washington now welcomes global deflationary forces since they are keeping the US economy from overheating in the midst of extremely tight labor markets. How long will the welcome mat remain out, and what will follow? You'll see in Chapter 25.

CHAPTER 25

TRADE WARS ARE A RISK

Asia and, to a lesser extent Europe as well, are competitively devaluing against the dollar, as you saw in Chapter 16. It's like the competitive devaluations of the 1930s with one big exception—Washington is condoning it, at least so far. Of course, the Administration makes periodic but rather soft utterances about the yen falling too fast, but like Japanese officials, they appear to be commenting for the public consumption of American protectionists. Other than that, the Administration, especially Treasury Secretary Rubin, has consistently stated that a strong buck is in America's best interest.

Why should the Administration accept competitive devaluations against our currency? After all, they promise a flood of imports, adding to the already leaping total. Since a strong dollar and collapsing domestic demand in Asia will also be very discouraging to US exports, the net effect will be to add to the large increasing current account deficit (Chart 12-14).

Hands Across the Sea?

To be sure, a huge American trade deficit is a big help for the rest of the world. As shown in Chart 16-7, the US is the only country with a sizable merchandise trade deficit, $200 billion, while many others have large surpluses. We're the happy dumping ground for the globe's excess production, the country that is providing the world's only major foreign stimulus.

Without the gigantic US excess of imports over exports, other leading economies would be plunging. Recall from Chart 5-11, exports account for 25% to 30% of GDP in Europe, but on average, about 100% of the GDP growth in the last two years. In other words, without the stimuli of export-generated incomes and spending, major foreign domestic economies would have contracted, even without any downward multiplier effects. Many developing countries in Asia are even more dependent on exports (Chart 16-6), and without the US market, their economies would be in deep trouble, especially now that their domestic activities are plunging from boom to bust.

Washington has never been willing to help the rest of the world unless the required actions are at least neutral if not supportive of domestic policies. Despite her global dominance, the US remains domestically oriented, both economically and politically. Generation upon generation of Federal Reserve Board members have told me that they will only assist foreign nations if such actions would not be adverse to their domestic policies. My observation is that successive Administrations, left or right, Democrat or Republican, are in the same camp.

The Domestic Policy Angle

With this in mind, it's clear why the strong buck and deteriorating US trade balance are accepted by the Administration—they promote its current domestic policy as well. As discussed in Chapter 18, the US labor market is now exceedingly tight, so many businesses are constrained by a lack of skilled labor. Help-wanted ads haven't been this strong for years. The risk is that declining unemployment will continue to push labor costs (Chart 25-1) to the point that a general wave of inflation breaks out.

CHART 25-1

US Real Employment Cost Index

Year/Year % Change

Deflated by the consumption price deflator

Source: ISI Group

Chapter 3 mentioned that the Fed, unlike me, is more concerned about renewed inflation than deflation, and the Administration is well aware of it. They also know that when the Fed gets worried enough over imminent inflation to tighten credit, it almost always embarks on a series of interest rate hikes that ultimately precipitate a recession. The impact of the Asian crisis and leaping greenback, of course, is tailor made to keep the US economy from overheating. So why shouldn't the Administration accept, even celebrate, the strengthening dollar?

Financing Treasuries

And one more thing. As I explored in Chapter 22, an appreciating buck makes US investments more valuable to foreign investors in their own currency terms. For some strange reason, the Treasury Secretary is interested in foreigners' holdings of Treasury securities, which have climbed to almost $600 billion (Chart 25-2). He may be especially interested, now that the Japanese and other Asian central banks appear to be selling Treasuries to raise dollars to support their local financial institutions.

At best, any such liquidation of Treasuries is a short-run and limited issue. As you saw in Chapter 22, foreigners have no choice but to invest the equivalent of the US current account deficit in American assets. Furthermore, rising US trade and current account deficits in the near term mean that even more dollars will be recycled into US investments than earlier, and I suspect

CHART 25-2

that Treasuries will get more than their share of new foreign-owned dollars in these uncertain times. Nevertheless, a strengthening buck will make all US investments, Treasuries included, even more attractive to foreigners. The man who runs the Treasury may no longer have big federal deficits to finance, but he still has lots of maturing Treasuries to roll over, so why shouldn't he back the buck?

A Parting Of the Ways?

At present, then, deteriorating US trade accounts and a rising greenback help foreign economies while aiding Washington's domestic goals. But what if the US economy softens in the next year or so, as we expect? What if we're right and the effects of Asia go beyond keeping the US economy from over-heating? What if they squeeze profits to the point of precipitating a big bear stock market which destroys considerable portions of individual wealth and scares consumers into retrenchment and a recession? Alternatively, suppose we're wrong and Asia has little impact on the US economy, but then fear of inflation-threatening tight labor markets drives the Fed to tighten credit and, as usual, touches off a recession?

Washington's attitude would, no doubt, shift 180 degrees as unemployment leaped. The Administration probably couldn't do much to arrest the dollar's upward climb, but it surely could deflect voter frustration by blaming domestic woes on foreigners, especially those with big trade surpluses and restrictive trade practices. You can write the script. Japan, with over a $56 billion trade surplus with the US would be Public Enemy #1, and China with $50 billion (Chart 25-3) would be #2. By that time, China's growing surplus may well be bigger than Japan's, so she would advance to the #1 spot, but what's the difference when scapegoats are needed? As discussed in Chapters 14 and 15, both countries remain committed to growth through mercantilistic export-oriented policies. Both still have considerable non-tariff barriers to trade. Both now have surpluses of exports over imports that are too big to escape notice by the US when her economy suffers from unemployment.

Trade Wars?

Trade wars? Impossible in today's world, you're thinking. After all, official trade liberalization conferences are so plentiful today as to keep a large army of bureaucrats busy, as noted in Chapter 23. NAFTA has been a ringing success. Japan is opening her financial institutions to foreign ownership. The IMF is forcing the Asian lands it bails out to curb import and export cartels, and to open ownership of financial and nonfinancial firms to foreigners. But, note a few sobering facts.

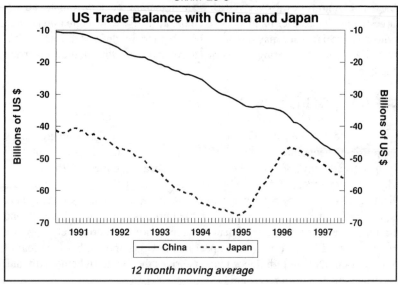

CHART 25-3

US Trade Balance with China and Japan

12 month moving average

To begin, free trade is not the way God made the world. In fact, free trade is not natural to human beings and seems to require a single dominant global power who sees free trade in her interest. In recent centuries there have been only two such periods—one when Britain ran the world from the middle of the 19th century through World War I, and the other as the US has dominated since World War II. Otherwise, protectionism, sprinkled with trade wars, prevailed.

The US seems likely to remain the only super power, at least for some years, but is free trade any longer in her interest? It definitely was during the Cold War since it allowed Europe and Japan to concentrate on economic development and remain free of Communist control. Often, this rebuilding came at the expense of the US since other countries were more closed to foreign capital and imports than America. This was especially the case in Japan. Still, despite the huge American cost of militarily shielding Japan and Europe, it was a lot cheaper than garrisoning large numbers of US troops around the world.

Now, however, the Cold War is over and the Russian elite are busy joining the capitalist class, not plotting its overthrow. The need to favor Japan is gone, including the acceptance of her mercantilism policy. We've seen Washington's fight against Japanese trade restrictions accelerate since the Berlin Wall came down. Recent publically-stated requests for stronger domestic growth in Japan are notably blunt. And China is no great favorite either, now that Beijing has made it clear that she wants to reduce US influence in Asia and promote her own—American business involvements in China not withstanding. The potential is there for economic warfare to replace military confrontation.

Simmering Protectionism at Home

Furthermore, US protectionist forces may now be subdued in an economy where anyone with any skills has multiple job offers, but what if a job surplus turns into a job glut? Pat Buchanan and Ross Perot on the right and Dick Gephardt on the left are beating opposite sides of the same protectionist drum, and their thumps will be heard much more clearly when the economy slumps.

Recall that only several years ago, when American jobs were much scarcer, organized labor was demanding that Washington cut off those slave labor-produced goods at the border so we could all go back to the lives we knew and loved. Note also, the ongoing polarization of American incomes discussed in Chapter 17 (Charts 17-19 and 17-20). By the early 1990s, middle-class families had run out of options to achieve the living standards they thought they deserved. Most wives were working and many teenagers as well. Debts were at crushing levels.

To add insult to injury, the struggling middle class saw itself going down in a leaky barge in the swamp while upper-income folks were sailing into the sunset in a beautiful new party yacht. It's no great surprise that the 1990 and 1993 federal tax hikes were "soak the rich" affairs. And the middle class has also lashed out at the other end of the income spectrum with the more recent anti-affirmative action zeal.

A Tough Political Problem

Although now disguised by the economic boom, the middle class frustration over income stagnation will remain one of the biggest post-Cold War problems, in my view, especially in the deflationary economy and the difficult transition to it that I foresee.

Democrats, typically, believe that middle-income growth can be revived by more education and training and by income redistribution through the tax system. Despite repeated attempts since the 1930s, tax changes to shift income have never worked. Also, it's doubtful that many of those now suffering and likely to suffer income losses have the necessary ability or inclination to substantially upgrade their skills. In addition, there is a long-term surplus of college-educated people in the US that is now buried in the strong economy.

Furthermore, how does training more computer programmers raise American incomes if Indians, working by satellite, will do the jobs for US companies at less than a quarter of American pay levels? Our analysis also suggests that even if all the high value-added professional and technical jobs in the world were captured by Americans, it would not be enough to revive middle-income growth. Approximately 5,000 people work in one auto plant, but that number of software engineers can do a lot of the world's available work.

Republicans, in contrast, propose reduced government regulation and spending, balanced budgets, and tax cuts to spur faster US growth and more capital for investment. Faster growth would no doubt create more high-paid jobs, but probably not enough to solve the problem. At the same time, much of the lower-skilled work would still be done in more cost-effective places abroad. Balanced government budgets and increased saving will reduce our dependence on foreign capital to fund domestic investment, but it is far from clear that more domestic saving will promote adequate domestic investment and high-end American jobs. Capital is already plentiful here and abroad, and will be even more plentiful with deflation. But as noted earlier, it can move freely across national boundaries, and in the production of many goods and services, its most profitable application is often found outside the US.

A Difficult Social Problem, As Well

The decimation of the American middle class is not only a difficult political problem, but a severe social issue as well. The genius of America, especially compared to Europe, has been her lack of class distinction and her social mobility, which are made possible by economic mobility. In the past, Americans believed that they would live higher on the hog than their parents and retire rich, and many rose from the bottom to the top of the economic heap by diligent hard work—and some luck, of course. As a result, Americans have traditionally favored enlarging the economic pie with the conviction that they would get larger slices. In contrast, in the UK before Prime Minister Thatcher's reforms, labor and management saw themselves as class bound in an "us versus them" zero-sum game. They were so consumed with fighting over the pieces of the pie that little attention was given to making it bigger.

Furthermore, many of America's high-paid but low-skilled jobs that are being automated away or shifted abroad used to be important stepping stones in economic mobility. A Southern share cropper may not have had much education, but he did have enough mechanical skills for a well-paid job in a Detroit assembly plant. From that setting, his children could move on to college and the professions. Also, before suspension of the draft, service in the military and GI Bill of Rights-financing of college educations were important stepping stones for many. Today, the economy is moving toward two classes of people—the well-paid executive or professional who is having his bags carried up to his hotel suite and the unskilled bellman carrying the bags. This is a huge skill and occupation gap, without much in between.

Recent Storm Clouds

The threat is that income polarization will lead to social class distinctions and the end of the American Dream for many, the dream that is of tremendous significance for American thinking and culture. Deflation can only intensify this problem, as it has in the past.

Middle-income purchasing power stagnated in the 1920s and 1930s. The response back then was repeated attempts to redistribute income by tax changes, as noted earlier, and protectionism. And despite the current exuberant job markets, we're now seeing some warning harbingers of protectionism. Note the recent concern of many Americans over immigration, despite the nation's traditional openness to newcomers, mentioned in Chapter 16. California, often the leader in trends, recently passed a proposition that would deny medical and other aid to illegal aliens with the obvious aim of discouraging them from coming in the first place. In the past year, Washington has also tightened up on immigration, both legislatively and administratively. For example, new arrivals will be much more carefully screened for past criminal records in their home countries.

Bear in mind that the benefits of free trade are subtle, broad, and long term, and often get lost as we all, as human beings, credit ourselves and not our environment for our economic good fortune. Setbacks, however, are someone else's fault, and it's easy to blame outsiders for job loses and stagnant incomes. Politicians find foreigners, who can't vote in US elections, especially easy targets.

Note also that even with strong support from the Republican majority and Fed Chairman Greenspan, President Clinton failed to win congressional approval for fast-track trade legislation last summer. As mentioned in Chapter 16, Congress seems reluctant to provide more money to the IMF to bail out Asia's financial woes and the majority of Americans agree, according to polls. Many argue that taxpayer money should not be used to bail out international bankers and Asians who threaten American jobs with cheap imports. Some even advocate the building of economic barriers to insulate the country against the Asian flu.

Less Internationalism in Europe

Memories of the destruction that protectionism wrought in the 1930s may well remain vivid enough to prevent a major rerun in the years ahead in the US, but we are not alone among developed countries. Europe, except the UK, has traditionally been much more protectionist than America, and the further consolidation around a common currency will magnify these tendencies. As more trade is carried on among the European users of that currency, they will be less internationalist in orientation. And it's a short step from being less internationalist to being more protectionist, especially in a deflationary world in which every nation wants more exports and none wants competing imports. Already we see in Europe arch protectionists like Jean-Marie LePen in France and the far right in Austria.

Elsewhere, note that the South American Mercosur trade bloc is being hurt by the Asian meltdown, especially its larger members, Argentina and Brazil. So the bloc is raising its common external tariff to 23% from 20%. Even our good Australian friends recently blasted the US for her offer to guarantee payments on US agricultural exports to Indonesia that would back out Australian cotton and wheat. The Aussies, of course, said they'd match the US offer. And not to be left out, Japan will discontinue import-duty cuts on 122 goods from South Korea, Taiwan, Singapore, and Hong Kong, as well as from her arch trading rival, New Caledonia, because of the increased competitiveness of those products.

No Winners

Any widespread protectionism and even trade wars in the years ahead will slow economies globally and obviously augment deflation. No country wins in that exercise, but the US would be in the best shape, relatively. During shortages, the producer reigns, but in times of surplus, especially when accompanied by significant protectionism, the consumer is king. As the globe's biggest consumer and importer, America has the clear advantage. The dollar and Treasuries as global safe havens would benefit, adding to the other favors bestowed on them during deflation. I'll tell you more about interest rates as well as corporate earnings in a deflationary world in Chapter 26.

CHAPTER 26

INTEREST RATES DOWN, PROFITS
SO-SO IN DEFLATION

As deflation becomes established, interest rates will obviously fall, but how far? The Fed won't hesitate to cut the short-term rates it controls once deflation is obvious, even though, as discussed in Chapter 18, lower borrowing costs probably won't do much to stimulate business or consumer spending. Chart 26-1 shows that US short rates have been all over the place since 1835, and they can go low, virtually to zero, as they did in the deflationary 1930s and during World War II.

CHART 26-1

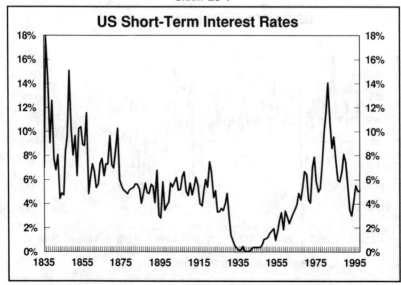

US Short-Term Interest Rates

Low Short-Term Interest Rates

I don't expect short rates to go to zero, but they could well fall to the 1% to 2% range in the 1% to 2% deflation we see ahead. That would put real short-term rates in the 2% to 4% range, not unusual by historical standards (Chart 26-2). Notice that in the pre-World War II era real short rates were not only higher on average but more volatile. Historical data compiled by my good friend Jim Bianco of Bianco Research supports the range I'm forecasting. Real short rates have averaged 3.6% since 1831 and 1.3% in the post-war period (Chart 26-3). In periods of mild deflation, when price declines were in the zero to 4% range, however, real short rates were 7.4% since 1831 and 2.0% since World War II. You may not believe it, but since World War II, there have been 26 year-over-year monthly periods, the measure used in Jim's study, when the CPI fell. Deflation isn't a *complete* stranger.

Lower Long-Term Interest Rates

Real long-term interest rates were also much more erratic before World War II (Chart 26-4) and generally higher, especially in times of deflation. In fact, the gyrations we've all sweated out since the tranquil 1950s and 1960s ended pale before earlier volatility. The 1970s were a big shock to bond investors as surging inflation and the financing of big private and government

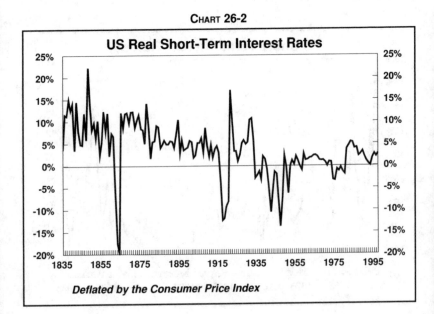

Chart 26-2

Deflated by the Consumer Price Index

borrowing pushed real long-term Treasury bond yields negative not once but twice (Chart I-8). Investors got a double dose of pain. They were hurt first as nominal bond yields rose (Chart 26-5) and the prices of existing bonds in

CHART 26-3

US REAL MEDIAN SHORT-TERM INTEREST RATES

	ALL PERIODS	PERIODS WITH MILD DEFLATION (CPI YEAR/YEAR 0 TO -4%)
1831-1997	3.6%	7.4%
1831-1913*	6.4%	8.7%
1913-1997**	1.3%	4.0%
1945-1997***	1.3%	2.0%

*Before creation of the Federal Reserve

** After creation of the Federal Reserve

*** Post World War II

Source: Bianco Research

CHART 26-4

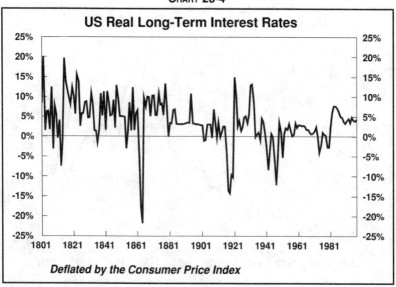

US Real Long-Term Interest Rates

Deflated by the Consumer Price Index

their portfolios fell, and then a second time as those higher yields failed to offset inflation. Not wishing to come back for thirds, they demanded, and got, real yield protection—9% in the early 1980s—which has slowly declined as concerns over resurgent inflation have proved unjustified. Nevertheless, real yields have not fallen as much as inflation has abated.

Consequently, real yields on high quality bonds, now about 4%, are not low by historical standards. They averaged 4.5% in the 196-year period since 1801 and 8.2% in the mild deflation years, as shown in Chart 26-6, again using Jim Bianco's insightful data. Since the Fed was formed in 1913, real bond yields have run 2.5% in all the rolling 12-month periods and 5.1% in those when the CPI was flat to falling 4%. In the postwar period, the average was 2.5% overall and 3.5% in mild deflation years. Maybe the Fed has, on balance, helped to reduce real long- as well as short-term interest rates.

If deflation in the years ahead is in the 1% to 2% range and real bond yields run at the 5.1% average for mild deflation periods since 1913, nominal Treasury bond yields would be 3.1% to 4.1%. The 3.5% real yield average for the postwar era would push them even lower, to the 1½% to 2½% range.

This latter range seems too low for future years, however, even with deflation accompanied by higher consumer saving and little if any new government borrowing. Even in the 1930s, and then during World War II when interest rates were pegged by the Treasury and the Fed, long-term Treasury yields dipped below 2% only in 1940 (Chart 26-7). In my judgment, the 3%

CHART 26-5

CHART 26-6

US REAL MEDIAN LONG-TERM INTEREST RATES

	ALL PERIODS	PERIODS WITH MILD DEFLATION (CPI YEAR/YEAR 0 TO -4%)
1801-1997	4.5%	8.2%
1801-1913*	7.2%	8.7%
1913-1997**	2.5%	5.1%
1945-1997***	2.5%	3.5%

*Before creation of the Federal Reserve
** After creation of the Federal Reserve
*** Post World War II

Source: Bianco Research

CHART 26-7

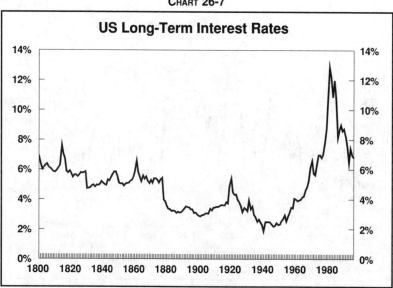

US Long-Term Interest Rates

target we've been using since the early 1980s for the final low for Treasury bond yields still seems valid after deflation is established. With 1% to 2% deflation, that would produce real yields of 4% to 5%.

Profits in and after the Transition to Deflation

In contrast to bonds, a not so funny thing will happen to US corporate profits on the way to deflation. As noted in Chapter 18, the Asian flu will probably squeeze US corporate earnings, and if not, recent exuberant profits growth may prove disappointingly unsustainable, as discussed below. As either precipitates a serious stock market slide, which slashes individual assets and induces consumer retrenchment and recession, profits will be depressed further. Alternatively, even if the Asian crisis proves to be a non-event for the US, it's only a matter of time until tight labor markets push the Fed to tighten credit to the recession-triggering level. The anticipating bear market would have the same net effect on individuals' portfolios and spending, and ultimately, on corporate earnings. One way or the other, the transition to deflation will involve a setback for profits.

After the Transition

But what happens to corporate earnings after that recession if American consumers remain cautious and chronic deflation continues? We constructed

CHART 26-8

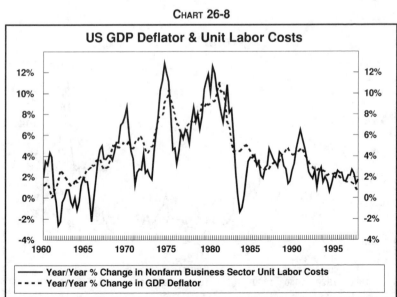

US GDP Deflator & Unit Labor Costs

——— Year/Year % Change in Nonfarm Business Sector Unit Labor Costs
- - - - Year/Year % Change in GDP Deflator

a statistical model which relates pretax corporate profits to real GDP, the GDP price deflator, and unit labor costs. The model may seem simplistic, but it does pick up the major determinants of earnings. Also, simplistic models have worked at least as well as much more complicated ones in my decades of experience (see Chapter 6). Real GDP and the deflator are, together, a proxy for total corporate sales. Unit labor costs represent compensation, the lion's share of business outlays, after offsets from productivity. According to our model, a 1% rise in real GDP increases profits by 2.9%, quantifying the well-known leverage effect of production on earnings. Similarly, a 1% hike in the GDP price deflator raises nominal profits by 2.1%, all other things being equal. Of course, higher unit labor costs have the opposite effect, with a 1% rise depressing profits by 2.4%.

It's not surprising that the effects on profits of the deflator and unit labor costs are offsetting and similar in magnitude. The first represents the prices of goods and services sold, and the second, the costs incurred in producing those items. So, the two would be expected to move in parallel (Chart 26-8). Higher unit costs are usually pushed through to higher prices, pretty much one-for-one.

Chart 26-9 shows various model simulations. The top row depicts no inflation, with both the GDP deflator and unit labor costs unchanged year-by-year. To get to zero inflation would probably require a somewhat more restrained consumer than in recent years and, as a result, slower real GDP growth. We assume a 2.0% annual rise compared with 2½% in the past decade. As

CHART 26-9

US PRETAX CORPORATE PROFIT IN DEFLATION
ANNUAL CHANGES

	GDP DEFLATOR	REAL GDP	UNIT LABOR COST	NOMINAL PROFITS	REAL PROFITS
	0	2.0%	0	4.4%	4.4%
	-1%	1.8%	-1%	3.2%	4.2%
	-2%	1.8%	-2%	2.4%	4.4%
1992-97	2.4%	2.8%	1.9%	11.8%	8.8%

shown, our model translates these assumptions into a 4.4% nominal profits increase.

What If Prices Fall?

If true deflation sets in and the GDP deflator and unit labor costs each fall 1% per year (Line 2), the general decline in the prices of goods and labor will probably be accompanied by an even slower growth in consumer spending. As discussed in Chapter 18, if consumers really get serious about saving, they may well increase their saving rate by about ½% per year for the next decade, a switch from the roughly ½% decline per year of the past two decades. This, as that chapter explains, will reduce real GDP annual growth from the 2½% average of the last decade to the 1½% to 2% range. I think 1.8% is a reasonable growth number for real GDP. Using these inputs, profits' annual rise drops to 3.2% (Line 2 of the chart). With the same GDP growth but 2% deflation per year and a 2% annual decline in unit labor costs, profit growth declines further to 2.4% per year.

In deflation, of course, real corporate profits grow faster than nominal earnings, about 4% to 4.5% per year, as shown in the last column. Still, both nominal and real growth are a far cry from the results of recent years (Line 4). In addition, our simulation results might be on the high side for a condition of deflation. Our model is based on the 1982-to-present era, one that saw corpo-

CHART 26-10

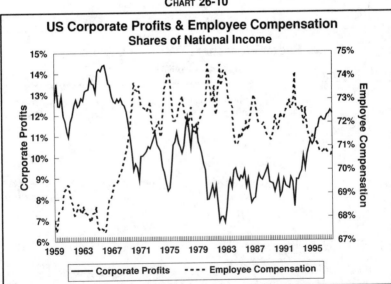

rations enjoy a substantial rise in their share of national income (Chart 26-10). This climb might be difficult to sustain in deflation due to the implied pinch in labor compensation's share.

Furthermore, slow sales growth during deflation would limit the spreading of overhead costs, and this may not be adequately reflected in a model based on a period of much more rapid sales gains. Also, as we've seen recently in Japan, deflation uncovers a multitude of corporate sins that were previously hidden by inflation. In addition, our model's 15 year sample period, except for the last two, was one of a weak dollar and currency translation gains for US firms with foreign operations. So, our model forecasts do not really reflect the switch of those gains to losses as the greenback continues to rise.

Unsustainable Profit Margin Gains

In addition, some of the other forces which have pushed profits ahead recently may not be sustainable. Some interesting work by *The Bank Credit Analyst* concludes that much of the recent growth in after-tax profits and margins is due to lower effective tax rates (Chart 26-11) and declining depreciating expenses and interest costs (Chart 26-12). Without these factors, profit growth in recent years would have been much lower (Chart 26-13).

CHART 26-11

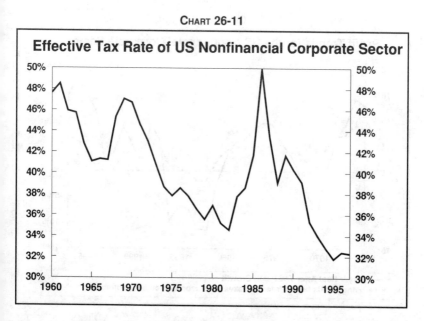

Effective Tax Rate of US Nonfinancial Corporate Sector

Will these salutary but non-operating influences on corporate earnings continue? Interest rates will continue to fall and cut interest expenses as deflation unfolds, but the bulk of the rate decline that commenced in the early

CHART 26-12

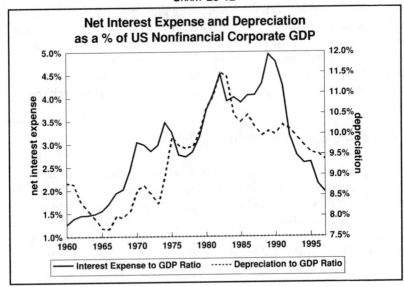

Net Interest Expense and Depreciation as a % of US Nonfinancial Corporate GDP

Interest Expense to GDP Ratio ⋯⋯ Depreciation to GDP Ratio

CHART 26-13

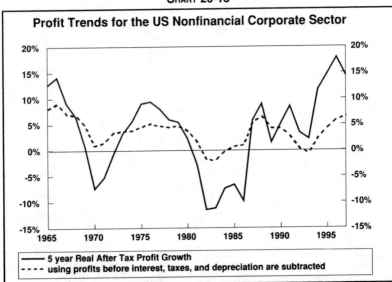

Profit Trends for the US Nonfinancial Corporate Sector

—— 5 year Real After Tax Profit Growth
- - - using profits before interest, taxes, and depreciation are subtracted

1980s is behind us. Also, corporations have been using much of their tremendous cash flow in recent years to pay down debt and to fund new capital spending without commensurate new debt. The likely squeeze on earnings in future years will severely restrict this contributor to lower interest costs. Tax rates have fallen, among other reasons, because corporations paid 29% tax on profits from leaping export sales in recent years, compared to about 35% on more slowly growing domestic earnings. With weaker growth in exports in prospect, effective tax rates may even rise unless US corporate tax rates are cut.

Depreciation has been falling in relation to gross corporate product (essentially corporate sales) in recent years due to earlier big writeoffs of obsolete plants and equipment. That removed old investments from balance sheets and, therefore, further depreciation on them. But most of those writeoffs are over, and depreciation ratios may not fall a great deal further, even if deflation retards capital spending .

Running Fast to Stand Still

When taxes, interest, and depreciation are stripped away, the rise in fundamental profit margins in recent years has been less than stellar. This suggests that American business has been running very fast just to stand still. It means that the tremendous restructuring that began in the early 1980s has been necessary to meet ongoing foreign and domestic competition. This is a sobering thought, since many believe that all the diligent earlier work by American business has finally begun to pay off. It's confirmed, though, by the spread between overall prices and unit labor costs, a rough measure of corporate profit margins (see Chart 26- 8) which has actually gone from positive to negative in recent years. Deflation will intensify this competition and necessitate even more aggressive restructuring, which in turn will fuel deflation.

Now that you've learned about the forces that are promoting deflation in Chapters 1 through 18 and its effects in Chapters 19 through 26, you're all set to delve into strategies for investors, businesses, and individuals who want not only to survive but to thrive in this new but perhaps not so brave world. Investors come first in the next chapter.

CHAPTER 27

INVESTMENT STRATEGY
FOR DEFLATION—
13 ELEMENTS

In some ways, the investment strategy for a deflationary world doesn't differ greatly from what we suggested for disinflation back in 1982 in our first book, *Is Inflation Ending? Are You Ready?* But in some ways, deflation demands a quite different approach. The combined strategy has a lot of elements, a baker's dozen to be exact. This makes it a large chapter, so be forewarned.

1. Bonds Are Beautiful, Especially in the Transition to Deflation.

With chronic deflation of 1% to 2%, I foresee 30-year Treasury bond yields returning to 3%, as discussed in Chapter 26. If so, then what we dubbed "the bond rally of a lifetime" back in the early 1980s is still underway (Chart 26-5). Of course, you might think that the action is largely over since these long bond yields have fallen from over 14% in 1981 to about 6%. What's another three percentage points on top of a decline of eight already? Think again. A one percentage point decline from 14% to 13% increases the price of a 30-year bond by 7.5%, but a drop from 4% to 3% appreciates it by 19.6% (Chart 27-1). To explain this phenomenon in over-simplified terms, a decline from 14% to 13% reduces interest rates by 7.1% while a fall from 4% to 3% is a 25% decline. As shown in this table, the cumulative effect of the nosedive in yields from 14% to 6% was a 116.5% gain, but a further fall to 3% would add another 61.7%.

Treasuries will also be aided in the transition to deflation by the limited new supply if balanced federal budgets persist, while the current account deficit rises due to more imports from Asia and elsewhere and fewer exports. Years

CHART 27-1

30-YEAR TREASURY BOND

COUPON @ EACH INTEREST RATE LEVEL	PRICE APPRECIATION FOR EACH 1 PERCENTAGE POINT DECLINE IN YIELD	CUMULATIVE PRICE APPRECIATION	
		FROM 14%	FROM 6%
14%			
13%	7.5%	7.5%	
12%	8.0%	16.1%	
11%	8.7%	26.2%	
10%	9.4%	38.0%	
9%	10.3%	52.2%	
8%	11.3%	69.4%	
7%	12.4%	90.4%	
6%	13.7%	116.5%	
5%	15.4%		15.4%
4%	17.3%		35.3%
3%	19.6%		61.7%
2%	22.3%		97.8%
1%	25.7%		148.5%

ago, Washington's formula was to run a big current account deficit when running a big federal deficit to force foreigners to finance it as they recycled their surplus dollars, as discussed in Chapters 22 and 25. Until consumer saving increases cut the current account deficit substantially (Chapter 12), large foreign demand for Treasuries will not be matched by new supply. So bond prices should rise and yields fall.

Once deflation is fully reflected in bond yields, of course, the bond rally fun is over, since fairly steady yields can be expected to continue as long as economy-wide prices fall 1% to 2% a year. Notice in Chart 26-7, that after deflation was established in the post-Civil War period, long term bond yields remained fairly steady until inflation flared with the Spanish American war at the end of the century. Real bond yields, similarly, were quiet in that long deflationary era (Chart 26-4). Nevertheless, 4% to 5% real returns on long-term Treasuries that I foresee after deflation becomes established will still be attractive, and much higher than the postwar average of 2.5%. Furthermore, on a risk-adjusted basis, those real returns are excellent because of Treasuries' three sterling qualities—they are the best credits in the world, highly liquid, and they cannot be called by the issuer, which can thereby limit price appreciation when interest rates fall.

Avoid Junk Bonds

There are bonds and then there are bonds. With the bond rally in recent years, many investors have been so hungry for yield that they charged into junk bonds, thereby compressing the yield spreads in relation to Treasuries. Both professional investors and individuals through mutual funds, have participated, and between them they own $300 billion in these low-quality instruments. I'd avoid them in the world I foresee. Like any fixed income investment, junk bonds are obligations to make regular interest payments, but their ability to do so is sometimes questionable due to the high financial leverage and uncertain business prospects of their issuers. Consequently, in times of turmoil, they tend to trade more on company earnings prospects then in relation to interest rates. This is especially relevant now, at least until deflation is fully established and its effects much better understood.

I don't expect a 1930s-style US financial collapse, as emphasized in Chapter 22, but it's interesting to see what happened to yields on Baa bonds back then compared to Treasuries (Chart 27-2). They exploded as investors doubted the viability of their issuers. Although that degree of US financial crisis is unlikely, lesser problems could result in similar effects, especially for issuers hit hard by the Asian crisis and other deflationary forces. Note, too, that Baa's were back then, and are today, much better credits than their newer and less reputable cousins, junk bonds.

2. Utility Stocks Are Interesting

Utility stocks are aided by declining interest rates because of their high borrowing levels, but ongoing deregulation complicates the outlook, especially in the electric utility and telephone segments, as noted in Chapter 9. So, too, does the reality that many electric utility managements have no better understanding of the competition that deregulation brings than did S&L managements when those institutions were deregulated. As you'll recall, most S&Ls were wiped out by poor investment decisions made in a newly competitive and volatile environment.

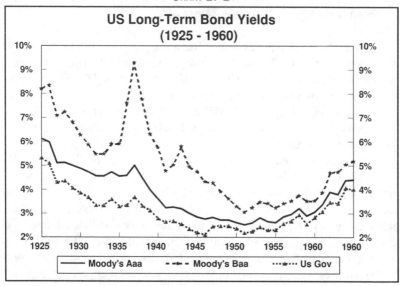

CHART 27-2

US Long-Term Bond Yields
(1925 - 1960)

Moody's Aaa — · — Moody's Baa · · · · · Us Gov

Utility officers who are very good at dealing with regulators in rate-setting hearings and at being model civic leaders are not necessarily skillful in meeting competitors who can suddenly invade their territory. Furthermore, there's uncertainty over how regulators, state-by-state, will split stranded costs (the earlier investments in nuclear and other unprofitable facilities) between the electric utilities and their customers. Similarly, regulators and telephone companies are still wrestling over access to local and long distance markets.

In this turmoil of utility deregulation lies investor opportunity, but also risks. I suspect that the winners will be utilities led by managements which understand, and embrace, competition, and which are also operating in a reasonably hospitable regulatory climate. In the case of electricity, the industry is separating into generation, transmission, and distribution components, and competition can be expected in all three areas. In addition, firms like Enron are managing final customers' total energy needs—natural gas or electric—and buying and trading whatever generation, transmission, and distribution services it takes to get the job done. While telephone companies compete among themselves, they will also continue to collide with cable TV, satellites, wireless, PCs, and other telecommunications services.

Even after interest rates stabilize when deflation is firmly established, the transition to utility deregulation will still be going on.

3. Stocks Overall Are Hurt by the Transition to Deflation, Reasonably Attractive Thereafter.

Overblown US equities may suffer a major fall of 40% to 50% in the transition to deflation. The spillover effect from Asia will seriously hurt corporate profits, as discussed in Chapters 18 and 26. Also, US firms with exports and foreign business will experience currency translation losses as the dollar continues to rise. And if Asia doesn't do the job, the ever inflation-wary Fed will, as it raises interest rates to head off wage inflation and ends up precipitating a recession.

Few are prepared for a major stock market decline, as discussed in detail in Chapter 18. It's as hard for those who have never sweated through a prolonged bear market to envision their physiological reaction to it, as it is for anyone who's never been in combat to mentally visit a foxhole with live bullets whizzing by. Nevertheless, I've suggested to some individual investors, for whom the next bear market will be their first, that they take themselves aside and try to picture their reaction to a 40% decline in their stock portfolio and no end of the sell-off in sight. Would they accept it as part of the game? Would they worry about their retirement, especially if their holdings of stocks and mutual funds directly and through 401(k) accounts are the bulk of their net worth? Would they be willing to buy more stocks, borrowing if necessary to do so because they were then so cheap? Professional investors who are veterans of bull markets only might ask themselves similar questions.

Stock Returns in Deflation

Beyond the transition lies deflation itself and, to many, this means curtains for stocks. They are undoubtedly thinking about the bad 1930s-style deep deflation and don't realize that stocks did well in the moderate deflation days of the post-Civil War era and the 1920s.

Misconceptions over the effects of overall price changes on stock performance aren't uncommon, though. Soon after I joined Merrill Lynch in 1967, we developed a statistical model to explain stock price movements. We used all the usual suspects as inputs—sales, profits, interest rates, and even a measure of speculation provided by my good friend Bob Farrell, now Merrill Lynch's Senior Investment Advisor. We also tried inflation rates, and much to our surprise, the model said that inflation was negative for stocks.

I say, surprise, because at the time, stocks were considered to be a great inflation hedge. Merrill Lynch even had graphs on posters mounted in its offices to remind investors that in the postwar era up until then, consumer prices and stocks had risen in parallel. Well, that was in 1967. It wasn't long

CHART 27-3

REAL US STOCK INDEX RETURNS SINCE 1802* (AVERAGE ANNUAL RETURN)	
1802-1997	4.29%
1802-1913	4.30%
1913-1997	4.27%
1945-1997	4.03%
1974-1997	5.15%

* *without dividends*

Source: Bianco Research

until we found out why our model was correct as rampant inflation killed stocks (Chart 5-1).

As noted in Chapter 26, with 1% to 2% steady deflation, corporate earnings will probably rise at around 2½% to 3½% per year in nominal terms and 4% to 4½% adjusted for inflation. Similar real appreciation in stocks seems likely, and interestingly, this is in line with historic returns as compiled by Jim Bianco (Chart 27-3). Notice how extraordinarily consistent the CPI-adjusted returns of 4¼% without dividends are for the Dow Jones Industrial since 1885 and earlier indexes compiled for stocks back to 1802. This is amazing. In the early 1800s, the US was an agrarian economy concentrated in the East Coast. Canals and river boats had yet to open up the interior east of the Mississippi. The heyday of railroads and the Industrial Revolution was still half a century away. Stocks were highly speculative and ownership was narrow. Anything that consistent over so much time and spanning so many big economic changes has got to get your attention!

Notice, too, the above-norm performance since 1974. This, in effect, made up for the miserable results during the earlier high-inflation years, mentioned in Chapter 18, since the total postwar result (1945-97) of 4.03% was about in line with previous history. The make-up aspect of the ongoing stock rally is also shown in Chart 27-4 which separates the postwar period into three parts, the initial post-Depression, postwar era of recovery and growth (1947-68); the years of inflation that slaughtered stocks (1968-82); and the period of disinflation (1982-97). The average annual nominal gain for the total postwar era, 8.5%, is close to the 9.3% of the 1947-68 pre-inflation years

CHART 27-4

POSTWAR S&P 500 INDEX RETURNS*

	NOMINAL		REAL	
	CUMULATIVE % CHANGE	% CHANGE AVERAGE ANNUAL RATE	CUMULATIVE % CHANGE	% CHANGE AVERAGE ANNUAL RATE
Jan. 1947- Dec. 1968	600.1%	9.3%	322.8%	6.8%
Dec. 1968- July 1982	2.7%	0.2%	-62.4%	-7.0%
July 1982- Dec. 1997	779.8%	15.1%	417.3%	11.3%
Jan.1947- Dec. 1997	6227.2%	8.5%	720.0%	4.2%

*without dividends

(Column 2), leaving the pounding stocks took during inflation (1968-82) to be offset by the subsequent disinflation-related rebound. Notice also the 4.2% real total return over the entire period (Column 4) with declines during inflation and the subsequent recovery. The rebound has been spectacular but so was the preceding decline. From December 1968 to July 1982, the real S&P 500 fell 62% (Chart 5-1) to below its real 1929 level.

Inflation comes and goes and it all averages out, apparently. In any event, our forecast of 4% to 4½% real stock appreciation, once deflation is established, is right in line with history.

Two caveats, however. Historically, the US has been largely an internally oriented country, and only recently have major American corporations earned 50% or more from foreign business. So currency translation gains or losses weren't generally important until the last decade or so, and during that time, except for the last several years, they have been gains, as noted in Chapters 18 and 26. But as the dollar continues to appreciate in steady state deflation, currency translation losses will persist and be substantial. Current thinking is quite to the contrary.

Note that when recent translation losses have been announced with no forewarning by the likes of IBM, Coca-Cola, 3M, Kodak, and GM, their CEOs have said, in effect, "I'm shocked, shocked to learn that we lost money when the dollar rose." Then equally shocked Wall Street analysts shutter and the stocks drop. If the dollar continues to rally, CEOs and analysts will eventually accept translation losses as an ongoing reality. In the meanwhile, shareholders will suffer from these shocks.

Second, as discussed in Chapter 26, US corporate profit margins have been boosted in recent years by declining interest costs and falling depreciation expenses as well as lower effective tax rates. Few investors seem to be aware of these salutary but unsustainable special factors.

Nominal Total Returns in Deflation

How about total returns, including dividends, in deflation? Many have almost forgotten about dividends in the ongoing 15-year stock rally, and with dividend yields below 2% (Chart 18-9), they hardly count when stocks are jumping 30% per year. But dividends have mattered in the past and will again. In fact, most of the total return on stocks in the postwar era has come from reinvested dividends. A 3% constant dividend yield on a stock that has risen 10 fold now is 30% of its original price.

Nominal profits are likely to grow by 2½% to 3½% per year in deflation (see Chapter 26). With an interim stock market decline of around 40%, current dividend yields would rise to about 3%. Combined with profit growth, this would give a nominal total return of about 5½% to 6½%, assuming that price earning ratios (P/Es) remain unchanged. This, too, is in line with Jim Bianco's historical data going back to 1801.

To be sure, lower interest rates should push P/Es higher in the normal fashion, but bear in mind that I'm talking here about stock returns *after* deflation is established and *after* the decline in interest rates is over. At that point, P/Es should be steady. In the transition to deflation, falling interest rates will boost stocks, but the effects will be more than offset by a key ingredient in that transition —the squeeze on profits, probably initiated by the Asian crisis but related to a recession in any event. This is, of course, nothing new. Stocks normally fall well into recession as earnings weakness overpowers the decline in interest rates that typically starts soon after the downturn commences.

It seems reasonable, then, that the total nominal return to stocks during a steady state of deflation will be in the 5½% to 6½% area, and in real terms, 1% to 2% higher. Again, this is normal by historical standards, but could be a big shock to investors accustomed to the 30% returns of recent years. It may be even more of a shock when they find that there is no return to the earlier investment salad days even after they have suffered through a severe bear market.

Nevertheless, in the long run, interest in US stocks will be strong because of the higher rates of consumer saving (Chapters 17 and 18) and the

CHART 27-5

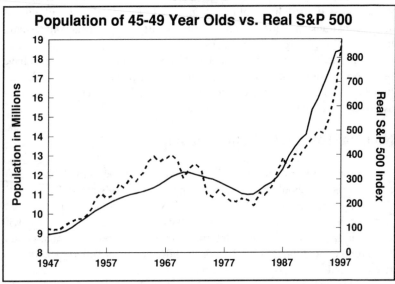

limited alternative investments in a deflationary world. Although the postwar babies' need to save for retirement is only one of many reasons for much higher saving in future years, it's fascinating to note the high correlation between US stock prices and number of people in the 45-49 age bracket (Chart 27-5).

Bonds vs. Stocks

It's abundantly clear that I favor bonds over stocks in the transition to deflation. A possible 60% appreciation in 30-year Treasuries compared with a 40% to 50% fall in the S&P 500 makes the choice simple.

Bonds still look relatively attractive once deflation sets in. To be sure, at that point a 5½% to 6½% total return on stocks compares favorably with a 3% yield on bonds, which are unlikely to experience further meaningful appreciation. Nevertheless, on a risk- adjusted basis, the spread narrows considerably. As noted earlier, nothing beats the high quality or liquidity of Treasuries. And, deflation may provide weaker profit growth than I'm assuming here, serving up some other unpleasant corporate surprises in the process.

4. Forget Global Diversification

No one diversifies his portfolio to hold down his returns. Yet many accept the lower returns that diversification normally brings in the name of reducing volatility, and especially in the hope of offsetting big losses.

As an undergraduate major in physics, I learned a lot about the law of large numbers. Let's say you flip a perfectly symmetrical coin. You know that the probability of its landing with heads up is 50%, but if you flip it only once, the results will be zero or 100% heads. Further flips could give the same result —that's the hope that attracts people to casinos despite the unfavorable odds—but the law of large numbers says that the more you flip the coin, the closer the results will be to 50% heads. Note, however, one very, very important thing. There is absolutely no relationship, causal or otherwise, between one flip and another. The dice have no memory, as gamblers say.

Interrelated Economies and Bonds

This last point explains why global diversification of bond and stock portfolios is much less successful than its proponents believe. Relationships

CHART 27-6

do exist among markets. This is clearly true for government and other high-quality bonds issued by developed countries. Developing country bonds are something else, either the residue of previous financial disasters, like Latin American Brady Bonds, or pieces of paper priced largely by the whims of the local potentate or the economy's stage in its boom-bust cycle.

Charts 27-6 and 27-7 show that G-7 bond yields generally move in close correlation. You invest in one, you've invested in all—not surprising, since they're all affected by the same major forces. Inflation in the 1970s pushed up yields on G-7 bonds. Disinflation and the recent universal zeal for lower deficits and control of government spending pushed them down. Sure, there are some significant differences but they are usually transitory. The Continental countries went into recessions in the early 1990s, later than English-speaking countries, and they recovered later, with some small differential effects on yields. Canadian yields were above the pack in earlier years when Quebec separatism was a serious threat; Italian yields jumped in the early 1990s when it looked like every politician, and half the rest of the country, were destined for jail during the anti-corruption binge; and Japanese bonds strayed because of the strong yen and the 1990s deflationary depression there. But these are exceptions.

Furthermore, as global economies become increasingly interdependent, the value of global bond diversification will fall further. It's sort of like foreign travel. Outside of scenic wonders (like in the American West, the Andes,

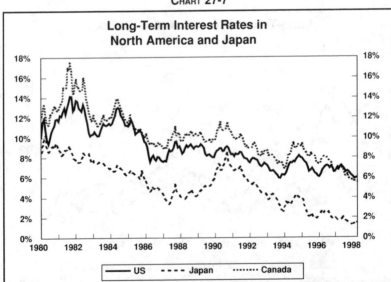

CHART 27-7

Long-Term Interest Rates in North America and Japan

Legend: —— US   - - - - Japan   ········ Canada

and the Alps) or historic sites (like London and Athens), the only places you want to visit are underdeveloped countries with strange, exotic cultures.   Who wants to visit a modern city like Frankfurt with virtually no historic buildings left after World War II and inhabited by folks who look a lot like you and me? Ireland is still interesting, but becoming less so as trucks and cars replace horse-drawn carts.   As economic development rolls on, the list of exciting tourist destinations shrinks. Antarctica, anyone?

Arbitrage and Inflation Differences Limit Spreads

G-7 bond yields also tend to move in lock-step due to arbitrage. Any openings of the normal spreads among bonds of similar quality issued by governments with similar policies and running economies on similar tracks don't last long.

These yields are even more closely correlated (Chart 27-8 and 27-9) when inflation differences are removed, as they should be since these differences in inflation rates are normally reflected in exchange rate movements. If the UK has bond yields one percentage point above US yields, it's probably because inflation rates there are one percentage point higher as well and sterling is falling 1% against the buck per year, thereby removing the yield spread advantage for US bond holders. This phenomenon was especially true for

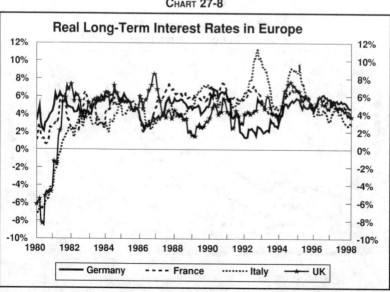

CHART 27-8

Japanese bonds for years. Lower inflation rates there than in the US spawned lower than normal government bond yields, but the rising yen against the dollar made up the difference for American investors.

CHART 27-9

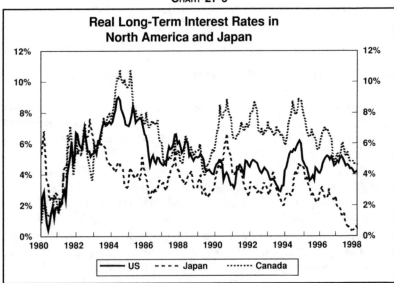

CHART 27-10

Source: ISI Group

G-7 Stocks Move Together As Well

For similar reasons, G-7 stocks also move in close correlation (Chart 27-10), and it probably explains why the Morgan Stanley EAFE index of major foreign stock markets had an almost identical gain as the S&P 500 from the end of 1969 to the end of 1997, 12.5% versus 13.0%, respectively. Note, also, that in recent years global diversification by US investors has been less than rewarding (Chart 27-11).

This isn't to say that US stocks have always been world beaters. In the 1970s, they had a total gain of just 5% while Chilean equities soared 2,351% as that country shook off socialism (Chart 27-12). In fact, virtually all equity markets, except Southern Europe, beat the US in that miserable decade of major inflation. The unwinding of inflation and restructuring pushed the US's rank up in the 1980s. Even in the 1990s, however, Brazil, Chile, Mexico, Hong Kong, and Switzerland outshone the excellent results in the US in the equity department.

Where Are Low Correlations When You Need Them?

Furthermore, there is evidence (Chart 27-13) that year-by-year performances in some high-flying foreign stock markets have relatively low corre-

CHART 27-11

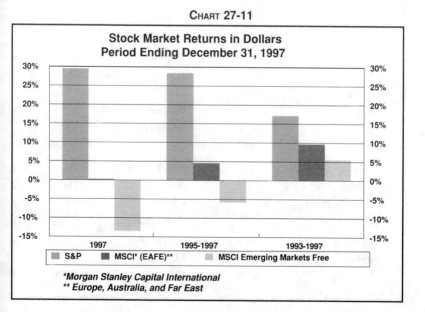

Morgan Stanley Capital International
** Europe, Australia, and Far East

CHART 27-12A

STOCK MARKET RETURNS BY DECADE IN DOLLAR TERMS

1970s		1980s	
Chile	2351%	Taiwan	2379%
Hong Kong	598%	Japan	889%
S.Africa	543%	Sweden	732%
Taiwan	456%	Portugal	572%
S. Korea	362%	S. Korea	550%
Japan	336%	Finland	525%
Mexico	325%	Italy	418%
Singapore	315%	Spain	357%
Switzerland	159%	Brazil	351%
Austria	156%	Austria	297%
Finland	136%	Singapore	286%
Belgium	101%	UK	276%
France	98%	Germany	255%
Norway	96%	India	252%
Ireland	89%	Ireland	252%
India	87%	France	249%
Argentina	86%	New Zealand	245%
Germany	71%	Norway	243%
Sweden	63%	**US**	**213%**
Canada	60%	Mexico	197%
UK	45%	Belgium	173%
Brazil	37%	Australia	134%
Greece	36%	Canada	125%
Philippines	21%	Hong Kong	103%
Australia	12%	Switzerland	102%
New Zealand	11%	Chile	92%
US	**5%**	Argentina	50%
Spain	-46%	S. Africa	26%
Italy	-57%	Greece	23%
Portugal	-65%	Philippines	-10%

CHART 27-12B

STOCK MARKET RETURNS BY DECADE
IN DOLLAR TERMS

1990-1997		CUMULATIVE 1970-1997	
Brazil	491%	Chile	19450%
Chile	316%	Taiwan	7815%
Mexico	289%	Hong Kong	5133%
Hong Kong	270%	Mexico	4809%
Switzerland	246%	Brazil	3557%
US	166%	Sweden	2361%
Germany	125%	Finland	2278%
UK	114%	Singapore	1807%
Ireland	113%	Switzerland	1712%
Norway	106%	Japan	1706%
India	103%	Ireland	1315%
Argentina	94%	Norway	1290%
Greece	86%	Germany	1266%
Belgium	82%	India	1236%
Sweden	81%	UK	1061%
Finland	61%	Austria	939%
Spain	57%	France	924%
France	48%	Belgium	893%
Canada	34%	US	777%
Australia	31%	Argentina	439%
Singapore	19%	Canada	384%
Portugal	16%	New Zealand	320%
New Zealand	10%	S. Korea	317%
Italy	6%	Spain	284%
Austria	2%	Australia	242%
Philippines	-4%	Greece	209%
Taiwan	-43%	Portugal	177%
Japan	-58%	Italy	134%
S. Africa	-79%	S. Africa	67%
S. Korea	-86%	Philippines	5%

CHART 27-13

GLOBAL STOCK MARKETS 1969-1997 (IN LOCAL CURRENCIES)

	AVERAGE GAIN	CORRELATION WITH US	STANDARD DEV. OF GAIN	STANDARD DEV. AVERAGE GAIN
Australia	11%	0.54	26%	2.4
Canada	11%	0.60	17%	1.5
France	15%	0.45	29%	1.9
Germany	15%	0.39	30%	2.0
Hong Kong	30%	0.43	52%	1.7
Italy	12%	0.39	40%	3.3
Japan	18%	0.18	37%	2.0
Mexico	25%	0.18	50%	2.0
Netherlands	19%	0.75	19%	1.0
Singapore	21%	0.27	51%	2.4
Spain	14%	0.19	32%	2.3
Switzerland	17%	0.54	26%	1.5
UK	17%	0.56	30%	1.8
US	14%	1.00	16%	1.2

lations with US equities. Hong Kong, for example, grew 30% per year on average between 1969 and 1997, compared with 14% in the US (Column 1), and had a correlation coefficient of 0.43 (Column 2). Mexican stocks had a 25% annual rise and an even lower correlation, 0.18.[1] This suggests that you can get better performance in some foreign markets without compounding the volatility of your US portfolio. But there's no such thing as free lunch. Like many other soaring stock markets, Hong Kong's was much more volatile than America's. Its standard deviation of annual market growth, 52%, was much higher than the 16% in the US (Column 3), and Mexico had a similar standard deviation, 50%. The ratio of the standard deviation to average annual growth (Column 4), a good measure of risk-reward, shows that you paid 1.7% in volatility in Hong Kong for every 1% of appreciation, and

---

[1] A zero coefficient means no statistical relationship between two markets; 1.00 would signify complete year-by-year lock-step movement in the two stock markets, while -1.00 would mean complete offsets in volatility.

even more in Mexico (2.0%), compared with 1.2% in the US. From this standpoint, the Netherlands' market would have been better —19% annual growth and a 1.0 ratio. But Dutch and American stocks were much more highly correlated, with a 0.75 coefficient, so bad years in Dutch stocks were usually bad years in Wall Street. Still no free lunch.

I obviously love that phrase, there's no such thing as free lunch. I'm going to have it engraved on my tombstone, not only because I believe it's true, but also because it sums up the essence of all economics—the allocation of scarce, *i.e.*, not free, resources.

In addition, these annual averages over the past 28 years hide a lot of variations, and some real cliffhangers. A study by researchers at Hautes Etudes Commerciales, a leading French university, shows that the correlations among US and foreign stock markets are low when market volatilities are low. These are often times of steadily rising stock prices, like the rampant bull US market in the 1990 to mid-1997 years, the longest stretch with no setbacks of 10% or more in over a century. But that's the time you'd like to have all markets in sync, so wonderful gains in the US won't be offset by the fall of over 50% in your Japanese stock holdings in that period.

Even worse, much worse, correlations among markets jump to the sky in periods of big volatility—read, during bear markets. That certainly was true in the 1962 and 1973-74 bear markets and, of course, in the 1987 crash, which started in the US and precipitated a global meltdown. Some of us can remember that they simply shut down the Hong Kong market on October 19, the day of the crash and let everyone sweat it out for seven days until it re-opened 33% lower. More recently, Russian and Eastern European stock markets were shut when stocks worldwide were being dumped with gay abandon last October. When the Russian market reopened, it promptly fell 20% more.

A One-Way Street

Diversification doesn't work for American investors because bear markets tend to be global but bull markets aren't as consistently so. In other words, global stock diversification works when you don't want it and doesn't work when you do. The Hautes Etudes Commerciales research found that in the 1973-74 and 1987 sell-offs, the correlations between the US and major foreign markets jumped to 70%, and even more so for the Hong Kongs of the world.

None of this should really surprise you. When financial difficulties are absent, investors can concentrate on country-by-country differences in economic growth, business regulations, and other factors that lead to lower correlations among stock markets around the world. But crises, regardless of where they start, tend to spread globally in today's financially-interconnected world. Also, when any market slides, the investors' urge for liquidity results in selling everything in every market at any price, and with today's telecommunications, they can do so almost instantly. Limited liquidity in some markets adds fat to the fire. If an investor has a big position in Hong Kong stocks and can't get out because of low liquidity, he'll dump US shares to reduce his overall portfolio risk.

The law of large numbers doesn't apply because stock markets around the world aren't independent. Ironically, the widespread use of global stock diversification has increased the interrelations of markets and, therefore, is largely responsible for its useless, even lethal nature.

Hedging Problems

Global stock diversification also encounters currency risks. Normally, when there is trouble in the world, even if the US starts it, the dollar benefits. If stocks fall globally as well, foreign losses can turn to disasters in dollar terms. Chart 16-13 shows the punishing US investors took when Asian stocks nosedived and their currencies collapsed as well. Currency hedging is possible against developed countries' money and a few others, like the Hong Kong dollar. But it's difficult against many other thinly-traded emerging country currencies, and impossible against controlled currencies like the Chinese yuan. Outside of the yen, few Asian currency exposures are hedged by professional portfolio managers.

In any case, as noted in Chapter 18, hedging is an expensive insurance policy. Sure, it's relatively cheap when all is calm. You pay a reasonable premium when your house isn't burning. But what happens to the premium when your neighbor's house is ablaze and yours is downwind? The guys selling you the hedge aren't stupid. As the flames and wind rise, they probably charge you about as much for the hedge as you'd lose without it as foreign currencies drop, plus a risk-enhanced profit. Again, no free lunch.

There are several other risks in global diversification, especially in developing-country markets. Company disclosure of key financial data is often nonexistent, if not distorted. So, deteriorating conditions can be hidden until it's too late for investors to exit with anything left. In some countries, companies can't be forced into bankruptcy, so managements can run them down to the last won or rupiah or dong.

Here's another problem. South Korea earlier limited foreign ownership of a company's stock to 26%, so shares available to outsiders sold at premiums of as much as 50%. That average disappeared when Korean stocks tanked and foreigners dumped their stocks. Another double whammy. The same was true for investors in emerging debt markets. Earlier, tranquility lulled them into leveraged positions to magnify their yields. It also magnified their losses when Asia came unglued and those bonds collapsed. The pain intensified further as banks that had lent as much as 90% on developing country bonds cut their limits to about 75%, and forced investors to sell out or come up with the difference. The IMF and investor pressures may remove some of these pitfalls, as noted in Chapter 13, but that remains to be seen.

Finally, don't confuse global diversification with foreign investing. Those with superior knowledge of developments abroad that will influence security prices seriously can achieve superior results. But this is far different from diversification solely to reduce volatility.

5. Favor New Technologies.

New technologies are great generators of deflation, as you saw in Chapter 6. They will also be great beneficiaries of deflation, especially in relation to old technologies whose sales will be muted as buyers wait for lower prices. In effect, deflation will further separate the sheep from the goats by further opening the sales and profits growth gaps between new and old technology industries.

Many new tech companies are no strangers to deflation. Also lower prices, far from reducing sales and profits, open up new markets that increase volume so much that earnings grow robustly. It is very similar to the post-Civil War era when huge declines in prices vastly expanded markets to include those who, for the first time, could afford manufactured products. The drop in the price of a Model T runabout from $500 in 1913 to $260 in 1924 had a similar effect. As in earlier times, the process of high tech advances leading to lower prices and expanding markets and profits should persist in the years ahead. It's true in semiconductors and computers. It will also probably prove true in telecommunications and biotechnology.

Obsolescence - Planned and Real

Another advantage that new tech companies will carry into deflation is the rapid obsolescence that rapid technological advances bring. This, too, is nothing new. The launching of the British battleship HMS Dreadnought a century ago instantly reduced the value of the rest of the world's battle wagons to scrap metal. The speedy technological advances in autos in the early decade of this century meant that even though prices were falling, buyers couldn't wait for still lower prices. Who wanted to keep cranking the old Tin Lizzy by hand after cars with electric starters were available?

To be sure, Detroit tried to keep the game going long after its technological advances slowed by instituting planned obsolescence. A new tailfin here, a few port holes there, and earlier models were supposed to look hopelessly out of date. But American car buyers, aided and abetted by the VW Beetle and then high-quality Japanese imports that seldom changed designs, finally got wise to Detroit. It's fascinating that Volkswagen is now reintroducing the Beetle. As I mentioned earlier, my wife is mad that the design and features of her eight-year-old Lexus haven't changed enough to warrant a new one.

In contrast, look at your own PC. You know from years of experience that you'll get more computer power per buck next year, but you can't wait until then to give your current machine to the church rummage sale and buy a new one, or at least replace a lot of its guts. By then it will be hopelessly obsolete. I know why first hand from my own shop.

Our in-house computer czar trots into my office every month or so to announce that we need to upgrade a machine or two. "Why?" I ask. "Are we going to make better forecasts and more insightful portfolio decisions with more powerful and faster machines? I don't think we're calling' 'em any better than 20 years ago when we didn't even know what a Wang was."

In reply, he carefully explains that the new machines have lots more memory which we may not need, but that the software boys use in writing their new programs. In the process they abandon updates on our current software, which, for reasons known only to them and to God, develops bugs over time. Have they taken a leaf from Detroit's book on planned obsolescence and built in time release viruses? Regardless, we have no choice but to jack up the old machines and run new ones under them—and you don't either.

6. Avoid Old Technologies.

Unfortunately for their makers, autos are now old technology with relatively few big advances, regardless of how much the industry's annual advertising blitz tries to convince you that anything produced earlier is of Flintstone vintage. They, and other old technology goods and services, have no rapid technological advances to create instant obsolescence and no big price declines to open new markets. Their form and function remain relatively static. In fact, as you saw in Chapter 8, American auto producers have extended car loan repayment periods and resorted to leases to disguise the fact that vehicle prices have consistently risen faster than average American incomes. Henry Ford, where are you when Detroit needs you most?

The Gap Widens

Chart 6-1 drives home this existing disadvantage of old tech versus new from an investment perspective. Old tech still dominates overall industrial production, which has hardly grown in the last two decades compared to new tech.

The gap between old technologies—flat to rising costs because of limited technological advances and aging work forces, and slow growth in saturated markets—and new technologies—declining costs because of rapid technological advances which open big new markets, and swift obsolescence—is nothing new. What is new is deflation. It will further open the investment gap between them. New technology industries won't be much different. But old technology industries will suffer as buyers expect lower prices and wait for them.

7. Consumer Discretionary Spending Loses, Especially Old Tech Products.

The disadvantages of old technologies will be especially true for consumer discretionary items, as people turn down their spending flames and add fuel to their saving fires. Goods like cars, appliances, extra big and fancy houses, and nonessential apparel, are obviously destined for disappointing sales and earnings. Even with quotas in place, imports have already virtually eliminated the ability of the apparel industry to offset sales weakness with price increases (Chart 27-14). US auto makers will be noticeably vulnerable as consumers save more, wait for lower prices, and see their suspicions confirmed as rising dollar-inspired cheaper imports force Detroit to follow suit.

CHART 27-14

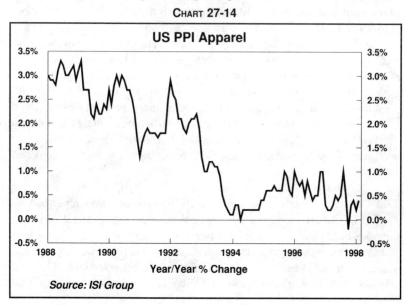

Ducking Henry Ford's Reality

As I mentioned in Chapter 21, Henry Ford paid his Model T assemblers an unprecedented $5 per day, so they could afford to buy the cars they were building. Many American producers of consumer discretionary goods and services have been able to avoid Ford's reality in recent years. They have restructured and, along with many other employers, curtailed wages and middle-income purchasing power in the process. But they have not been faced with the weak demand that could have followed. Consumers have continued their spending spree, regardless of their income growth, and have covered the gap by reducing saving and increasing borrowing, (see Chapter 17).

This situation is unsustainable. I'm not suggesting that American companies involved in the domestic production and distribution of nonessential consumer items should or will increase employee compensation to provide the wherewithal to buy their products. That might be in their best interest, and it might work if they were organized as cartels and walled off from imports, but foreign and domestic competition won't allow it. Instead I'm saying that those firms will find that the years of middle-income stagnation spawned in part by their restructuring will come back to haunt them.

Consumers will not only stop increasing their spending faster than their income growth, but will cut back spending and increase saving rates to make up for past year's excesses (see Chapter 18). This will be very rough on the sales and earnings of the firms involved. As spelled out in Element 12 of this investment strategy, meaningful sales growth is necessary for good profit performance. Continual restructuring alone can't do the job.

Chart 27-15 lists the changes in various categories of consumer spending in the 1973-75 recession, the worst since the 1930s, and it may give a rough guide to the nature of future consumer entrenchment. Notice the weakness in autos, appliances, foreign travel, clothing, and even tobacco. Utility spending rose due to surging oil prices, and medical spending was still out of control back then. What's interesting is the switch from foreign to domestic air travel in times of consumer caution and the movies—cheap entertainment and escape from economic worries. But how about movies for worried economists?

Services are just as discretionary as goods. Maybe more so. Just ask my Dad who started practicing dentistry in 1931 in Toledo, Ohio, reportedly the hardest hit American city in the Depression. Postponing dental work was common back then. As you're well aware, we expect no depression, but even if service prices don't drop enough to encourage people to wait to buy, consumers will still postpone or even eliminate the nonessentials. They will probably hold back on dining out and vacations, to the detriment of restau-

CHART 27-15

% CHANGE IN US REAL CONSUMER SPENDING IN NOV. 1973 TO MAR. 1975 RECESSION

Total	-0.9%
Movies	37.9%
Medical	6.8%
Household Utilities	6.4%
Domestic Air Travel	3.7%
Video, Audio, & Computing Equipment	2.7%
Alcohol	2.5%
Home Prepared Meals	0.6%
Dining	0.6%
Spectator Sports	-1.8%
Clothing & Shoes	-2.3%
Books & Maps	-2.8%
Foreign Travel	-3.5%
Tobacco	-5.5%
Kitchen & Other Appliances	-13.0%
New Cars	-27.4%

rants, gasoline sales and oil companies, hotels and motels, middle-brow cruise ships and their builders, and airlines and aircraft manufacturers. Note that, like any other capital-equipment maker, Boeing gets a magnified effect from any fall off in demand for the goods or services that utilize its equipment. If airline traffic falls and excess airline capacity mounts, new aircraft orders will collapse.

Naturally, retailers and related firms will benefit from declining costs of goods, especially imports and domestic products that complete heavily with imports. But those who handle consumer discretionary items will see their volumes and profit margins squeezed, as increasingly thrifty consumers wait for still lower prices. Furthermore, as consumers switch from borrowing and spending to saving, credit card issuers will be damaged.

8. Consumer Spending—A Few Winners

Even with increased saving among individuals, there will be some winners in the consumer spending area. Among them are imports which will decline in cost but are essential to consumers. Also included are goods and services with strong brand identifications or patent protection that will limit competitive price erosion, and proprietary products and luxury goods with status appeal. This group would include the high-priced items preferred by those with the bucks, as the national income continues to move into higher-income hands. Lower-cost status symbols may also sell well to those who can't afford much but want the very best of what they can afford. Surveys show that lower-income people often drink higher-priced liquors than those with higher pay and more assets. Upscale recreational travel and other services that higher-income people favor will also be winners. So, too, will be financial services as consumers save more and need help in investing their funds.

With financial services, though, you've got to distinguish between the climate in a steady deflation state and near-term developments. For now, regional banks will probably continue to be bought as the banking industry consolidates, although many are currently selling at prices you would expect to see only in takeover premium bids. Mutual fund advisors are pursuing their shareholders by diversifying into brokerage and banking services. The insurance industry will continue to consolidate due to persistent intra-indus-

CHART 27-16

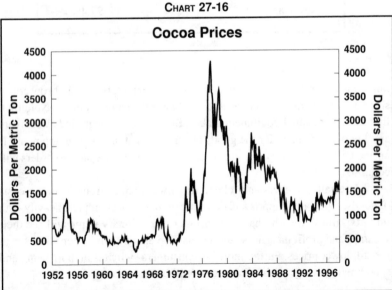

Cocoa Prices

try competition and expansion into insurance by banks, brokers, and other financial service providers, as discussed in Chapter 9. Stock insurance companies will keep buying one another and mutuals as well, as they become available for sale through mutual holding companies and demutualization. More mergers that cut across banking, insurance, and security industry lines can be expected, following the announced combination of Citicorp and Travelers Group.

Nevertheless, a major bear market in US stocks could disrupt many of these plans, especially for securities-related firms in and out of Wall Street. Virtually all of their activities depend on the stock market. Declining equity prices dry up trading volume and profits, causing investment banking and merge acquisition activity to atrophy as well. Bear markets ultimately drive individual investors out of managed accounts and mutual funds. Stocks of all of these firms are simply leveraged plays on overall equity prices, and they will fall much more than the average when stocks take a tumble.

9. Commodities Will Remain Weak.

Disinflation has cut commodities prices, in some cases dramatically, as a world of surpluses emerged in the last decade. Note the decline in commodities ranging from agricultural products like cocoa to industrial commodities like crude oil (Charts 27-16 and 27-17). Even prices of gold have collapsed, much to the dismay of its devotees (Chart 27-18).

CHART **27-17**

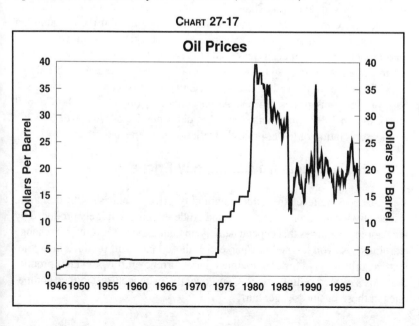

CHART **27-18**

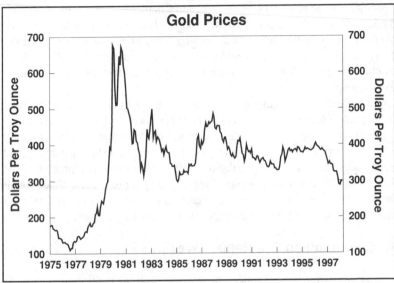

In fact, even the central banks now see gold as a non-earning asset—falling in price and tying up money that could be better spent balancing government budgets or earning a return. Many are slashing their holdings of 30% of the world's mined gold (Chart 27-19), but of course, not the gold-passionate French. Central banks in Europe may even sell more if the forthcoming European central bank, which will replace those of the common currency participants, decides it needs less gold than its predecessors and the host governments elect not to keep the excess. The World Gold Council reported that global demand for the yellow metal, especially for jewelry and coins, rose 9% last year even as prices fell and Asian demand dropped. Still the Council noted that in 1997 consumers "tended to defer purchases whenever possible in the expectation of lower prices." Deflationary expectations at work!

Deflation's Effects On Commodity Prices

Expect more of the same commodity price weakness with deflation, especially for materials like copper and crude oil that are largely produced by developing countries that depend heavily on their exports for foreign exchange earnings. As you learned in Chapter 13, those lands will produce more, not less, as prices fall in order to maintain hard currency inflows, even if production costs exceed selling prices. Consequently, even well-disciplined companies in these businesses get hurt.

CHART 27-19

NATIONAL GOLD HOLDINGS
(IN BILLIONS OF US DOLLARS)

	1980	1997	% CHANGE
US	264.3	261.9	-0.9%
Germany	95.2	95.1	-0.2%
Switzerland	83.3	83.3	0.0%
France	81.9	81.9	0.0%
Italy	66.7	66.7	0.0%
Netherlands	43.9	27.1	-38.3%
Belgium	34.2	15.3	-55.3%
Japan	24.2	24.2	0.0%
Portugal	22.2	16.1	-27.5%
Austria	21.1	9.3	-55.9%
Canada	21.0	3.1	-85.2%
Britain	18.8	18.4	-2.1%
Spain	14.6	15.6	6.8%
Australia	7.9	3.2	-59.5%
Sweden	6.1	4.7	-23.0%

Source: The IMF and The Bank of Canada

The OPEC oil cartel remains especially vulnerable and may disappear. Regardless, it's rapidly becoming irrelevant to the energy scene as its share of global output falls. What a difference from the frightening early 1970s days of the oil embargo, when the world quaked at every Saudi whisper. Oil producers will not prosper in this climate, assuming no new major Middle East war or other big oil supply disruptions.

Agricultural prices are also likely to weaken further as deregulated US farmers plant fence-row to fence-row. Where are the pheasants I love to hunt going to find cover? Other developed countries will also expand output and exports as agricultural deregulation spreads, albeit slowly, to Europe and Japan. And, of course, developing lands will produce sugar, palm oil, soy beans, and other export crops flat out to keep people employed and to earn foreign exchange. To be sure, the El Niño weather phenomenon, and his sister, La Niña, that may follow, could disrupt weather in the next year or so, but should be out of the way by the time chronic deflation sets in. In the meanwhile, global economic weakness will probably limit any resulting surge in agricultural prices.

Falling commodity prices are good news for ultimate consumers and business users that aren't forced to pass through all of the decreases in their materials costs. But they will be bad news for those who aren't so lucky, and also agricultural suppliers of farm implements and fertilizer companies as well as mining equipment manufacturers. The oil field equipment and services industry is more problematic since little drilling has been done since the 1980s and equipment is presently fully utilized, while promising new oil fields in the former Soviet Union and elsewhere are being developed. Nevertheless, caution is warranted there, as well, in deflation with weak energy prices.

10. Real Estate and Other Tangibles Generally Aren't Attractive.

Real estate excesses of the 1970s came to grief in the 1980s, as discussed in Chapter 22, but have since stabilized and revived. Foreclosures and write-downs cut the prices of many structures down to profitable size, especially those that are well-located, high-quality buildings with prime tenants. Think about it. As long as rent covers ongoing costs for utilities, maintenance, and repairs, the building is worth something. All that's needed to make it economically viable is to wipe out the mortgage, *i.e.*, give the lenders a bath and take the equity participants into the hot tub with them. Bulldozers take care of the remaining real estate excess.

Additional forces helped other real estate-troubled sectors revive. As noted in Chapter 22, government spending aided the agriculture and oil patch rebounds; the Midwest ceased to be the rust belt as manufacturers restructured and regained competitiveness against foreign invaders; and the East and West coasts bounced back as the late 1980s-early 1990s financial crisis and defense cutbacks were absorbed. More recently, the booming US economy has revived real estate demand, but not back to the heady days of the 1970s and early 1980s when it served as the hedge of choice against high inflation.

Nevertheless, real estate tycoons are buying up everything in sight, marking it up, and then redistributing it in REIT form to individual investors and financial institutions alike. Some aggressive REITs are borrowing with the intention of repaying in newly-issued stock which they hope will be selling at higher prices later on. But if their share prices fall, they will dilute their capital or be forced to pay out precious cash. Most REITs are now trading at about 20% premiums to their underlying asset values.

This strikes me as getting out of hand, especially the new-found real estate zeal of pension and endowment funds and other institutions. They previously owned real estate directly, but swore off after the 1980s debacle, citing, among other factors, its illiquidity. Now they're back, participating through REITs. But will those vehicles prove any more liquid if there is, for any reason, another rush for the exit? Once again they might yell, "Sell!," and their brokers would answer, "Sure, but to whom?"

Fundamentally, real estate, farm land, and other tangibles are not great investments in deflation, regardless of local pockets of strength. The same holds for companies involved in the business as lenders, developers, and builders. If the prices of everything else are falling, why should the prices of land and structures resist? Especially in a time of excess capacity when few need more of it; when businesses are looking for ways to put more people in a given office space and encouraging telecommuting and teleconferences in place of hotel-utilizing business trips; when consumers are visiting malls less frequently and buying less; when people are cutting down on discretionary leisure travel and the hotel and motel use involved; and when agricultural price supports are being phased out and farmers are free to overexpand production to their hearts' content.

Real Estate and Lower Interest Rates

Ah, but you may be thinking, lower interest rates will make real estate and other tangibles much cheaper to finance and, therefore, more attractive. That's what I heard from a group of real estate clients in the early 1980s when I first forecast 3% yields on 30-year Treasury bonds. I met periodically for dinner in Los Angeles with this group of developers, builders, and other real estate specialists, and they were so overjoyed with my forecast that one of them even offered to pick up the dinner tab.

But then I delivered the bad news. Sure, I acknowledged, lower interest rates would reduce the rates at which real estate is capitalized and therefore push prices up. But, I went on, the key to lower interest rates, then in double digits, was disinflation, and an important enabler of declining overall inflation rates would be a collapse in real estate prices. Those guys were assuming that real estate would continue to appreciate, with interest rates falling in a vacuum. It didn't quite work out that way, as California subsequently went through the real estate wringer.

If I'm right and long-term Treasury yields drop to 3%, mortgage rates will be about 4%. If overall prices are falling 1% to 2% annually, real estate prices in general will probably decline at about these same rates. They've tracked inflation rates closely in the past. Then the real cost of real estate financing won't be negative, as in the 1970s, but positive and quite high, 5%

to 6%. Recall from Chapter 26 that real long-term interest rates are likely to be about twice as high as the average of the earlier postwar years. A real estate investment will be profitable if the net income from it exceeds 5% to 6%, but its attractiveness will be based on income, not appreciation, which is likely to be negative.

Antiques and Collectibles

To be sure, the continuing polarization of American income will put more purchasing power in the hands of those high-income people who tend to be the buyers of coins, antiques, and artwork. But will they want to "invest" more of their increased saving in these items in a deflationary era? Are they, by and large, true appreciators of beauty for its own sake? Or are they quasi-appreciators who want to believe that their treasures will rise in value, irrespective of whether they ever intend to sell—or could sell at profitable prices, given the huge spreads between the bid and ask prices of many tangibles? Don't get me wrong. My wife and I love 18th century English and American furniture, but we see it as gorgeous furniture, not appreciating assets.

On Public Television's Antiques Road Show, people in various cities bring in their antiques to be evaluated by experts. The pros give lengthy and interesting discussions of the backgrounds of selected pieces, their designers, and where and when they were made. But the high point is always the same. The expert asks the owner how much she thinks her antique is worth and then shocks her with its huge value, as the video camera zooms in for a closeup of the overjoyed collector. I hope this fine program will survive in deflation days.

11. Manufactured Housing and Rental Apartments Win

We've been bullish on manufactured housing ever since we foresaw disinflation killing the investment appeal of housing many years ago. In the high inflation of the 1970s, people combined a great investment with a place to live. Get a bigger, more expensive house regardless of your needs, mortgage it to the hilt, and clean up as inflation propels the price, was the philosophy. But house prices are no longer zooming.

So people are now separating their abode from their investments, and manufactured houses fill the bill. They tend to be smaller than site-built houses, and with advances in design and quality, look almost identical when two or more units are attached and finished. Their improved quality has also led to the repeal of zoning restrictions in many locales, and they no longer have the trailer park image. More important, manufactured housing is about one-half the cost of site-built units, per square foot. They also appeal to retirees and middle income Americans, who continue to be restructured into tough economic straits, as well as those seeking moderately priced second homes.

Deflation and newfound consumer zeal to save will only add to the comparative advantage of factory-built over site-constructed housing. People will be much less likely to buy unneeded housing than before, but for those who need it, the choice seems clear to me—but then I'm a director of a major manufactured home company, Palm Harbor Homes.

Rental apartments will also thrive in an environment in which people increasingly separate their living quarters from their investments. Now, I'm not suggesting that Americans will give up on single family owner occupied housing. The idea of a single-family home of your own is just too deeply embedded in the American culture. Consider me as exhibit number one in that department. I'm a dedicated gardener and do-it-your-selfer who plans to be carried out of the suburban house we've owned, remodeled, and re-remodeled for 30 years—much to the consternation of my wife who'd love to move on, even into an apartment some day. Talk about remodeling, I even put heat under our driveway last year to melt the persistent New Jersey winter ice. Sadly, El Niño eliminated the ice needed to test the system last winter. Anyway, how could I keep my bees in an apartment?

But many who have no pride of home ownership and who would vastly prefer to yell for the "super" (New Yorkese for the building superintendent) than to apply a wrench to a leaky pipe have bought houses and apartments in past decades to participate in capital appreciation. If I'm right, they'll be more inclined in future years to occupy rental apartments. This might be especially true of empty nesters who don't like to mow their lawns and who decide to unload their money pits a few years earlier than when these single family houses were still appreciating rapidly. At the other end of the life cycle, young couples may decide that since houses are no longer great investments, there's no reason to strain their financial, physical, and emotional resources to buy big expensive houses as soon as possible. So, they'll stay in rental apartments a bit longer and wait until their kids are of the age that single family houses make sense.

It will take a surprisingly little shift in housing patterns to make a big difference in the demand for and construction of rental apartments. Today there are 116 million housing units in the US, about 46 million of them apartments of which 35 million are rental. If only 1% of total existing households decided to move to rentals, the demand for apartments would increase by over one million, most of which would need to be newly built, given current low vacancy rates. This is a big number compared to new apartment starts of 339 thousand last year.

Investors can participate in rental apartments, either through direct ownership or through REIT stocks. There are also REITs that concentrate on rental sites for manufactured houses. As noted earlier, though, I think the REIT craze has been overdone.

12. Productivity Enhancers Will Be Even More Attractive

The deflationary world that I see ahead will be even more competitive than the disinflationary climate we're leaving. So the need to cut costs and improve productivity will be even more pressing.

We first looked at this phenomenon from an investment viewpoint back in the mid 1980s and developed the concept, "bottom-line growth stocks." These were companies that would prove so effective at enhancing productivity and carrying the fruits to their bottom lines that investors would eventually perceive them as growth companies, even though they lacked the sales growth normally associated with growth stocks. As a result, their stock prices would gain from both rapid earnings growth and rising P/Es as investors awarded them growth-stock status.

We went so far as to conduct an extensive study of all major US industries, ranking them by such characteristics as evidence that they were already taking concrete restructuring steps, the proprietary value of their products, the pressure on the various industries to cut costs, the size of costs that could be cut, and the extent to which domestic and foreign competition might force them to run very fast in restructuring just to keep profits intact.

The concept seemed sound and the resulting industry, as well as company rankings, were intriguing. We found inorganic chemicals, rubber, photographic equipment, tobacco, aerospace, engines and turbines, aircraft, iron and steel, foundries, drugs, and communications equipment especially interesting. The complete list of all 52 industries, ranked from the most to the least likely to contain bottom-line growth stocks, is shown in Chart 27-20 for your historical amusement.

With the recession and slow economic recovery of the early 1990s, however, it became apparent that rapid and consistent profit growth cannot be produced by restructuring alone, even of the most heroic and persistent dimensions. It takes meaningful top-line growth as well, and many of our bottom-line growth stock companies did not, and probably cannot, produce that growth consistently.

Consequently, we didn't abandon the concept but shifted to the other side, to those that help others restructure, cut costs, and promote productivity. Even if their customers end up running very fast to stand still, these productivity enhancers will thrive, assuming they're not servicing only failing industries.

When I think about this category, computers, telecommunications, and many of the other new-technology industries discussed above in Element 5

CHART 27-20

INDUSTRIES LIKELY TO CONTAIN BOTTOM-LINE GROWTH STOCKS (RANKED FROM MOST TO LEAST LIKELY)

1. INDUSTRIAL INORGANIC CHEMICALS
2. Tires & Inner Tubes
3. Photographic Equipment & Supplies
4. Cigarettes
5. Guided Missiles, Space Vehicles, & Parts
6. Engines & Turbines
7. Aircraft & Parts
8. Iron & Steel Foundries
9. Drugs
10. Communications Equipment
11. Electrical Industrial Apparatus
12. Measuring & Controlling Devices
13. Nonferrous Rolling & Drawing
14. Electronic Components & Accessories
15. Household Appliances
16. Newspapers
17. Metalworking Machinery
18. Blast Furnace & Basic Steel Products
19. General Industrial Machinery
20. Motor Vehicles & Equipment
21. Medical Instruments & Supplies
22. Cutlery, Hand Tools, & Hardware
23. Weaving Mills, Cotton
24. Soap, Cleaners, & Toilet Goods
25. Periodicals
26. Electrical Lighting & Wiring Equipment
27. Metal Forgings & Stampings
28. Preserved Fruits & Vegetables
29. Industrial Organic Chemicals
30. Grain Mill Products
31. Knitting Mills
32. Paper Mills, Except Building Paper
33. Misc. Converted Paper Products
34. Plastic Materials & Synthetics
35. Paperboard Containers & Boxes
36. Toys & Sporting Goods
37. Concrete, Gypsum & Plaster Products
38. Fabricated Structural Metal Products
39. Glass & Glassware, Pressed or Blown
40. Commercial Printing
41. Misc. Plastic Products
42. Household Furniture
43. Sawmills & Planing Mills
44. Construction & Related Machinery
45. Millwork, Plywood, & Structural Members
46. Office & Computing Machines
47. Meat Products
48. Men's & Boy's Furnishings
49. Women's and Misses' Outerwear
50. Footwear, Except Rubber
51. Primary Nonferrous Metals
52. Petroleum Refining

certainly come to mind. But so do low-tech or even no-tech sectors. Temporary help agencies that provide workers at only the times of the day or seasons of the year they're needed certainly are productivity enhancers. So, too, are consultants that often achieve economies of scale in communicating research, expertise, best business practices to a wide variety and number of clients. First and foremost in the category are, naturally, good economic consultants, and please don't think that's an oxymoron like honest politicians.

13. The Dollar Will Rally.

Chapter 12 spells out all the reasons I expect a strong greenback for many years. Ok, but how do you invest in it? One way is to favor the stocks of domestically oriented companies which are often, but not always, smaller. At the same time, avoid the multinationals that usually need global markets to accommodate their size, and will be constantly beset by currency translation losses, weak exports, and perhaps depressed sales in developing economies for some years to come. Also, as noted in Element 4, currency hedging can be prohibitively expensive. But watch out for domestic firms that compete with imports. An import may have only 1% of the US market, but force the 99% share that is domestically produced to match its declining price. Or it can be worse. Note that imports have virtually wiped out the domestic production of TV sets and many other consumer electronics in the US.

You can, of course, also take advantage of dollar strength directly through currency futures and forward markets. I see the yen and Continental currencies in long-run bear markets, but am much less convinced that the Anglo-Saxon group—British sterling and the Canadian, New Zealand, and Australian dollars—will fall against the greenback.

Winners and Losers

Our first book, written back in 1982, discussed and then listed the winners and losers in a disinflationary era with a strong dollar. You might find these lists interesting, even amusing (Charts 27-21 and 27-22). Please bear in mind that they were drawn up 16 years ago. Since 1982, many of our winners, such as stocks and bonds, have won, and many of the losers on the list, like real estate and other tangibles, have lost.

What struck me in preparing this book was how many on our 1982 lists are on our 1998 lists (Charts 27-23 and 27-24 for investments, 28-1 and 28-2 for business, and 29-1 and 29-2 for personal strategy). Perhaps this isn't surprising since in some ways deflation is an extension of disinflation. But in many ways, deflation is different, as you'll notice in comparing the lists.

Be aware that the new lists refer to a steady state of deflation, after the rough transition that may produce quite different interim results. For example, as noted in Chapter 28, a major bear market in US stocks in the transition will be devastating for Wall Street firms, but during deflation they should thrive as they help individuals invest their rapidly-rising savings. Similarly, agricultural commodities should fall in deflation, but may rise in the nearer term due to El Niño weather disruptions, followed by the reverse, La Niña.

I've listed 13 elements in an investment strategy for deflation, and I hope that 13 doesn't turn out to be an unlucky number. In any event, investment and business strategies in deflation are similar in some ways, but in other ways, they differs, as you'll see in Chapter 28 where my business strategy has 18 elements. I hope that's *your* lucky number.

CHART 27-21

WINNERS IN A DISINFLATIONARY ERA
1982 LIST

Savers
Businesses with little or no debt
Quality stocks and bonds
Producers of proprietary products, where competition
  will not erode pricing power
Low-cost producers
Venture capitalist
Research and development
Efficiency and quality control experts
Entrepreneurs
Companies that derive profits from increased volume
  rather than higher prices
New products and those with the talents to develop them
Pensioners and others on fixed income
Marketing and production people
US-made automobiles
Conservative investment practices
The US dollar
Strict family budgeting
Specialized education, continuing education for
  professional people, and trade schools
Consumers with low debts, high savings, and
  productive jobs
Renters
Money market funds backed by US government
  securities
Importers
US tourists abroad
Consumers of imported goods
Users of internationally traded commodities

CHART 27-22

LOSERS IN A DISINFLATIONARY ERA
1982 LIST

Individuals and businesses heavily in debt
Municipalities
Art auctioneers
Real estate and commodity brokers
Commodities and commodity producers
Housing speculators
Farmland investors
Investors in hotels, office buildings, and shopping centers
Producers of farm equipment
Collectibles, objets d'art, antiques and their dealers
Previous buyers of tangible asset-rich companies
Investment letters which stress trading and speculation
Publications geared toward instant gratification
Luxury, foreign-made automobiles
Non-US government money market funds
Publications oriented toward real estate speculation
French wines and other foreign-produced "collectibles"
Foreign investments with an emphasis on natural resources
Companies that earlier bought their stock and ran down liquidity
International commodity cartels
Counties with high external debts denominated in US dollars
Noncompetitive businesses that were shielded from competition by inflation
Undercapitalized businesses
Advertising activity
Bureaucracy, corporate staffs, overhead and staff functions
Regulation-oriented lawyers and publications
Unionized labor in previously regulated industries
Washington consultants and lobbyists
Creative finance people
Conglomerates
Merger and acquisition specialists and activities
Arbitrageurs
Those who were over indexed to inflation
The federal government
Newly deregulated industries such as airlines and trucking (initially)
Many tax shelters
Firms that merely mark up costs
OPEC
The United Kingdom, Mexico and other non-OPEC oil exporters
Executive recruiters
Those who rely on government bailouts
Companies with long-term, fixed-rate supply contracts
Leveraged buy-outs and those who specialize in them
Joint venture partners of OPEN countries
Employees of local governments
Businesses that depend heavily on municipal spending

CHART 27-23

INVESTMENT WINNERS IN DEFLATION
1998 LIST

High quality bonds
Utilities with competitive-minded managements and reasonable
    regulatory climate
US stocks in general
New technologies such as

- Semiconductors
- Computers
- Telecommunications
- Biotechnology
- Internet related

Imports of consumer essentials and their distributors
Strong brands and popular products that are consumer essentials
    and their distributors
Goods with effective patent protection
Goods and services appealing to upscale consumers

- Foreign and upscale domestic travel
- Upscale recreation
- Luxury goods and services

Small luxuries
Financial services for savers and investors
Manufactured housing
Rental apartments
Productivity enhancers

- Productivity-oriented plant, equipment, and software
- Temporary help agencies
- Consultants, especially economic

The dollar

CHART 27-24

INVESTMENT LOSERS IN DEFLATION
1998 LIST

Bonds of weak currency countries
Junk bonds
Stocks of weak currency countries
Old technologies, especially consumer discretionary goods
    and services

- Autos
- Appliances
- Site-built housing
- Airlines
- Aircraft manufactures

Industrial commodities

- OPEC

Agricultural commodities
Real estate and tangibles except some oriented toward productivity
    enhancement and upscale consumers

- Builders and contractors
- Developers
- Lenders

Plant and equipment that increases capacity rather than productivity
Multinationals
Farm equipment producers
Credit card issuers

CHAPTER 28

BUSINESS STRATEGY
FOR DEFLATION—
18 ELEMENTS

If you've read this book up to this point, you are probably already aware of much of the business strategy that is needed to survive and indeed thrive in a deflationary atmosphere in future years, and in the difficult transition to it. Nevertheless, you might find it useful to see all of the elements assembled with brief explanations.

1. Continue to Cut Costs and Push Productivity.

The need for ruthless cost cutting and aggressive productivity enhancement is obvious in the transition to deflation, considering the troubled economies and financial markets in developing countries, gyrating foreign exchange rates, surging imports at substantially lower prices, weak American exports, and a major bear market in US stocks, followed by consumer retrenchment and a recession. Enough said?

Continuing restructuring will also be necessary in the steady state of deflation that lies beyond that transition. This deflation will be driven by excess supply rather than collapsed demand, but it still means excess capacity and wrenching competition in most businesses.

2. Anticipate Deflation.

Prepare for deflation by avoiding unnecessary investments in plant and equipment that may burden you with excess capacity. Wait for lower prices before investing if at all possible. Keep the pressure on suppliers for lower prices. Continually search for lower-cost sources and production sites abroad as currency devaluations against the dollar present opportunities. And, oh yes, be prepared for pressure from your customers to reduce your prices.

3. Avoid Excess Capacity.

There is a tremendous urge to increase capacity in anticipation of fondly-hoped-for market expansions. No one wants to lose customers to competitors because he doesn't have the capacity. But there also seems to be an innate business zeal to expand, to increase sales and market share regardless of the consequences. The Japanese have been notorious for this trait and it worked as long as their targeted markets grew rapidly.

American CEO's have contracted a milder strain of the bug. Most are aware of increasing global glut, but each plans to be one of the shakeout's survivors. It may work for a few, but it can't work for all. CEOs are accustomed to winning, and the battle for market share is one more fight to test their mettle. In addition, they hope to get big enough to scare competitors away. Some hope that the mere announcement of new capacity plans will do the job. Good luck in a deflationary world, guys!

4. Keep Inventories Slimmer than Bare Bones.

If you can remember the 1970s days of high inflation, you'll recall that holding inventories wasn't all it was cracked up to be. Sure, if inflation drove the value of your stocks up 20%, that was pure inventory profits. But if you paid a 40% tax rate on that profit and, say 10% interest to finance your stocks, your net after-tax gain was slashed to 6%. And after the goods were sold, you had to replace your inventories at the new higher price, kick in more net cash, and pay more interest to finance the higher dollar value of your inventories.

In deflation, holding inventories is worse, much worse. Even if you aren't among those with a warehouse full of PCs which are now falling in value by 1% per week as obsolescence rages, your inventories will be very expensive. If your inventory value dips a mere 10% per year, you start with a pretax 10% loss. Of course, a 40% tax rate cuts that to 6% after tax, but if your borrowing rate is 5%, you have a net after-tax loss of 9%. You can replace your inventories after they've sold at the lower prices, and your cash flow increases a bit, but you still lost money.

The moral of this exercise is simple. Inventories are assets which will generally decline in value in deflation. The fewer you have, the better.

5. Emphasize New Technologies, Not Old.

New technologies like semiconductors and computers are well acquainted with deflation, create rapid obsolescence for their products, and open vast new markets as prices fall, as you saw in Chapters 6 and 27. But buyers will wait for lower prices before purchasing the output of old technology industries, especially if they produce postponable discretionary consumer goods and services like autos and airline travel.

6. Go for Volume.

If your selling prices are falling, you need significant volume growth to achieve decent earnings. Ongoing restructuring alone won't do the job, as discussed in Chapter 27. That chapter also gives a few clues as to where volume growth may be found in deflation: Financial services that help zealous savers and investors. Productivity-enhancing capital equipment. New technology industries. Deregulated and expanding utilities. Manufactured housing and rental apartments. Consumer luxury items, both big and small, may offer exciting volume growth opportunities, as well as other upscale consumer goods and services.

7. Develop Proprietary Products.

Volume growth is easier in products with patent protection or brand identification which will be more sheltered from domestic and foreign competition—and from price erosion.

8. Explore Niche Businesses.

Niche businesses can be safe havens from the nonstop onslaught of foreign competition in basic commodity-producing industries, and from domestic competition as well. They may involve the production of special sizes and shapes, businesses where high service content or fast delivery time is important, or areas where fad or fashion changes so fast that it would be impossible to get the items made in Asia and shipped to the US before demand for them disappears. Domestically-oriented businesses with limited import competition also fit this category.

9. In Commodity Businesses, Be the Low-Cost Producer or Get Out.

Businesses in which the technologies are universally available and the products are indistinguishable are difficult at best in deflation. In a world of surpluses and strong competition, the key to success is being the low-cost producer, and the cost differences often boil down to labor and transportation, since raw materials and other costs are similar for all producers. To achieve this status, it may be necessary to move production to cheaper areas in the US or abroad, merge to cut overhead, and innovate lower-cost production techniques. If a firm can't become the low-cost producer, it should seriously consider exiting the business, unless other considerations, such as the need to produce a complete product line, prevail.

10. Get into the Productivity-Enhancing Businesses.

Productivity-enhancing businesses are all-time favorites of mine. It doesn't matter whether it's high tech, low tech, or no tech, any good or service that can measurably and significantly enhance others' productivity or help cut their costs is a sure winner. As mentioned in Chapter 27, economic consulting is a superb example.

11. Watch Out for Protectionism.

Only Buchanan, Perot, Gephardt, and Detroit are beating the protectionist drums now, but many more will join them when the US economy cools and unemployment rises. (See Chapter 25). US protectionism may impede imports that compete with your products, but exports and foreign operations of US firms will suffer as other countries retaliate. Don't automatically assume that you can avoid the effects of protectionism. If you aren't directly in its hair sights, your customers or suppliers may well be.

12. Be Prepared for More Competitive Devaluations.

As noted in Chapter 14, China may well join the devaluation crowd and touch off another round in Asia in the currency-cutting race for the bottom. Hedging is difficult in many developing countries and expensive everywhere, as discussed in Chapters 18 and 27, even prohibitively expensive if it's a complete hedge. Perhaps the best defense against losses from foreign currencies is big enough profit margins to absorb a lot of decline. In any event, if you have foreign operations, anticipate currency translation losses and treat them like depreciation, a continuing deduction from revenues in deriving earnings. Your stockholders may well applaud your realism and the reduced risk of nasty surprises.

If falling foreign currencies will help you, I wouldn't worry about hedging against their revival. Most foreign currencies are unlikely to rise appreciably against the dollar beyond dead cat bounces.

13. Stick to Businesses You Know.

Business strategies come and go, but the current trend is clearly toward divesting nonessential activities of secondary importance in order to devote full management attention to the firm's principal business. This certainly makes sense in the deflation era we see ahead and the tough transition to it.

14. Emphasize Service to Customers.

Everyone agrees that the customer comes first, but not all businesses act that way. In any event, deflation and the intensified competition it brings to many industries will increase the necessity of attending to customers' needs and wants. Furthermore, customer-driven businesses are much quicker to understand important and even critical changes in the market place than those who simply wait to fill the orders that filter back to them.

Without question, an all-out customer orientation can turn a mundane commodity business into a proprietary niche. A friend of mine sells stationery and envelopes, a highly price-sensitive commodity business. Yet he thrived by having a thorough understanding of his customers, even their personal activities. Before calling on a prospect, he gathers information on that person to the point that at their first meeting he can discuss specific areas of mutual interest, be they sports, colleges attended, or charitable activities.

My late father-in-law, Ed Bloete, sold business forms, another highly competitive commodity business. Yet for years, he prospered and was the principal supplier for all of Avon representatives' order forms because of his service orientation. Among other things, he was willing to get up at 3:00 a.m. to deliver a needed shipment personally, while his much larger competitors waited for regular business hours. As you saw in Chapter 8, his daughter followed in her father's footsteps.

15. Share Company Risk with Employees and Pay More from the Bottom Line.

In times of inflation, it's relatively easy to correct a mistake in paying an employee too much or to handle one whose productivity has slipped. As noted in Chapter 5, you just don't give him any more pay increases and let inflation erode his real compensation back to the proper level. That can't be done in deflation. In fact, real salary and benefit costs go up even if nominal pay remains flat. Consequently, firms need to be much more careful in hiring and promoting—and more aggressive in terminating overpaid people who can't be made cost effective.

You should also pay as much of total compensation as possible in bonuses and other incentives linked to your firm's success. This can take the form of productivity sharing, pay for knowledge, profit sharing, or stock options, among others. That not only inspires diligence and productivity, but also permits pay to be more closely linked to changing internal and external conditions, including deflation.

Sure, nobody likes to take pay cuts and reducing ongoing wages and salaries is extremely difficult, as explored in Chapter 24. Nevertheless, in a deflationary world, whenever business turns down without the cushion of inflation, pay cuts may well be necessary, and at other times as well. Paying people substantial amounts from the bottom line means that those compensation reductions are effective immediately, with the arguing done later and not while the company is still paying oversized amounts. And it's certainly easier than cutting salaries.

More compensation linked to company results is also needed for middle as well as upper management. As the need for cost control and restructuring continues to bring about departures of people on all levels in big and small companies alike, job security in large corporations no longer exists. Earlier, many top-flight employees balanced their shot at higher rewards but with higher risks at smaller companies, against the less likely crack at the brass ring but greater job security at large corporations. Since career risk is now prevalent throughout the spectrum, incentives for valued managers at all levels are needed, and in large firms as well as smaller ones.

It's often easier to share the risks with employees in the fringe area than with cash compensation. Meaningful employee co-payments and medical savings accounts not only reduce costs, but also cut out what I call "recreational medicine"—an afternoon off work to see a physician when an employee feels any ache or pain and isn't paying much of the cost. Shifting from defined-benefit pension plans, in which the company is responsible for pension payments irrespective of the investment success of the funds set aside, to 401(K) and other defined contribution plans, with the employees responsible for the investment results, also shares more risks with them, as noted in Chapter 5.

16. Build Financial Strength.

Fortress-like balance sheets are certainly appropriate in the uncertain transition to deflation, and on into the era of generally declining prices. Financial strength protects against squeezes on earnings and also provides the wherewithal to buy some of the attractive but distressed companies that will be served up by deflation.

17. Adapt to Higher Real Interest Rates.

Nominal interest rates may be lower, but both short- and long-term real rates are likely to be higher in deflation than they were in the earlier postwar era, as discussed in Chapter 26. In other words, stated rates may seem low, but if your selling prices are falling, borrowing is expensive. Obviously, this means that falling selling prices must be taken into account in calculating the returns needed to justify capital investment, especially if it is financed by borrowing.

18. Wait to Issue Bonds, but Float Stocks Yesterday.

History shows that in periods of declining interest rates, most corporate bonds are issued well before the bottom in yields. This probably reflects human nature. Corporate treasurers who sweated out the preceding jump in rates want to grab the money before rates return to their old highs, and cost them their jobs. Also, most underestimate the extremes in rate swings, both up and down. The recent rash of corporate bond issues indicates that this historical pattern continues. But if deflation is in the cards, it's still far too early to rush new bonds to market, about three percentage points too early.

Stocks, on the other hand, are selling at near record-high P/Es. Those levels may prove justified by lower interest rates once deflation is firmly established, but in the recessionary transition to deflation, declining earnings will do a lot of damage to stock prices. Furthermore, P/Es will probably fall as speculation evaporates and individual investors are punished by losses and lose faith in stocks. In my judgment, any firm contemplating equity financing should do so immediately or be prepared to delay its financing plans for some years. Recent heavy insider selling in a number of companies suggests that many corporate officers and directors agree.

Just as deflation has significant ramifications for investors and business people, so too does it impact people in their personal lives, as you'll learn in Chapter 29. But first, have a gander at my lists of business winners and losers in deflation, Charts 28-1 and 28-2. You may also enjoy comparing them with the lists we drew up in 1982 (Charts 27-21 and 27-22).

CHART 28-1

BUSINESS WINNERS IN DEFLATION
1998 LIST

WINNERS WILL BE FIRMS THAT:

Cut costs and promote productivity ruthlessly

Have competition-oriented managements in deregulating industries

Anticipate deflation

Are involved in new technologies

Avoid excess capacity

Profitably expand volume

Hold low inventories

Produce proprietary and branded products

Are niche oriented

Are the low-cost producer especially in commodity businesses

Produce small and upscale luxuries

Concentrate on goods and services preferred by upscale consumers

Are involved with imported consumer essentials

Help others enhance productivity

Are concentrated in industries they know

Are customer-service driven

Share risks with employees

Build fortresses-like balance sheets

Adapt to high real interest rates

Are domestically oriented in industries with limited import competition

Are relatively immune from protectionism

Can benefit from a strong dollar

Chart 28-2

Business Losers in Deflation
1998 List

Losers will be firms that:

Fail to adapt to deflation

Rely on regulation that is fading

Believe that high inflation will return

Don't cut costs and pursue productivity aggressively

Remain in old technologies

Don't control capacity

Are in commodity business unless they are the low-cost producer

Have slow volume growth and falling selling prices

Are high-cost producers

Are widely diversified

Are production, not customer driven

Have inflexible compensation structures

Have weak balance sheets

Have high inventories

Have high financial leverage

Have high exposure to foreign currencies and developing country markets

Compete directly with imports, especially from developing countries

Are exposed to protectionism

Are involved in real estate and tangibles, with some exceptions

Are oriented to agriculture outside of biotech

Chapter 29

Personal Strategy
For Deflation—
5 Elements

The last 15 years of disinflation have drastically altered the personal economic climate for Americans, and most have adapted to it, at least in part. Few still view real estate and other tangibles, the darlings of the inflationary 1970s, as great investments. The vast majority now admire financial assets, especially stocks. Not many any longer expect automatic pay increases that are designed to offset inflation and then some. Many know first hand what restructuring can do to disrupt employment.

As disinflation turns into deflation, much of this climate will remain, but much will change even further and some new storm clouds will gather. If you pursue the following five elements in your personal strategy, you will probably avoid getting drenched.

1. Wait for Lower Prices before Buying.

Deflationary expectations are an important part of our forecast of widespread and chronic price declines, so join the happy throng. Hold off on buying nonessentials, especially imported items and their domestically-produced competitors. On big-ticket items like cars, you may save a bundle. And don't forget deflation in service prices. With full seats in recent years, airline fares have leaped in some markets, but remember the fare wars a short while back when they were empty? Those days will be back in spades. I don't recommend, however, postponing purchases of aspirin until you expect deflation to be worry free.

I am, however, trying desperately to wait for lower prices in an area of critical importance—tools. As a heavy duty do-it-yourselfer, I am, quite naturally, a tool junkie. I have tools I've yet to find a use for, much less use. In my workshop at our beach house sit a jointer and a lathe that are yet to be uncrated a decade or more after I bought them. There are very few woodworking, electrical, or plumbing tools that I don't desperately need. Yet, I recently, and painfully, delayed my semi-annual big order with one of my favorite tool supply houses, Harbor Freight. Many of their tools are made in Asia, and the American-made equipment they handle competes with Asian imports. I'm eagerly awaiting my next Harbor Freight catalog to see how much I've saved by waiting.

Delaying purchases until prices fall in deflation isn't just for the thrills of saving money. It will also be a necessity for many as their income rises little if at all in current dollar terms. The only way for them to enjoy rising living standards will be to take advantage of falling prices.

2. Save More.

A switch by American consumers from their decades-long borrowing and spending binge to a saving spree is also part of our deflation forecast. I suggest you lead this parade, especially if you've saved little out of your ongoing income in recent years and are relying on your stock portfolio to put the kids through college or finance your retirement. Look at the table in Chart 18-11 to see what I mean. The stock market gains on your saving over the years could largely evaporate in the next big bad bear market, whenever it comes—and it will, sooner or later. In fact, you might consider a more conservative investment stance now, like more cash and bonds and fewer stocks.

Once stock and bond markets have adjusted to deflation, you'll want to return to stocks as well as continue to hold some bonds, as observed in Chapter 28, but that could be some time off.

Increased saving also makes sense now because there will be rainy days, no doubt lots of them, as restructuring-related layoffs intensify and the impending recession takes its toll. Be assured that the current economic atmosphere for Americans is about as good as it can get. Close to zero inflation. Strong economic growth. Multiple job offers for anyone with any skills. A soaring stock market.

3. Reduce Your Financial Leverage.

Deflation generally pushes up the real value of financial assets, so you want more of them. It also increases the real burden of debts, so you want less. And don't be misled by the siren call of lower nominal borrowing rates to finance either assets or liabilities. As noted in Chapters 27 and 28, real interest rates are likely to remain high even as nominal rates fall. In other words, even if mortgage rates drop to 4%, it doesn't do you much good if the market price of your house is falling 2% or more each year.

Financial leverage works both ways, as many homeowners (*i.e.*, former real estate speculators) in California, Texas, and elsewhere learned painfully in the 1980s. If you put down 20% on a house with a 10% mortgage and the price leaps 15% a year, you make a cool 35% on your investment per year. But with the same down payment and a 4% mortgage, you lose 26% each year if the market value of the house falls only 2% per annum.

Not all interest rates adjust with inflation. Credit card rates are notoriously stable and have declined little in recent years as inflation and market interest rates have plummeted. Deflation provides a further incentive to pay off debts on the plastic. It's a lot more onerous to pay 20% rates when your pay hardly rises year after year than if your compensation is climbing 6% or 8% per annum.

Finally, unless you've got great investment to finance with borrowing, it's always better to a lender than a debtor be. And that will be the case in the world I foresee, especially after deflation gets established. Sure, I see a continuation of "the bond rally of a lifetime" we first dubbed in the early 1980s when long-term Treasuries yielded over 14%, but after they rally to a 3% yield in the transition to deflation, well, 3% is 3% (See Chapter 27). Stocks will probably take a header in the transition and then provide total returns of 5½ to 6½ percent. This is good, but, risk adjusted, not worth mortgaging your house at 4% in order to buy more equities. Real estate and other tangibles don't do well in deflation. What's left to make you want to borrow big time?

My dad tells a great story about a trip by car that he, my mom, and his parents took many, many years ago to visit one of my uncles in Wheeling, West Virginia, some 200 miles away. With the condition of the roads back then, 200 miles was a full day's drive. All the way down and all the way back, Grandpa Shilling delivered a nonstop lecture to my dad that had one and only one point. If you're borrowing money, you pay 5% interest. If you're lending money, you get paid 5% interest. The difference between paying 5% and receiving 5% is 10%, a huge net gain back then—and in the deflation years ahead. That's more clearly true now that income tax rates are much lower than in the earlier postwar era and for the first time in decades, a saver in the top tax bracket gets a positive after-tax, after-inflation return, even on Treasury bills (See Chart 17-22).

4. Add Value to Your Employer.

An old friend, Don Bein, then at A. O. Smith, used to tell me that, in any business, value added *must* exceed cost. And that applies not only to capital investments and software, but to employees. Restructuring has driven this point home to many people. They're aware that layers of paper-shuffling middle management are gone. They've seen the exit, with varying degrees of employer encouragement, of older employees whose pay was raised beyond their economic value by managements that wanted to buy employee peace with excessive annual raises.

Deflation adds another dimension to the necessity of being worth at least as much to the boss as he's paying you. As you saw in Chapters 5 and 28, in deflation when few pay increases are justifiable, employers have to be very careful about over paying people. If they do, there's no inflation that can be used to erode their real cost back to realistic levels. In fact, as the firm's selling prices fall, the real cost of even a steady wage rises.

There's not much point in my giving you a definitive list of ways to increase your value to your firm, or more importantly, to your firm's customers. It's all the usual suspects. Harder work. Smarter work. More education and training. More attention to the needs of customers, etc. But you also might want to avoid jobs in firms that may now *think* your value added exceeds their costs, but the market for the company's goods and services doesn't agree, or soon won't. I'm not just thinking of failing firms or those in industries with falling volume or excruciating downward pressure on prices. I'm also thinking about jobs that will no longer be protected as deregulation introduces the bracing winds of competition, and union jobs in an era of accelerating outsourcing to nonunion shops here and abroad.

5. Aim for Income Guarantees—Maybe.

In Chapter 28, I advised employers to keep compensation as flexible as possible and pay more from the bottom line. As an employee, however, you should think—but maybe only think—about doing the opposite. I'm simply reflecting the fact that deflation raises the purchasing power of any fixed payment, including a salary. If nominal pay isn't likely to rise, except for those who add more value and are therefore worth more, the greater the portion of compensation in fixed form, the better for the employee. People on fixed pension, private or social security, obviously make out like bandits in deflation.

Note, however, that I said you should "maybe only think" about getting more of your pay in fixed form. In an uncertain era of intensifying restructuring, employers want more, not less flexibility. Since cutting wages and salaries remains taboo in most companies, fixed compensation arrangements encourage layoffs when costs need to be pared. On the other hand, if a lot of pay is linked to performance and profits, employees may suffer with their firm's misfortune, but still keep their jobs.

Furthermore, the greater the portion of compensation that is fixed in wage and salary form, the lower the total amount will be, or at least should be. When I'm negotiating compensation with a prospective employee in our firm, I point out that the total has three components—the salary, the benefits, and the bonus. The total is the firm's cost of the employee's services, and there is absolutely no distinction between a dollar paid in salary and a dollar contributed to our 401(K) plan and a dollar of bonus. They're all fungible, except for the element of uncertainty. The more of the total paid in salary, the more the risk is on the firm's shoulders. The more that goes into bonus, the more the employee assumes the uncertainty over its size. Higher risks must be compensated with higher rewards. Our employees who are less demanding on salaries not only get bigger bonuses, they get bigger total compensation.

Check out Charts 29-1 and 29-2 for my lists of personal winners and losers in deflation. See how they compare with the lists we drew up in 1982 (Charts 27-21 and 27-22).

Finally, finally, finally, thanks for reading this book to its conclusion— if you did so. I hope it was a good investment of your time and thinking, and will help as you face the challenges and opportunities in deflation.

CHART 29-1

PERSONAL WINNERS IN DEFLATION
1998 LIST

PERSONAL WINNERS IN DEFLATION WILL BE:

Those who wait for lower prices before buying
Savers and lenders
Those with low financial leverage
Well educated and trained people
Customer-oriented employees
Employees whose value to employers vastly exceeds
  their cost
People on social security / fixed private pensions
Renters
Those not looking for free lunch
US tourists abroad
Those who take the advice of A. Gary Shilling & Co.
  and subscribe to *Insight*

CHART 29-2

PERSONAL LOSERS IN DEFLATION
1998 LIST

PERSONAL LOSERS IN DEFLATION WILL BE:

Impulsive buyers
Big spenders with huge credit card debts
Those with high financial leverage
Net debtors
Poorly trained and educated people
Over-payed employees
    •   Union members
Government employees
Those who believe the customer be damned
Those who believe in free lunch